# A WRITER'S WORKBOOK

## An Interactive Writing Text for ESL Students

# A
# WRITER'S
# WORKBOOK

## An Interactive Writing Text for ESL Students

**TRUDY SMOKE**

*Hunter College*

*St. Martin's Press*
*New York*

**To**
**My Mother and Father**
**and**
**Especially to**
**Alan**

Library of Congress Catalog Card Number: 86-60732
Copyright © 1987 by St. Martin's Press, Inc.
All rights reserved
Manufactured in the United States of America
1098
fedc
For information, write St. Martin's Press, Inc.
175 Fifth Ave., New York, N.Y. 10010

Cover design: Darby Downey
Cover photograph: "Rensselaerville, New York, 1983," by Victor Schrager
Book design: Suzanne Bennett
Illustrations: Alan Robbins

ISBN: 0-312-89435-X

**Acknowledgments**

Dena Kleiman, "Language Barrier Is Thwarting Young Vietnamese Immigrants in Elmhurst." Copyright © 1982 by The New York Times Company. Reprinted by permission.

From *Language Two* by Heidi Dulay, Marina Burt, and Stephen Krashen. Copyright 1982 by Oxford University Press, Inc. Reprinted by permission.

Ernest Hemingway, "A Day's Wait" from *The Short Stories of Ernest Hemingway*. Copyright 1936 Ernest Hemingway; copyright renewed © 1964 Mary Hemingway. Reprinted with the permission of Charles Scribner's Sons.

Maria L. Muñiz, "Back, But Not Home." Copyright © 1979 by The New York Times Company. Reprinted by permission.

Charles Olson, "These Days," *The Maximus Poems*, © 1982. The regents of the University of California.

Acknowledgments and copyrights continue at the back of the book on page 356, which constitutes an extension of the copyright page.

# Contents

# Grammatical Categories

## III. SENTENCES

## IV. PUNCTUATION

# Rhetorical Considerations

# Preface

**A** *Writer's Workbook* presents ESL students with a wide variety of thinking, reading, and writing experiences that expand their communicative skills. The many interactive exercises, derived from the context of the reading selections that open each chapter, show students the many dimensions of language, ranging from the smaller considerations of words, word choice, and sentence form, to the larger issues of meaning, implications, and essay form. Students read, speak, and write; since the more students write, the better their skills become, *A Writer's Workbook* particularly promotes writing.

The book is organized into five units, each focused on a different aspect of life: language and communicating; coming of age and knowing ourselves; relationships; working; and establishing the self. Each unit contains three chapters organized around a specific type of reading selection. The first chapter in each unit begins with a selection from a piece of journalistic writing (a newspaper or a magazine), chosen for its high interest and cultural insight. The second chapter opens with an excerpt from a textbook. Exposure to this style of writing and the accompanying exercises will make future studies more successful. The third chapter begins with a short story, or an excerpt from a novel or an autobiography. These literary pieces were selected because of their themes and the quality of their writing.

Following each reading selection are exercises in vocabulary development and questions to guide in the analysis of the text. In this section, journal writing begins, starting with the dialogue journal. The student writes to the teacher, and the teacher responds without correction of grammar and/or spelling errors. The exchange establishes honest communication between a student and teacher. As the term progresses, many students keep a private journal, a forum for ideas and feelings not to be shared. This book encourages the student to write as much as possible in order to become more proficient in expressing ideas in English.

The next three sections of each chapter—word skills, sentence skills, and paragraph skills—deal more with the surface problems of writing. In other words, these sections address the aspects of writing that are often redmarked as errors: the editing problems of punctuation, tense, agreement, grammar, and so forth. Each student should do only as many exercises as are necessary to improve editing skills, for that is the final goal. Although there are no perfect writers, there are many excellent editors; this section of the book prepares students to edit carefully.

The final section of each chapter, "Essay Skills," concerns itself with how to begin writing, how to be creative, and how to write more formally. In addition to containing writing exercises, the section includes "Suggested Writing Topics" at the end of each chapter that are designed to produce a variety of rhetorical modes, most particularly, description, narration, and persuasion. This text is not arranged around rhetorical modes, although some exposure to rhetorical design is important for non-native speakers. The "Essay Skills" section concludes with exercises in revising, urging the writer to experiment, to try different techniques. Each writer is unique and each writer's process is unique as well.

I want to express my gratitude to friends, family members, and colleagues who encouraged and supported me throughout the writing of this text. Andrew Robinson, Chair of the Department of Academic Skills at Hunter College, City University of New York, made every effort he could to facilitate the development of this book. A special thanks must also go to the hundreds of students whose insights and discoveries as they studied English greatly influenced the creation of this text.

I would like to thank the following reviewers for their insightful criticism and much appreciated encouragement: Phyllis Cindy Gould, Wayne State University; Denis A. Hall, American Language and Culture Center, New Hampshire College; Alexandra Krapels, University of South Carolina English Program for Internationals; Jorge R. Luis, Army Staff College, Argentina; Carolyn Raphael, Queensborough Community College, City University of New York; Amy

Sonka Sales, Boston University; Maria Thomas-Ruzic, University of Colorado; Benné Willerman, University of Texas at Austin.

There would be no book, however, if it were not for three extraordinary people. Susan Anker nurtured and encouraged me throughout this entire project. She was thoughtful, knowledgeable, and always available and understanding. Anne McCoy showed creativity, dedication, and perseverance during the editing and production of the book. I especially appreciate her careful supervision of its elegant interior design. Above all, however, my thanks must go to my husband, Alan Robbins, for his unending patience and gentle advice. His illustrations give life to this book. His love and belief in me brought me through all the trying times and helped me to see that it was all worth it.

T.S.

# A
# WRITER'S
# WORKBOOK

## An Interactive Writing Text
## for ESL Students

# Language and Communicating

# CHAPTER ONE

# Language Barrier Is Thwarting Young Vietnamese Immigrants in Elmhurst

*The following is part of a series of articles published by the* New York Times *about the lives of immigrants in New York. This article, by Dena Kleiman, "Language Barrier Is Thwarting Young Vietnamese Immigrants in Elmhurst," deals with some of the difficulties faced by a young Vietnamese family trying to adjust to a new language, a new culture, and a new way of life.*

**S**he stays up half the night copying over the notes she took in class, hoping the repetition alone will help her absorb the English. She keeps long lists of vocabulary words and has not missed a day of school since she began. She gets all of her assignments done early—including the report on "Death of a Salesman," but after reading the play at least four times, she is still not sure who the salesman is. 5

And Khan Duong, who is 20 years old, is failing at Newtown High School.

There are few at Newtown, in Elmhurst, Queens, who know about Miss Duong—how she is already in charge of a household of five, that in addition to school she works stuffing Chinese-style steam buns in a factory and practices the piano two hours a day instead of eating lunch. 10

Few know about her arrival here—how she and her cousins set off in a small boat three years ago from Vietnam, leaving their parents behind—and that today they live on their own. Most at school only know that Miss Duong, who gave herself the name "Matina" 15

because she thought it sounded American, is having trouble with
English.                                                                    20

Yet even those who have been in her class 40 minutes a day, five
days a week, do not understand the scope of the problems linked to
her troubles learning English—her fear of getting lost on the sub-
way, the loneliness of being unable to make friends, the frustration
of missing jokes.                                                           25

Hers is not a unique story for Newtown High School, or for anywhere else in Elmhurst, the city's most ethnically diverse° neighbor-

°varied

hood, where the struggle to understand English is often among the
most baffling challenges to newcomers to this country. What makes
her story and that of her cousins different, however, is that they are   30
so young and are facing this challenge entirely on their own.

"Nobody teach you," said Miss Duong. "Find out by yourself."

Miss Duong and her cousins live in a cramped° but tidy two-

°crowded

bedroom apartment. Three of the cousins sleep on mattresses on the
floor. The living room serves as entertainment center, dining room     35
and study hall, organized so that each of the cousins has a desk facing away from the television set.

It is quite different from the homes they lived in north of Saigon,
children of well-to-do parents with businesses and live-in help.

There was little in their childhood to prepare them for their jour-   40
ney to America, which included 45 days on a ship without a chair or
a bed and often no water. There was little, too, in their past to prepare them for their lives here.

"I die already," Miss Duong said. "Now I am reborn again."

The five cousins, who range in age from 12 to 22, spend much of   45
their time together. Since they are afraid to go outside at night, they
remain indoors even on weekends. Because money is tight, they rarely
get to Manhattan and have been to a movie only once in three years.
Ashamed of their English, they do not talk to their neighbors.

"We don't know anyone," said Miss Duong, who believes she and   50

°contradiction

her cousins are among the few foreigners around. The irony° is that
almost everyone else in the building and many in her school are
newcomers to this country, too.

Lac Hua, 22, the eldest of the cousins, earns the money to pay
the bulk of the family's expenses—including the $453 a month they   55
pay for rent—by driving a truck. All five contribute for food, including Vinh Hua, 12, and his sister, Thuong Hua, 19, who receive public assistance.

Since Vinh, who came here at the age of 9, is the only one who
does not hold even a part-time job, he is also responsible for dusting   60
the floor, changing the water in the fish tank and doing the wash.

Spend an evening with this young family, and one is moved by
their energy and sense of structure. Miss Duong and Miss Hua do

°complexly

the cooking. Vinh washes the dishes. Ky Trung, 17, the fifth cousin, scrubs the pots. They sit in a circle and have dinner together as a family—American or Vietnamese specialties ranging from spaghetti to intricately° spiced rice, but always with chopsticks, even when the menu features "Shake and Bake" chicken. 65

Then at about 9 o'clock, the activity comes to a halt and it is time for study until 1 in the morning. 70

°cannot be seen

" 'Invisible,'° I don't know what that means," Miss Duong said the other night, picking up her assignment: the prologue to *Invisible Man* by Ralph Ellison. She reached for a dictionary, but found no help. She asked Miss Hua, who is also a senior at Newtown and is doing better than Miss Duong. But Miss Hua shrugged her shoulders. 75

°qualified

Miss Duong, who has already been at the high school three years, is afraid that unless her English improves soon she may be denied a diploma. Under New York state law, students are entitled to a free public education until the age of 21. While she would be eligible° for alternative academic programs, this may be the last year she can graduate from a regular high school. 80

"If I miss now, then what?" said Miss Duong, adding that in Vietnam she received high marks.

# Vocabulary Development

**prefix *re-***

A recent study of successful Americans was aimed at discovering what one aspect of knowledge they all had in common. After many tests, the study found that they all had very well-developed vocabularies. One of the goals of this book is to help you develop skills that will increase your vocabulary. One technique for increasing vocabulary is to be aware of the use of prefixes and suffixes on words you already know. The prefixes and suffixes change the meaning of the words. For example, in this article, Khan Duong says that she had died already and that she was reborn when she came to the United States. We add *re* to the word "born" and the new word "reborn" is created. Based on the reading, what does "reborn" mean? _____
Some other words that can use this prefix to change their meaning are listed below. Can you figure out the meaning of each of these words without using the dictionary? To find more words like these, you may want to look in the dictionary.

reappear means _to appear again after an absence_  *it was gone.*

reapply means _to apply again_

reappoint means _to choose again for a position_

rebuild means _to make again_

recharge means _to pay asked for a payment again_

recirculate means _to move or flow again_

recopy means _to make a thing like the another again_

rediscover means _to find something again_

reestablish means _to start something again_

reuse means _to consume again_

Try using each of these words in a sentence.

# Reading and Thinking Skills

## Comprehension Questions

1. What are some of the problems Khan Duong has had to face since she came to the United States?

2. How does her life now differ from her life in Vietnam? Be specific. Use examples from the article.

3. According to the article, Khan Duong studies very hard. What are some of her techniques for studying English?

## Discussion Activities

### Analysis and Conclusions

1. Question 3 in the preceding exercise looked at some of Khan Duong's study techniques. Despite all her hard work, she is not doing well in school. Do you think there is anything wrong with the way she is studying English? Can you suggest any ways in which she might improve her study techniques?

2. Why did Khan Duong change her name to "Matina"?

3. According to the article, why is it ironic that Khan Duong is afraid to make mistakes speaking English with her neighbors?

4. Do you think Khan Duong speaks English outside the classroom? Use examples from the article to support your point of view.

**Writing and Point of View**

1. Dena Kleiman reports about Khan Duong and her family. She does not give her opinions or make suggestions. Why not? For whom was this article originally written?

2. Why is the second paragraph of the article only one sentence long? How does this make you as the reader feel? What in the article makes you think it was written for a certain audience?

3. Are there any words or details that make you feel the author is sympathetic to Khan Duong and her family? What are they?

4. How would you rewrite this article in order to argue that better programs are needed to help people learn English? What would you add and/or delete?

**Personal Response and Evaluation**

1. Compare Khan Duong's typical daily schedule to your own schedule and that of your classmates. You may want to answer such questions as "What time do you get up in the morning?"

2. Is the way Khan Duong and her family eat dinner similar to the way you eat dinner at home? Describe a typical meal for you.

## Creating Questions

What questions do you think the interviewer asked Khan Duong? Write some of the questions in the following blanks.

1. What _____

2. When _____

3. How _____

4. _____

5. _____

## Role Playing

1. Act out the interview between Khan Duong and Dena Kleiman. Interview a classmate using some of the questions from the ex-

ercise above and questions of your own. (Some of these interviews might be taped and played back for the class.)

2. Have several members of the class play Khan Duong and her cousins and act out dinnertime in their home. Then act out dinnertime in your own home. Move your desks together to create the feeling of eating together.

## Journal Writing

Keeping a journal will be a major part of your writing experience while you use this book. Your journal will be a place where ideas count, not spelling or grammar. You may be able to use some of these ideas in other writing assignments; even more important, you will use them to get to know yourself better and to get to know your teacher. We will use dialogue journals, in which you write to your teacher and he or she writes back to you. However, you may enjoy writing in a journal so much that you will also want to keep your own private journal every day. Each chapter includes suggestions and questions to write about in your journal, but you may also decide to write about something very different that is important to you. Sometimes the topics will simply point you in a direction and you can explore as many or as few as you choose.

After reading about Khan Duong and her family, think about your own experiences learning English. Close your eyes and think about the word *home*. What thoughts come to your mind? Think about the word *school*. When you are ready, begin to write down your thoughts. Do not worry about writing complete, grammatically correct sentences. Write, and the writing itself will help you become a better writer.

# Word Skills

## Idiomatic Expressions

When we write or speak, we often use expressions that cannot be understood simply by looking them up in the dictionary. They are best understood in the context (the parts that come before or after) in which they appear. Each of the following paragraphs contains a context clue that will help you understand some of the expressions used in the article. Underline these context clues; the first one has been done for you. Then use the expressions when you answer the questions at the end of each paragraph. The page and line indicators show you where to find the expressions in the article.

*in charge of* (page 3, line 11)

Khan Duong is the person who <u>has responsibility for</u> her family. She makes sure they study for school, keep the house clean, and have enough food to eat. She is also the person who tells everyone what to do. She is in charge of her family. At what age do you think people should be in charge of their own lives?

*in addition to* (page 3, line 12)

Khan Duong goes to school full-time. In addition to going to school, she works in a factory and practices the piano two hours a day. She is also in charge of her family. In addition to going to school, what other responsibilities do you have? (Note: In this expression, "to" is followed by an *-ing* verb.)

*live on their own* (page 3, line 17)

Khan Duong and her cousins left Vietnam and their parents, and now they live on their own. Many young Americans look forward to the day they can be independent and live by themselves away from their families. Do you think it is a good idea for young people to live on their own before marriage?

*well-to-do* (page 4, line 39)
*live-in help* (page 4, line 39)

In Vietnam, the Duong family was well-to-do. Because they were wealthy, they could afford live-in help, that is, people who lived with them to do the housework. Do you know any people who were well-to-do and had live-in help in their country but who had to change their lifestyle when they came to the United States?

## Prepositions

**in**

Review the article and notice how often the preposition *in* is used. This exercise will help you become familiar with the use of *in* in place expressions. Two examples have been chosen from the article. Find three more examples and write them in the blanks.

in class

in Elmhurst

_____

_____

_____

These examples show that *in* is used to give the feeling of being inside or within something, whether it be a country, city, apartment, or box. We use the following expressions:

in class
in a factory
in a small boat
in the fishtank
in the car
but *not*
*in* the floor

What is the difference in meaning between

| | |
|---|---|
| *in* the refrigerator | *on* the refrigerator |
| *in* the desk | *on* the desk |

However, there are some special expressions that use *on:*

| | |
|---|---|
| *on* the train | *on* the plane |
| *on* the bus | *on* the ship |

**EXERCISE**      Fill in the blanks in the following sentences with either *in* or *on.*

1. The cousins live _____ Elmhurst, _____ a two-bedroom

   apartment _____ the third floor.

2. Every afternoon Khan Duong gets _____ a bus to go to work

   _____ a factory where she puts filling _____ Chinese-style
   steam buns.

3. When Khan Duong puts her hands _____ the piano keyboard,
   she feels happy.

4. Thuong Hua used a potholder to reach _____ the oven to check the chicken; then she looked at the soup pot _____ the stove.

5. The cousins stay _____ their apartment on the weekends because they are afraid to get _____ the train to go to New York City.

## Uses for *Make* and *Do*

The words *make* and *do* have very special uses in English. Read the following paragraph and underline *make* and *do* each time they appear and the words that directly follow them. The first two have been done for you.

Every evening Khan Duong and Thuong Hua <u>do the cooking</u>. They <u>make an effort</u> to <u>make a meal</u>* that everyone will enjoy. Usually it takes a while to make dinner, but at other times they make do with leftovers. After dinner, Vinh does the dishes. They do without television so they can begin to do their homework early. The family tries to make time to do the housework too, but they usually have to wait for the weekend. Then they do the wash in the laundromat. They do all the floors; they mop the kitchen and bathroom and vacuum the living room and bedrooms. Soon it is Monday morning again. When the alarm rings, they get out of bed, do a few exercises, make their beds, and make breakfast. Then they rush off to school and, as usual, try to do their best in all their classes.

*In some parts of the United States, people say "fix a meal" or "fix dinner."

Make a list of the *make* and *do* phrases you underlined. The first two have been done for you.

| *Make* | *Do* |
|---|---|
| make an effort | do the cooking |
| _____ | _____ |
| _____ | _____ |

_____     _____

_____     _____

_____     _____

_____     _____

_____     _____

Write five sentences using *make* and *do* to describe things that you typically do at home.

**Note:** There is no final *s* in "homework" or "housework." For example: I do my homework for all my classes after I finish dinner. He does all his housework on Saturday.

Fill in the blanks in the following sentences with *homework* or *housework*.

_____ is school work, assignments for classes.

_____ is cleaning work done in a person's home.

## Commonly Confused Words

### they're/there/their

This exercise focuses on words that are often confused in writing because they are spelled differently but pronounced the same. These words are called homonyms. Looking at these words in context should help you understand how they are used.

*There* are many reasons why Khan Duong and her cousins find life in the United States difficult. *They're* afraid to talk to new people because of *their* English. They do not realize that *they're* not alone; many people in the United States are learning English as *their* second language.

Examining this paragraph should help you complete the following definitions.

_____ means "they are."

_____ means "belonging to them."

_____ means "in that place or at that point."

Fill in the blanks in the following sentence with *they're, there,* or *their.*

Khan Duong and her cousins would like to succeed in _____

education so _____ trying very hard, but _____ are many problems and responsibilities that are making it hard for them.

Now write sentences of your own using each of these words.

# Sentence Skills

## Simple Present Tense

The article we have just read is written mostly in the present tense. The author tells us about the habitual or routine activities of Khan Duong and her family. The simple present tense is often used to describe habitual or routine activities. Let's examine some of the sentences from the article.

The following sentences are all in the present tense. Draw a rectangle around the subject of each sentence and a circle around the verb. The first sentence has been done for you.

1. Khan Duong and her cousins live in a cramped but tidy two-bedroom apartment.

2. The living room serves as entertainment center, dining room and study hall.

3. Three of the cousins sleep on mattresses on the floor.

4. She stays up half the night copying over notes.

5. They sit in a circle and have dinner together as a family.

6. Vinh washes the dishes.

In the following spaces, list the subjects and the verbs from the preceding sentences. Some of the verbs end in -*s* and some do not. If the verb ends in -*s*, list it in the left column. If it does not end in -*s*, list it in the right column. (The first two have been done for you.)

| Subject | -*s* ending | Subject | no -*s* ending |
|---|---|---|---|
| The living room | serves | Khan Duong and her cousins | live |
| _____ | _____ | _____ | _____ |
| _____ | _____ | _____ | _____ |

Look at the subjects and verbs you have listed. Is the subject singular or plural when the verb has an -s ending? Is the subject singular or plural when the verb does not have an -s or -es ending? Now complete the sentences in the box.

---

In the present tense, when the subject is plural, the verb

_____ an -s ending. In the present tense, when the subject
has/does not have

is singular, the verb _____ an -s or -es ending.
has/does not have

---

# Paragraph Skills

## What Is a Paragraph?

A paragraph is a guide for the reader. It shows what the writer thinks is important, what belongs together, and where a new idea begins. Paragraphs help the reader digest writing, just as breaking up a meal into courses such as soup, salad, main dish, and dessert helps in the digestion of a meal. If all the food from a meal was piled on the table in front of you at once, you might not know where to begin to eat. When writers do not use paragraphs, readers often cannot understand the big blocks of sentences piled up in front of them. So a clear, considerate writer breaks up ideas into paragraphs.

*A paragraph begins with an indented line.* This makes it stand out from the rest of the text. A paragraph is not too long, usually not more than 250 words, but you do not have to count the number of words. You can use your judgment. *When your ideas are changing or when you want to divide a general concept into smaller parts, you should begin a new paragraph. A paragraph is a group of sentences related to a single subject.*

*A paragraph usually has a topic sentence or main idea* that tells the reader what the paragraph is about. *This topic sentence can appear anywhere in the paragraph. Sometimes it is implied, which means that it is not actually stated,* but the reader can find it by inferring or reading into what the author has written.

*A paragraph may have different purposes in a piece of writing.* It may explain a concept introduced in a topic sentence. It may illustrate a point or give support to an argument. Each paragraph works together with the rest of the paragraphs in a letter, essay, story, or book to help the reader understand the writer's point of view.

Fill in the following blanks with the seven characteristics of a paragraph emphasized above.

_____

_____

_____

_____

_____

_____

_____

Paragraphs make writing easier to read. They help the reader know how the writer thinks. The following piece of writing would be easier to read if it were divided into paragraphs. Read it with a classmate and decide where new paragraphs should begin. Remember that each time you begin a totally new thought, you should indent for a new paragraph. Most writers agree that there should be three paragraphs in the following exercise.

The article about the Vietnamese immigrants made me think of my experiences learning English when I first moved to the United States. I was thirteen, very shy, and afraid to meet new people. So when I began school, I sat way in the back of the room. I spent most of my day staring at the gray floors, hoping my teacher would not call on me. When he did, I would get all mixed up, and I even forgot things I had practiced at home. Sometimes I had trouble understanding the way he pronounced words. Everything changed the day I met Cynthia. She sat near me in class, and one day she talked to me on the way to the cafeteria. She spoke slowly and I understood her. We had lunch together and that was the beginning of our friendship. She taught me many words, and she introduced me to other people. I began to use English, and after a while it didn't even bother me if people laughed a little when I made a mistake. Cynthia helped me with my homework too, and I started to understand more. I didn't have to stare at the floor anymore. I even began to raise my hand to ask some questions. It seems to me that if someone wants to learn a language, the person has to use it a lot. It also helps to practice with a friend. I probably would have learned English one day anyhow, but Cynthia certainly made it easier for me in the beginning.

## Editing Skills: Plurals

One common problem in editing writing and looking for surface errors is recognizing plural forms. Test your knowledge of plurals in the next paragraph. There are twenty missing plurals in this paragraph. Can you find them all?

Thousands of man, woman, and child have left Vietnam to come to the United State. They have had to leave their parent, friend, and family behind. When these person arrived, they suffered many crisis; often they found their life were difficult. They had to attend class to learn the new language, and they usually had to move to overcrowded city in order to get job opportunity. Traditionally, person have come to the United State from country all over the world. Despite the many difficulty of adjusting, these immigrant give a vitality to the country and the country offers many possibility to these newcomer.

Turn to page 342 to check your answers. If you had more than two mistakes, you should review the following rules.

### regular plurals

The regular plural of a word is usually formed by adding an -s to the singular form. The article about Khan Duong and her family has many examples of regular plurals.

| Singular | Plural |
|----------|--------|
| cousin | cousins |
| parent | parents |
| newcomer | newcomers |

Can you find three more examples of regular plurals in the article? List them with the singular forms on the left, as shown above.

|         |         |
|----------|--------|
| _____ | _____ |
| _____ | _____ |
| _____ | _____ |

**special rules**

There are also many words that follow special rules to form their plurals.

Words that end in a consonant (*b,c,d,f,g,* and so on) plus *y* form their plurals by changing the *y* to *i* and adding *es*.

| | |
|---|---|
| body | bodies |
| country | countries |
| baby | _____ |
| library | _____ |
| city | _____ |
| family | _____ |

Words that end in a vowel (*a,e,i,o,u*) plus *y* form their plurals by adding *s*.

| | |
|---|---|
| monkey | monkeys |
| turkey | _____ |
| ashtray | _____ |
| boy | _____ |
| highway | _____ |

Words that end in *s, sh, ch, ss, zz,* or *x* usually form their plurals by adding *es*.

| | | | |
|---|---|---|---|
| plus | pluses | mattress | _____ |
| brush | brushes | wish | _____ |
| patch | patches | watch | _____ |
| class | classes | business | _____ |
| fizz | fizzes | buzz | _____ |
| wax | waxes | tax | _____ |

Words that end in one *z* usually double the *z* and add *es*.

quiz    quizzes    whiz    _____

Words that end in *o* usually form their plurals by adding *es*.

tomato    tomatoes    hero    _____

veto    vetoes    mosquito    _____

Many words that end in *f* or *fe* form their plurals by changing the *f* to *v* and adding *es*.

life    lives    housewife    _____

knife    knives    yourself    _____

leaf    leaves    wolf    _____

calf    calves    half    _____

There are some exceptions to this rule, however.

roof    roofs
belief    beliefs

### irregular plurals

Some words have irregular plurals. This means that the plurals have special forms and do not use the regular *-s* form we have already learned. Some examples of irregular plurals are:

man    men    woman    women
child    children    foot    feet
tooth    teeth    goose    geese
mouse    mice    ox    oxen

Here are some other words with special plurals:

crisis    crises (crucial turning point in politics, story, play, or everyday life)

criterion    criteria (standard or rule to judge something by)

axis    axes (fixed or center line about which things are arranged as in a graph or a globe) medium        media (means or agency; instrument of communication)

**special words**

There are some words that always end in *s*, yet they are not plural. These words are treated as singular in sentences. They are followed by the singular form of the verb, as you can see in the following examples.

news         No news is good news.
                     The news is on television at six o'clock.

measles      Measles is a very contagious disease and many children get sick from it.

mumps       Even though it is usually not a serious sickness for children, mumps is often dangerous for adult males.

There are also a few words for which the plural form is the same as the singular form.

sheep       There is one sheep who got lost from the flock.
                There are thousands of sheep in New Zealand.

fish          The shiny silver fish is swimming downstream.
                They saw hundreds of fish in the aquarium.

deer         The deer is a very graceful animal.
                Many deer live in the woods.

moose       The moose is a large animal that looks like a deer.
                Moose have large antlers.

**EXERCISE**

In the following paragraph there are twenty missing plurals. Using what you have just practiced, make the corrections.

Khan Duong and her family are not all that unusual. There are many family of young man and woman and sometimes even child from many country all over the world who are living in and trying to adapt to the big city of the United State. At first, they get lost trying to find bus that will take them to job, library, movie, and school. They have many difficulty communicating with their new neighbor. Eventually though, their life begin to make sense again. The successful one start their own business, make new friend, find new responsibility, and develop new strategy for living in their new country.

**EXTRA PRACTICE**

Here is an amusing poem that helps illustrate some of the problems of learning the rules for plurals in English. If you want some extra practice, circle all the acceptable plurals in the poem and put an *x* under the nonsense plurals.

### Why English Is So Hard

We'll begin with a box, and the plural is boxes;
  But the plural of ox should be oxen, not oxes.
Then one fowl is goose, but two are called geese;
  Yet the plural of moose should never be meese.

You may find a lone mouse or a whole lot of mice;
  But the plural of house is houses, not hice.
If the plural of man is always called men,
  Why shouldn't the plural of pan be called pen?

The cow in the plural may be cows or kine.
  But the plural of vow is vows, not vine.
And I speak of a foot and you show me your feet.
  But I give you a boot—would a pair be called beet?

If one is a tooth and a whole set are teeth,
  Why shouldn't the plural of booth be called beeth?
If the singular is this, and the plural is these,
  Should the plural of kiss be nicknamed kese?

Then one may be that, and three may be those,
  Yet the plural of hat would never be hose.
We speak of a brother, and also the brethren,
  But though we say mother, we never say methren.

The masculine pronouns are he, his, and him.
  But imagine the feminine she, shis, and shim!
So our English, I think you will all agree,
  Is the trickiest language you ever did see!

ANONYMOUS

## Editing Skills Paragraph

When editing your writing, look for surface mistakes, the kinds of mistakes that a writer makes in the first draft. One way to improve your editing skills is to practice. The following paragraph is a first draft. Read it carefully and make the necessary changes so that the paragraph is free of surface errors. Below is a list of the types of errors in the paragraph and the number of times each type occurs. If you have difficulty finding some of the errors, review the appropriate parts of the chapter.

| | |
|---|---|
| 4 subject/verb agreement errors | 4 plural form errors |
| 2 preposition errors | 1 *make/do* error |

All the student from Mr. Alexander's English class on Barrett College spends time on the library. Every week each student borrow a book and read it in order to make the homeworks. One student has read four books on child because she want to be a child psychologist. Another student has an interest in economic and has read many books on that subject. The whole class seems to be benefiting from its library experience.

Answers are on p. 342.

# Essay Skills

## Getting Started

**the use of the anecdote**

Most people find that the hardest part of writing is getting started. They feel that if they can just get those first few lines on the page, they will be able to write the rest of their piece with ease.

There are many techniques for getting started. Some are quite formal, such as outlining or following a particular model or pattern. Some are very informal, such as brainstorming, clustering, relaxation exercises, and/or visualizing. We will explore many of these techniques in this book, and you will find out what works best for you. There is no one correct way for all writers. Each of us has an individual pattern of writing. The more you write, the more you will learn about how you write best.

In this chapter, we will explore one way to start an essay. It is to begin with an anecdote or short story taken from your personal experience or from something you have heard. The anecdote should relate to the topic of your essay. This allows for a smooth transition to the body of your essay. You will notice that many magazine and newspaper writers use this technique. It is a good way to engage the reader, that is, to get the reader interested in reading what you have written. Audience engagement is an important aspect of successful writing. If the reader is interested in your writing, then communication is going on between writer and reader. This is the real purpose of writing.

If you look at the first paragraph of the article that begins this chapter, you will see an anecdotal introduction. The writer tells us a short story about Khan Duong's daily life. Notice that it is written in the present tense and, therefore, tells us what she does routinely. The second paragraph seems ironic at first. We ask ourselves how this hardworking student could possibly be failing. We are engaged; we want to read more.

She stays up half the night copying over the notes she took in class, hoping the repetition alone will help her absorb the English. She keeps long lists of vocabulary words and has not missed a day of school since she began. She gets all of her assignments done early—including the report on "Death of a Salesman," but after reading the play at least four times, she is still not sure who the salesman is.

And Khan Duong, who is 20 years old, is failing at Newtown High School.

**EXERCISES**

1. In a newspaper, school paper, or news magazine, find an essay or article that begins with an anecdote or short story and share it with the class.

2. If you have an essay that you have already written that begins in a different way, try rewriting the introduction using an anecdote. Share both versions with a class member and discuss which introduction seems more interesting and why. Which do you prefer and why?

## Suggested Writing Topics

One of the most important parts of writing comes before you even put your pen onto your paper. It occurs when you are thinking about what you are going to write. For some people this takes more time than for others. Some people close their eyes when they think, and some stare at the wall or at the person in front of them. Do whatever feels right for you, but be sure to allow yourself some time to think before you write.

Choose one of the following topics to write about. You may find it useful to look at your journal for ideas.

1. Tell a story about someone who has had problems learning English or getting used to living in a new country. What has this person learned from facing these problems?

2. Write a letter to Khan Duong telling her how you feel about her situation and offering her advice.

3. Compare your experience living in a new country and learning a new language with Khan Duong's experience. Use the article for information.

4. Many people say that learning a new language is easier for children than it is for adults. Do you agree or disagree? Explain your point of view, telling about yourself and people you have known or read about. Try to convince your audience.

## Revising

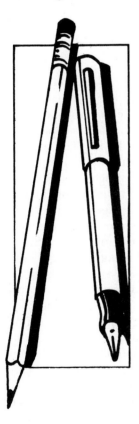

When you finish writing, you should look over your writing for surface errors, but that is only one part of your job as a writer. Another important part of writing is revising. This involves examining your work for its meaning. Writers naturally revise as they write; they look back at what they have already written and make changes. Writing involves much rereading and rewriting. When a piece is completed in its first draft, it is helpful to separate yourself from your work, even if you can only look away from it for a couple of minutes. Of course it is best if you can put your writing away for a day or so, but this is usually not possible in class.

When you do look at your writing again, do not focus on the surface errors. Instead, look to see if you have really said what you wanted to say. Is your writing clear? Are there enough examples? Could someone who didn't know you understand what you are trying to say? Is everything in a logical order? You may want to move things around or rearrange parts of your writing. You may want to add or cross out. You may decide to change words. Remember that all writers do this. In a *Paris Review* interview, Nobel Prize–winning writer Ernest Hemingway was asked how much rewriting he did.

Hemingway: It depends. I rewrote the ending of *A Farewell to Arms*, the last page of it, thirty-nine times before I was satisfied with it.
Interviewer: Was there some technical problem there? What was it that had stumped you?
Hemingway: Getting the words right.

No one writes perfectly the first time. See how much you can improve your writing by revising it. Imagine a piece of your writing in a room with a person who has never met you, and make your writing speak for you.

# CHAPTER TWO

# The Importance of Knowing a Second Language

*The following excerpt, "The Importance of Knowing a Second Language," comes from* Language Two, *a book that describes the process of acquiring a second language. It explains why knowledge of a second language is important in today's world.*

**O**ver a billion people in the world speak more than one language    1
fluently. In the Philippines, for example, many people must
speak three languages if they are to engage fully in their community's social affairs. They must speak the national language, Pilipino;
one of the eighty-seven local vernaculars; and English or Spanish.    5
In small countries, such as the Netherlands or Israel, most children
are required to study at least one foreign language in school, and
sometimes several. Most adults in the Netherlands speak German,
French, and English in addition to Dutch. Even in the United States,
whose inhabitants are notoriously unconcerned about languages other  10
than English, about 10% of the residents usually speak at least one
language in addition to English in the course of their daily lives (National Center for Education Statistics, 1978). Throughout much of
the world, being able to speak at least two languages, and sometimes
three or four, is necessary to function in society.    15

In business affairs, foreign language needs loom° large. Economic
futurists° say that knowledge of a foreign language will be among
the most sought after skills for business people from the 1980s on
into the twenty-first century. A 1979 editorial by Grace Hechinger
of *The New York Times* reminded American business people that most  20
Japanese merchants bring fluent English to their transactions in the
United States. Americans doing business in Japan, on the other hand,
are often encumbered° with the need for translators. This, according to Hechinger, may be one reason that Japanese companies are
so often more successful in the United States than American com-    25
panies are in Japan.

°appear large or threatening
°people who study the future

°burdened

Despite the evident need for foreign language skills, a survey of the top U.S. corporation executives with responsibilities in export development and overseas manufacturing revealed that less than half of those who were born in the United States spoke a language other 30 than English (Craighead, 1980). In contrast, 80% of the foreign-born executives spoke a language in addition to English, and 59% spoke three or more languages!

Survival language skills or business needs are not the only compelling reasons for learning a second language. Neurolinguistic re- 35 search is beginning to suggest that people who know more than one language make use of more of the brain than monolinguals do (Albert and Obler, 1978). Though the evidence is scant, it appears that the part of the brain that is used in second language functioning remains undeveloped in monolingual brains. Albert and Obler (1978) 40 reviewed a series of post-mortem studies on polyglot brains—brains of people who spoke from three to twenty-six languages—and found that certain parts of these brains were especially well developed and markedly furrowed.°

°wrinkled or filled with grooves

Psycholinguistic studies further indicate that people who control 45 more than one language are verbally more skillful than monolinguals, and they mature earlier with respect to linguistic abstraction skills. Lerea and Laporta (1971) and Palmer (1972) report, for example, that bilinguals have better auditory memory than monolinguals, and Slobin (1968) found that bilinguals are better at intuiting° 50 meaning from unknown words. Feldman and Shen (1971) discovered that low-income bilingual children were better at learning new labels than low-income monolinguals, and Peale and Lambert (1962) concluded that ten-year-olds who spoke both French and English demonstrated higher skill in linguistic abstraction than their mono- 55 lingual counterparts. Expanding mental abilities, therefore, may be reason enough to learn a second language.

°knowing without studying

# Vocabulary Development

### words dealing with language

This reading introduces many new words that deal with language. These are valuable words for you to be able to understand and use. All languages, including English, are constantly changing. New words are always being added. Some come from other languages, some from new technology, and some from adding endings (suffixes) or beginnings (prefixes) to base forms.

The word *vernacular* comes from the Latin word *vernaculus,* which means domestic or native. It refers to the native language of a place, the common everyday speech, the dialect. Many of you come from countries in which one language is taught in school and another is spoken at home or on the street. The language spoken on the street is the vernacular.

Another group of words comes from the Latin word *lingua,* which refers to the tongue. You have probably heard languages referred to as "tongues." Many words that describe language and language learning come from this base. A linguist is a person who studies language and language learning. There are special fields for studying language: a neurolinguist studies the effect of the brain and the nervous system on language; a psycholinguist studies how people learn languages and how the mind works in relation to language. A person who speaks only one language is monolingual. A person who speaks two languages with about the same proficiency is bilingual. A person who speaks many languages is multilingual, but is usually called a polyglot or a linguist.

*Mono-, bi-,* and *poly-* are commonly used prefixes. On the basis of what you have just read, can you figure out the meaning of the following words? A person who has one spouse (marriage partner) is monogamous. A person who has two spouses is _____gamous. And a person who has many spouses is _____gamous.

You can probably find many other words that use these prefixes in your dictionary. Learning base forms such as *lingua* and prefixes such as *mono-, bi-,* and *poly-* is one way to increase your vocabulary.

# Reading and Thinking Skills

## Comprehension Questions

1. What do economic futurists say will be the most sought after skill for business people from the 1980s on into the twenty-first century?

2. According to Craighead's 1980 study, what percentage of U.S. corporation executives who had responsibilities in export development and overseas manufacturing spoke a language other than English? What percentage of the foreign executives in comparable jobs spoke three or more languages?

3. According to the reading, what differences have been found between people who are monolingual and people who are bilingual or who are polyglots?

## Discussion Activities

### Analysis and Conclusions

1. In the first paragraph of the article, the authors state that people who live in small countries are required to study at least one foreign language in school. Why is it particularly important for people who live in small countries to be bilingual or multilingual?

2. "Economic futurists say that knowledge of a foreign language will be among the most sought after skills for business people from the 1980s on into the twenty-first century." What kind of jobs do you think people who speak more than one language are best qualified for?

3. Imagine a family in which the mother and father each speak a different language and belong to a different culture. What effects might this have on the development of their children?

### Writing and Point of View

1. In small groups of three or four students, discuss what this selection is about. Do the authors convince you that it is important to know a second language? How do they do this?

2. Compare the excerpt in this chapter with the article about Khan Duong in chapter 1. Do you notice any differences in writing style? What audience does this piece seem to be written for? Which piece of writing is easier to read? Why?

3. What is the purpose of this excerpt? If you wanted to rewrite this piece to convince people that they should learn a second language, what would you add and/or delete?

### Personal Response and Evaluation

1. The authors state that people in the United States are in general unconcerned with languages other than English. In your experience, have you found this to be true? If so, why do you think this is the case?

2. Using the telephone can be difficult if English is not your first language. Why is this so? How does body language help you to communicate? Describe some language experiences you have had on the telephone.

3. A famous linguist, Benjamin Lee Whorf, reported that in the Eskimo language there are ten different words for snow (see the list), depending on whether the snow is falling, has fallen, is soft, or is hard and crusty. One possible explanation for this is that

because of their environment the Eskimos observe snow more carefully than people in other countries need to do. Can you suggest any other explanations? Can you think of some ways in which your language differs greatly from English? Are there words that cannot be translated and ideas that are very difficult or impossible to express in English?

| | |
|---|---|
| sillik* | hard, crusty snow |
| nutagak | fresh snow, powder snow |
| aniu | packed snow |
| pukak | sugar snow (near ground) |
| auksalak | melting snow |
| akillukkak | soft snow |
| milik | very soft snow |
| mitailak | soft snow on ice floe covering open spot |
| kiksrukak | glazed snow in thaw time |
| katik sunik | light snow, deep for walking |

*Social Psychology*, 1974, p. 106

## Role Playing

Bilingual education means that students are taught in two languages. Subjects or content areas are taught in the students' first or native language, and English (or the language students are studying) is taught only in the English classroom. Some people think that bilingual education makes it difficult for a student to succeed in an English-speaking environment and, therefore, does not prepare the student for the outside world. Others believe that bilingual education helps the child to enjoy school and to succeed. They believe that the child will be motivated to learn English by living in an English-speaking environment.

Divide the class into two groups, one in favor of bilingual education and the other opposed. Debate the issues, using personal experiences and observations to support points of view. You might want to videotape or tape record this debate, and then review it and discuss what occurred.

## Journal Writing

You will write if you will write without thinking of the result in terms of a result, but think of the writing in terms of discovery, which is to say that creation must take place between the pen and the paper, not before in a thought or afterwards in a recasting. . . . It will come if it is there and if you will let it come.

GERTRUDE STEIN

What you write in your journal should come from you, from your heart. The following are some suggestions that may help you decide what you want to write. Think about your experiences learning English. Has it been easy for you? What kinds of problems have you had? Have you discovered anything new about yourself by learning a new language? Do you like English? Do you feel or act differently when you speak in English? When you dream, what language do you dream in?

One student wrote in his journal, "It hurts my ears to listen to English for a long time. The sounds are sharp and come by so fast that I get a headache listening to it." Have you ever felt this way?

# Word Skills

## Idiomatic Expressions

Each of the following paragraphs contains a context clue that will help you understand some of the idiomatic expressions used in the excerpt. Underline these context clues; the first one has been done for you. Then use the expressions when you answer the questions at the end of each paragraph.

### *at least* (page 24, line 7)

In the Netherlands, children are required to study at least one foreign language in school. They are permitted to study no less than one new language. This is not true everywhere in the United States. What do you think? Is it important for people to know at least one language other than their native language?

### *on the other hand* (page 24, line 22)

Most people agree that it is important to know as many languages as possible. On the other hand, or conversely, many people say that they do not have the time or the ability to learn a new language. Learning a new language is not easy, but in your experience, on the other hand, has it been worth it?

***with respect to*** (page 25, line 47)

Bilinguals and multilinguals seem to be more skillful with respect to verbal skills. In relation to communication, they have made a real effort to reach out to new people and new cultures. Do you think bilingualism adds to or enhances a person with respect to anything else?

***in the course of*** (page 24, line 12)

In the course of talking to someone, you do more than listen to that person's words. While the other person is talking, you pay attention to body language. You look at the person's face, watch his or her hand movements, and listen to the tone of voice. What clues to meaning do you look for in the course of a conversation?

Now use these idiomatic expressions in sentences of your own.

---

## Articles

**the**

In paragraphs 1 and 2 of the excerpt, find five country names. Copy them in the spaces provided below. If *the* comes before the country name, then copy it too. The first one has been done for you.

the Philippines

_____

_____

_____

_____

Notice that some place names occur with *the* and some do not. *The* does not occur with names of continents:

| | |
|---|---|
| Australia | Africa |
| South America | Europe |

In general, *the* does not occur with country names:

France      Turkey

Japan       Chile

unless the name of the country refers to a political union or association:

the Soviet Union                    the British Commonwealth

the United Arab Republic

or unless it uses common nouns plus a proper noun with an *of* phrase:

the Dominion of Canada                    the Kingdom of Thailand

the Union of Soviet Socialist Republics

or unless it is plural:

the West Indies      the United States

In general, *the* does not occur with names of cities:

New York      Paris

Bangkok       Caracas

For some cities, however, the article has become part of the name:

Las Vegas      Le Havre

*The* is used for names of mountain ranges:

the Himalayas      the Alps

but it is not used with the name of a single mountain:

Bear Mountain      Mount Everest

*The* is used with most bodies of water:

the Pacific Ocean                    the Red Sea

the Mississippi River

but it is not used with lakes and bays:

Lake Erie      Hudson Bay

unless they are plural:

the Great Lakes          the Finger Lakes

*The* is used with deserts, forests, and peninsulas:

the Sahara Desert          the Black Forest

*The* is used with the names of geographic areas and points on the globe:

the Northwest          the Midwest
the South Pole          the Equator

*The* is not used with names of languages:

Mandarin          Arabic
Spanish          Korean

These are some of the rules for using *the* with place names and languages. Apply these rules to the following sentences. Write *the* in the space if it is needed; otherwise leave the space blank.

1. _____ English is the primary language spoken in _____ Australia, which is located between _____ Indian Ocean and _____ Pacific Ocean.

2. The enormous land mass extending from _____ Russia in _____ north to _____ Iran in _____ south and eastward via _____ Afghanistan and _____ Pakistan to _____ northern India and _____ Bangladesh is predominantly Indo-European in speech.

3. The Malayo-Polynesian language family includes languages spoken in _____ Indonesia, _____ Madagascar, _____ Philippines, and other islands as far east as _____ Hawaii.

4. The Sino-Tibetan group is the second largest language family

in number of speakers; the major languages in this group are

_____ Burmese, dialects of _____ Chinese, _____ Thai and

_____ Tibetan. However, the majority of speakers in this group

speak _____ Mandarin and _____ Cantonese.

5. Some important language families are found on the continent of

_____ Africa and throughout _____ Middle East.

**EXTRA
PRACTICE**

Use the rules you have just learned to correct the six *the* errors in the following paragraph. In some cases you will need to delete *the*, and in others you must add *the*.

My best friend moved to the New Jersey from the Philippines three years ago. Now she lives in the Hoboken and she can see Hudson River and the boat that travels up to the Bear Mountain each day. She has learned to speak the English and she plans to travel to the Canada next year as an exchange student.

## Use of Modals

**must**

In paragraph 1 of the reading, we find the following:

. . . many people must speak three languages
. . . most children are required to study at least one foreign language.
. . . being able to speak . . . two languages . . . is necessary to function in society.

In the reading, underline these sentence parts. Notice that the meaning of "must," "be required to," and "be necessary to" is almost the same or synonymous. They all mean "have to."

$$\left.\begin{array}{l} \text{must} \\ \text{(to be) required to} \\ \text{(to be) necessary to} \end{array}\right] = \text{have to}$$

In the United States, each person *has to* pay taxes.
In the United States, each person *must* pay taxes.

In the United States, each person *is required to* pay taxes.
In the United States, *it is necessary for* each person to pay taxes.

Rewrite the following sentence in the places provided, using each of the patterns shown above.

In order to learn a new language, you *have to* practice every day.

_____

_____

_____

## Commonly Confused Words

### to/two/too

People in the United States are *too* ready *to* tell other people in the world *to* learn English, although the majority of Americans can speak only one language. Throughout much of the world, being able *to* speak at least *two* languages, and sometimes three or four, is necessary *to* function in society.

Examine how *to, two,* and *too* are used in the preceding paragraph. On the basis of what you observe, complete the following definitions.

_____ refers to the number 2.

_____ means "also" or "overly."

_____ means "toward" or is part of the infinitive verb form.

Fill in the blanks in the following sentences with *to, two,* or *too.*

1. Knowledge of _____ or more languages makes travel _____

   different countries more interesting and rewarding _____.

2. Scientists are beginning _____ believe that people who know

   _____ or more languages make more use of their brains than
   monolinguals.

3. Therefore, when it comes _____ languages, there is no such

   thing as _____ much knowledge.

Now write your own sentences using *to, two,* and *too.*

# Sentence Skills

## Simple Present Tense

In Chapter 1, we looked at how the simple present tense can be used to express habitual or routine activities. In the selection in this chapter, the authors use the simple present tense to express a general state of being. This means something that is a generally accepted fact or theory. It is thought of as almost timeless and includes the past, the present, and the future. Here are two examples: The sun rises in the east. The earth revolves around the sun. These are general truths.

Review paragraph 1 on page 24. Notice that each sentence refers to a general state of being and is written in the simple present tense. The following exercise is a review of subject/verb agreement in this tense. Draw a rectangle around the subject of each sentence and a circle around the verb. The first sentence has been done for you.

1. [Over a billion people in the world] (speak) more than one language fluently.

2. In business affairs, foreign language needs loom large.

3. Economic futurists say that knowledge of a foreign language will be among the most sought after skills.

**EXERCISE**

In the following paragraph, fill in each blank with an appropriate verb. Some verb suggestions are: *begin, seem, start, try, feel, think,* and *believe.* You may also choose other verbs; there are many correct possibilities. Experiment and see how changing the verb can change the meaning of the paragraph.

Many linguists _____ we can learn a lot about language from observing children. Every normal child _____ to learn language in a similar way. From birth on, a baby _____ to imitate language sounds. Then from about the age of two, a child _____ to speak in words and sentences. The child _____ to communicate. By the time a child is five or six, the child has constructed a grammar that is basically the same as that of most of the adult population.

The preceding paragraph tells about a generally accepted theory. It is timeless, so we use the simple present tense. Check the verbs you have written in and make sure you used the *s* ending when it was necessary.

## Point of View/Voice

Everything that is written is written from someone's point of view or perspective. When we write, we must decide who will narrate or be the voice for what we write. We have several voices to choose from; we refer to these as "persons."

There is first-person singular and plural, second-person _____ and _____, and _____-person singular and plural. First-person singular is *I.* First-person _____ is *we.* Second-person singular is *you.* _____-_____ plural is *you.* Third-person singular is *she, he, it, one,* or a singular subject. Third-person _____ is *they* or a plural subject.

In general, first person is more personal and third person is more formal. We rarely use second person for essay writing. Whatever person is used, it is important to maintain a consistent point of view. If a writer moves from person to person in a single piece of writing, it can be confusing to the reader. In the following paragraph, the writer did not maintain a consistent person. Change the paragraph so that it is consistent.

We can learn about language learning by observing yourselves. The problems that they have probably can be generalized to other language learners. Although they may think English is more difficult to learn than another language, David Crystal, a noted linguist, tells us in his book *Linguistics* that there is no such thing as a most complex language. "A thing is more difficult to do depending on how much practice we have had at doing it, and how used we are to doing similar things." Based on that statement, you can learn that if we really want to learn a new language, we must practice.

---

# Paragraph Skills

## Using Facts to Develop Paragraphs

An effective way to convince our readers that we know something about our subject is to use supporting facts and details. Facts contain proven or verifiable information about a subject. On the other hand, opinions tell what someone thinks or believes about a subject. Opinions are not yet proven.

**EXERCISE**

In the blanks provided, mark whether each of the following sentences is a fact or an opinion.

_____ 1. It is hard to learn a new language.

_____ 2. Most adults in Israel know more than one language.

_____ 3. One reason why Japanese companies are successful in the United States may be because most Japanese merchants know how to speak English.

_____ 4. A survey of U.S. corporation executives showed that less than 50% of them spoke a language other than English.

**EXTRA PRACTICE**

With a classmate, read paragraphs 1–3 on pages 24–25. Decide whether each sentence is a fact or an opinion.

---

## Transitions

**general to specific**

When we write, we try to connect our ideas so that our readers can follow our thinking. One way to do this is to use connecting or transitional words and phrases. We will examine various types of transitions throughout this book. One type of transition is from the general to the specific, from broad, large references to smaller, more specific ones. Paragraph 1 of the excerpt in this chapter is here adapted in a slightly changed form showing only the transitions from broad or general to narrow or more specific and then back to general again.

Over a billion people in the world _____

_____. In small countries, such as _____,

_____. Most adults in _____

_____. In the United States, the residents _____

_____. Large   countries,   such   as   _____,

_____. Throughout   most   of   the   world

_____.

Notice the pattern from general to more specific and then back to general again, which is further shown in the diagram.

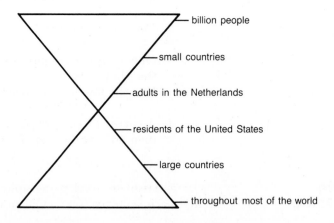

Using this model, try to create a paragraph of your own about any subject you are interested in. One example is shown here.

*Over a billion people in the world* are women. *In some small countries* such as Iran, there are special rules about how women should behave and be treated. *Most adults in these countries* respect these rules. *In the United States, the residents* believe that women and men should be equal. *In other large countries* such as Russia and China, women and men are usually treated as equals. *Throughout the world,* however, there are many countries in which women are treated differently from men.

## Capital Letters

When editing for surface errors, many writers have difficulty with capital letters. Test your knowledge of capital letters by trying to find the thirty missing capital letters in the following paragraph.

Sung Hee moved to massachusetts from korea. She attended boston university and lived in a dorm with her cousin. She began to work on saturday nights in filene's, a big department store, and she practiced english with her customers. on sundays Sung Hee usually rented a little chevrolet from avis. Carrying a tourist book called *inside massachusetts,* she visited such historic sites as plymouth rock and old north church. She spent hours at the boston public library looking at the john singer sargent murals. She met tony at a midnight showing of *casablanca,* and last christmas they said "i do." Now she is teaching tony korean and planning to travel home to introduce him to her family.

Turn to page 343 to check your answers. If you had more than two mistakes, you should review the following rules.

Capital letters are used for

*the first word in a sentence, names of people, and "I"*
My mother hopes that I will marry Eric soon.

*names of the months, days of the week, and holidays*
Miguel was born in November, on the fourth Thursday, Thanksgiving Day.

*names of particular places, languages, and nationalities*
The Brazilian girl in my class speaks French because she went to Le Havre High School in Montreal.
(*Do not use capital letters if the specific names are not used:*
He enjoys attending college and working in a store, but he likes to have time to visit museums and churches.)

*titles of books, magazines, newspapers, stories, articles, films, television programs, songs, and poems*
When I saw Aida she was carrying *The Silent Language, Psychology Today,* and the *Washington Post.*
She was going to see the movie *Salvador* with her class.

*first word in a direct quotation*
Tony said, "You can really do a lot if you try."

*brand names of products*
    The man bought Pampers and Pepsi-Cola in the A&P.
*names of religious and political groups, companies, corporations, and clubs*
    Françoise joined the Republican party when she was in college, but she became less active when she started to work for General Motors because she was very busy with her job, her commitment to Catholicism, and to Literacy Volunteers of America.

**EXERCISE**

    Below is part of paragraph 2 of the reading that began this chapter. All the capital letters have been removed. Using the rules above, fill in the missing capital letters. When you have finished, go back to the reading and check your answers.

    a 1979 editorial by grace hechinger of *the new york times* reminded american business people that most japanese merchants bring fluent english to their transactions in the united states. americans doing business in japan, on the other hand, are often encumbered with the need for translators. this, according to hechinger, may be one reason that japanese companies are so often more successful in the united states than american companies are in japan.

**EXTRA PRACTICE**

    The following paragraph has thirty-five missing capital letters. Can you find them all?

    when martin and fatima volunteered to work one afternoon in the westville college post office, they were in for a surprise. in one corner, there were many boxes piled high. they found three heavy cartons of english jam and jelly addressed to professor honey white, now of the ford foundation. she had left the school back in february and had moved to new jersey. fatima accidentally opened a box filled with the wordstar programs needed for the college ibm computers. "mr. smith, this post office is a mess," martin told the postmaster. "i know it, son. we just have to get a little more organized. the u.s. mail has to go through and we will do it. soon." martin and fatima left there wondering if the college mail would ever get through.

The answers are on page 343.

## Editing Skills Paragraph

All writers make surface errors in their first drafts. Sometimes it is difficult to find your own errors, but practice will help you improve your editing skills. Below is a first draft and a list of the types of errors it contains and the number of times each type occurs. Use the list to help you with editing this paragraph. Answers are on p. 343.

| | |
|---|---|
| 4 subject/verb agreement errors | 3 preposition errors |
| 4 *the* errors | 3 plural errors |
| 12 capital letter errors | 3 inconsistencies in person |

Marie learn languages very easily. She was born on haiti and has spoken the french and the creole all her lives. Now marie also know the english, spanish, and italian. She has a special technique that always work for her. At night you go to sleep by hypnotizing yourself as you stare at a poster of the stained glasses window in notre dame on the paris. Her sony walkman tape deck is in her head, and she listen to a different language tapes each night.

# Essay Skills

## Getting Started

**using observations**

Getting started is one of the hardest parts of writing. We looked at one technique in the last chapter; another useful technique to help you begin is simply to look around and closely observe your world. Many times a closer examination of your environment or your life can offer valuable insights that will make your writing richer and more interesting. Your reader may learn from what you have written. Just as scientists use observations to uncover facts, you too may learn more about your subject from your observations. For example, if you were writing about the college experience in the United States, you could observe your own classroom, the school cafeteria, the library, and the halls to create generalizations. Your observations may lead to more fully developed essays. A student begins:

I attend a large school in a big city. In all my classes, there are more female than male students. For example, in this writing class, there are fifteen female students and only nine males. Many of the female students are returning to school after raising their children. They are more mature than the average first-year college students. . . .

If you are writing about conformity, look around your classroom and count how many students are wearing jeans and how many are not. Quickly calculate the percentage and use it in your essay.

Seventy percent of the students in this writing class are wearing jeans. . . .

Information can also come by closely observing yourself and others, and then reflecting on those observations. For example, you may notice that male students raise their hands in class more often than females, or that female students do better on essay questions. You might also observe how you have learned English. At first, was it easiest to listen, speak, read, or write? How did your skills advance? If you have children or brothers and sisters, compare their learning of English with your own. Using your observations and reflections in your writing can add information that makes your writing more interesting to your audience.

The following introduction shows how observations can be used in an essay. It is taken from a student esssay about why the world should not be ruled by the majority.

In this classroom, twenty-nine of the thirty desks are made for right-handers. And it is true, there are a lot of right-handers. About 90% of the people I know are right-handed, but what happens to the other 10%? Watching them struggle with scissors, toasters, pencil sharpeners, etc., makes me realize the world is created for the majority, the average. The exceptional 10% is often neglected. What does this mean to the world?

Moreover, making observations and reflections starts you thinking about your subject and, therefore, gives you more to write about and lends support to your point of view. Observation is the beginning of the scientific method; it is the impetus for collecting and arranging data such as were used in the reading in this chapter.

**EXERCISES**

1. In a newspaper, school paper, or magazine article, find an essay or article that contains facts or observations and share it with the class.

2. As a class or small-group activity, develop a series of facts about your classmates. For example, how many of the students have short hair, long hair, curly hair, wear make-up, carry radios? How many of the students have mustaches, wear sneakers, chew gum? How many languages do your fellow students speak? What are they planning to major in? Calculate the percentages. Do you see any interesting patterns emerging?

## Suggested Writing Topics

Give yourself time to think before you write. Observe your classmates and yourself; you may even want to look in your journal for ideas. When you do begin to write, keep your audience in mind. Try to make your writing interesting to your readers as well as to yourself.

1. "Over a billion people in the world speak more than one language fluently." On the basis of what you have read in this article and your own observations, what are some of the reasons why people learn a second language? What are some of the advantages of knowing a second language?

2. Write a letter to your representative in Congress explaining why you feel bilingual education should or should not be funded— that is, financed. (See page 28 for an explanation of bilingual education.) Use your own experiences and observations to support your point of view.

3. Analyze the experience of learning English as a second language. What are some of the problems that many people face when learning English? What do people seem to learn most easily? What takes a long time to learn? You may want to interview some of your classmates and friends, or you might base your essay on your own observations and experiences.

4. Some people believe that all schoolchildren in the United States should be required to show competency in a second language before they can graduate from high school. Do you agree or disagree? Support your point of view with your own observations, experiences, or readings.

## Revising

Revising a piece of writing can be a very personal experience. However, writing is a communicative activity. One way to judge how well your writing is communicating is to share it with a peer. If you and a classmate exchange papers, it is important to show respect for each other's writing. Read slowly and carefully. Do not mark someone else's paper. Afterward ask each other questions and listen carefully to the answers. These answers can help you when you actually rewrite your paper. Some suggestions for questions are:

What do you think I am trying to say?

What did you like best about my essay?

Did any part of it make you stop and read it over in order to understand what I meant?

What do you remember most about my essay without looking at it again?

You will certainly think of more questions, but keep in mind that the purpose is the sharing of writing. You should not evaluate or judge each other's writing, but offer support and suggestions. After discussing your essay in this way, keep your peer's comments and suggestions in mind as you rewrite.

# CHAPTER THREE

# A Day's Wait

*Ernest Hemingway (1899–1961) was a famous American writer who often wrote about relationships. The story "A Day's Wait" is about one day in the life of a father and his young son who is suffering from the flu and a mysterious fear.*

**H**e came into the room to shut the windows while we were still   1
in bed and I saw he looked ill. He was shivering, his face was
white, and he walked slowly as though it ached to move.

"What's the matter, Schatz?"

"I've got a headache."   5

"You better go back to bed."

"No. I'm all right."

"You go to bed. I'll see you when I'm dressed."

But when I came downstairs he was dressed, sitting by the fire,
looking a very sick and miserable boy of nine years. When I put my   10
hand on his forehead I knew he had a fever.

"You go up to bed," I said, "you're sick."

"I'm all right," he said.

When the doctor came he took the boy's temperature.

"What is it?" I asked him.   15

"One hundred and two."

Downstairs, the doctor left three different medicines in different
colored capsules with instructions for giving them. One was to bring
down the fever, another a purgative,° the third to overcome an acid   20
condition. The germs of influenza can only exist in an acid condition, he explained. He seemed to know all about influenza and said
there was nothing to worry about if the fever did not go above one
hundred and four degrees. This was a light epidemic of flu and
there was no danger if you avoided pneumonia.

Back in the room I wrote the boy's temperature down and made   25
a note of the time to give the various capsules.

"Do you want me to read to you?"

"All right. If you want to," said the boy. His face was very white
and there were dark areas under his eyes. He lay still in the bed and
seemed very detached from what was going on.   30

°laxative, cleanser of the bowels

**45**

I read aloud from Howard Pyle's *Book of Pirates;* but I could see he was not following what I was reading.

"How do you feel, Schatz?" I asked him.

"Just the same, so far," he said.

I sat at the foot of the bed and read to myself while I waited for 35 it to be time to give another capsule. It would have been natural for him to go to sleep, but when I looked up he was looking at the foot of the bed, looking very strangely.

"Why don't you try to go to sleep? I'll wake you up for the medicine."

"I'd rather stay awake." 40

After a while he said to me, "You don't have to stay in here with me, Papa, if it bothers you."

"It doesn't bother me."

"No, I mean you don't have to stay if it's going to bother you." 45

I thought perhaps he was a little lightheaded and after giving him the prescribed capsules at eleven o'clock I went out for a while.

°frozen or partly frozen rain

It was a bright, cold day, the ground covered with a sleet° that had frozen so that it seemed as if all the bare trees, the bushes, the cut brush and all the grass and the bare ground had been varnished 50 with ice. I took the young Irish setter° for a little walk up the road and along a frozen creek, but it was difficult to stand or walk on the glassy surface and the red dog slipped and slithered° and I fell twice, hard, once dropping my gun and having it slide away over the ice.

°reddish brown dog often used for hunting

°slid, as on ice

We flushed° a covey° of quail° under a high clay bank with over- 55 hanging brush and I killed two as they went out of sight over the top of the bank. Some of the covey lit in trees, but most of them scattered into brush piles and it was necessary to jump on the ice-coated mounds of brush several times before they would flush. Coming out while you were poised unsteadily on the icy, springy brush 60 they made difficult shooting and I killed two, missed five, and started back pleased to have found a covey close to the house and happy there were so many left to find on another day.

°drove out of hiding
°flock or group
°large wild bird

At the house they said the boy had refused to let any one come into the room.
65

"You can't come in," he said. "You mustn't get what I have."

I went up to him and found him in exactly the position I had left him, white-faced, but with the tops of his cheeks flushed by the fever, staring still, as he had stared, at the foot of the bed.

I took his temperature.
70

"What is it?"

"Something like a hundred," I said. It was one hundred and two and four tenths.

"It was a hundred and two," he said.

"Who said so?"
75

"The doctor."

"Your temperature is all right," I said. "It's nothing to worry about."

"I don't worry," he said, "but I can't keep from thinking."

"Don't think," I said. "Just take it easy."

"I'm taking it easy," he said and looked straight ahead. He was 80 evidently holding tight onto himself about something.

"Take this with water."

"Do you think it will do any good?"

"Of course it will."

I sat down and opened the Pirate book and commenced to read, 85 but I could see he was not following, so I stopped.

"About what time do you think I'm going to die?" he asked.

"What?"

"About how long will it be before I die?"

"You aren't going to die. What's the matter with you?"                90

"Oh, yes, I am. I heard him say a hundred and two."

"People don't die with a fever of one hundred and two. That's a silly way to talk."

"I know they do. At school in France the boys told me you can't live with forty-four degrees. I've got a hundred and two."                95

He had been waiting to die all day, ever since nine o'clock in the morning.

"You poor Schatz," I said. "Poor old Schatz. It's like miles and kilometers. You aren't going to die. That's a different thermometer. On that thermometer thirty-seven is normal. On this kind it's ninety-100 eight."

"Are you sure?"

"Absolutely," I said. "It's like miles and kilometers. You know, like how many kilometers we make when we do seventy miles in the car?"

"Oh," he said.                105

But his gaze at the foot of the bed relaxed slowly. The hold over himself relaxed too, finally, and the next day it was very slack° and he cried very easily at little things that were of no importance.

°limp, not firm

# Vocabulary Development

**words relating to illness**

One method to develop vocabulary is to study related words. This gives you a context that helps you to remember them. In Chapter 2 we looked at words that dealt with language. In "A Day's Wait," we find many words that describe illness. Reread the story and under-line each word that either names an illness or describes a symptom. List these words in the spaces provided below; we found sixteen. Next to each word write a definition in your own words. You may find a synonym in the story itself, for example, influenza and flu. If you are not sure what a word means, ask a classmate. Then add other words you know that either name an illness or describe its symptoms.

*influenza*  flu, a contagious virus that causes muscular aches, headache, fever, respiratory problems, and sometimes intestinal problems.

_____  _____

_____  _____

_____  _____

_____  _____

_____  _____

_____  _____

_____  _____

_____  _____

_____  _____

_____  _____

_____  _____

# Reading and Thinking Skills

## Comprehension Questions

1. How does Papa know that Schatz is sick? What are the boy's symptoms? How does Papa know that Schatz has a fever?

2. When Schatz asks his father if "it" will bother him, what is "it"?

3. What is Schatz's confusion? Why does he think he is going to die?

## Discussion Activities

### Analysis and Conclusions

1. What is the relationship between the boy and his father? Did you think it was odd that the boy's mother did not figure in the story?

2. Why do you think Schatz didn't just tell his father what he was afraid of? Why wouldn't he want his father to know that he was afraid? What does this say about the father? about the son?

3. Does Hemingway help you to picture the boy or the father? How did you see them? Describe what the father looks like. Describe what the boy looks like. When you read, do you usually picture the characters inside your head? Does it help you if the author describes the characters carefully, or do you prefer to use your imagination?

### Writing and Point of View

1. For the first half of the story, we do not know who the narrator (teller of the story) is; in other words, we do not know from whose point of view the story is being told. When you began reading the story, who did you think "I" was? What clues did you have?

2. "He (Schatz) lay still in the bed and seemed very detached from what was going on." Hemingway uses the word *detached* to describe Schatz's behavior. Do you agree that in some ways this story keeps the reader "detached" instead of "engaging" or bringing the reader closer to the characters? Can you support your point of view with examples from the story?

3. Does this story seem masculine or feminine? Support your point of view with examples from the story.

4. Fiction creates a mood or a feeling. What is the mood of this story? What elements or parts of the story create this mood? Some things to think about are: In what season does the story take place? Where does it take place—the city or the country? What does the father leave the house to do? Are the boy and the father alone in the house? Do we meet any other characters?

### Personal Response and Evaluation

1. If you were Schatz's father or mother, how would you have handled the situation?

2. Have you had any similar experience with a child?

3. Why did Papa go out hunting that day?

4. If Schatz were a girl, how would the story change? Why?

## Creating Questions and Answers

In small groups, take turns asking each other the following question, changing the symptom each time: What do you do if you have a headache (backache, toothache, etc.)?

Your answer should follow one of these three patterns:

Complete response—If I have a headache, I take an aspirin.

Short answer, but complete sentence—I take a nap. (I go to sleep.)

Conversational style, not necessarily complete sentence—Take two Tylenol. (Massage my head.)

## Role Playing

Act out the short story with one student playing Papa, one student playing Schatz, and one student acting as narrator and reading the background information. You might want to record this and play it back for the class, or individual students may want to listen to review the story.

## Journal Writing

First, I do not sit down at my desk to put into verse something that is already clear in my mind. If it were clear in my mind, I should have no incentive or need to write about it. . . . We do not write to be understood; we write in order to understand.

C. DAY LEWIS, *The Poetic Image*

Writing in a journal, whether it is shared or kept for yourself, is powerful. It is a means of touching upon feelings and experiences hidden inside ourselves. Allowing the journal to really express our deepest selves will have a positive effect on all our writing.

"A Day's Wait" is about a fundamental fear in life, the fear of dying. It is about a boy's unexpressed fear and in some ways his unexpressed love as well. Have you ever felt afraid? Have you ever thought about dying? Did this story make you think about your parents and your relationship with them when you were a child?

# Word Skills

## Idiomatic Expressions

Each of the following paragraphs contains a context clue that will help you understand some of the idiomatic expressions used in the short story. Underline these context clues; the first one has been done for you. Then use the expressions when you answer the questions at the end of each paragraph.

***take it easy*** (page 47, line 79)

Schatz cannot take it easy; he cannot <u>relax.</u> All he can do is worry about dying. Sometimes when we have a problem, we cannot take it easy. Some people have special exercises such as yoga or meditation that help them to take it easy. What techniques help you to take it easy when you are nervous?

***after a while*** (page 46, line 42)

At first Schatz is very afraid. Then he finds out about the different kinds of thermometers; after a while, he feels a little better. After some time has passed, he knows that he will recover. After a while, did you begin to feel more comfortable speaking English? How long did it take?

***for a while*** (page 46, line 47)

Papa goes out for a while. He leaves the house for a short amount of time. Sometimes before we fall asleep, we may read for a while to help us relax. What do you do to help you relax for a while before you fall asleep at night?

***out of sight*** (page 46, line 56)

When Papa is hunting, he tries to shoot the quail, but some of them fly out of sight so that he can no longer see them. When we say goodbye to someone at an airport, we may wait at the window and watch until the plane is beyond where we can see it. What other experiences have you had of watching something until it was out of sight?

Now write sentences of your own using these idiomatic expressions.

## Prepositions

**in/on/at (place)**

In Chapter 1 (page 9), we looked at the use of *in* with places. We live *in* a country, a state, a city, a town, a neighborhood. *In* is also used to mean "inside." Notice how *in* is used in Hemingway's story.

We were still *in* bed.
The doctor left three different medicines *in* different colored capsules.
The germs of influenza can only exist *in* an acid condition.

When we want to be more specific about the location of something, we use *on*.

I live *on* Pacific Street, on the north side of town.
I live *on* the wrong side of the tracks.*

*"The wrong side of the tracks" is an idiomatic expression that means "the poor side of town."

When we want to be even more specific, we use *at*.

I live *at* the corner of Hoyt and Blair Streets.
I live *at* 3426 SE Columbia Avenue.
I met him *at* the Live Aid concert in Philadelphia in the summer of 1985.

However, notice the use of *in* and *on* in the following sentences:

I live *in* the gray house with the blue shutters. (*In* means "inside.")
I live *in* the attic apartment. (*In* means "inside.")
I live *on* the top floor. (*On* refers to the surface.)

In "A Day's Wait" Hemingway uses *on* to indicate the surface of something.

When I put my hand *on* his forehead I knew he had a fever.
It was difficult to stand or walk *on* the glassy surface.

To review the use of *in, on,* and *at,* fill in the blanks in the following sentences. *In* is often used to mean _____ a place. *On* often refers to the _____ of something. *At* is the most _____, in that it points out an exact location.

(Answers are on page 343.)

**PRACTICE EXERCISE**

Fill in the blanks in the following sentences with *in*, *on*, or *at*.

1. Schatz's family lives _____ a house _____ a part of the world where the winters are cold.

2. Schatz feels so sick that he has to stay _____ bed all day long;

   he cannot step out of bed and put his feet _____ the cold floor.

3. I have lived _____ the South Side _____ the corner of Boyd

   and Emerson Streets _____ a big red brick building _____ a

   small apartment _____ the third floor for six years.

## Articles

**a/an**

In "A Day's Wait" on pages 45–47 underline *a* and *an* each time they appear. Then, circle the first letter of the word that follows each *a;* do the same thing for the first letter of the word that follows each *an*. For example,

I've got a headache.

On the basis of the letters that you have circled, fill in the blanks in the following sentences.

> Use *a* when the word that follows begins with a _____. Use
>
> *an* when the word that follows begins with a _____. *A* and
>
> *an* are used before _____ words.

## Commonly Confused Words

**your/you're**

"You go up to bed," I said, "*you're* sick."
"*Your* temperature is all right," I said. "It's nothing to worry about."

Notice how *your* and *you're* are used in the preceding sentences. Now complete the following definitions.

_____ is a contraction of the words "you are."

_____ means "belonging to you."

Fill in the blanks in the following sentences with *your* or *you're*.

1. "Did you lose _____ wallet?" the waitress asked, holding it in her hand.

2. "_____ going to have to practice every day if you want to compete in the Olympics," the coach announced.

3. "_____ visiting the Sears Building on _____ trip to Chicago, aren't you?" Willie asked.

# Sentence Skills

## Simple Past Tense

"A Day's Wait" is written in the past tense. Many writers use the past tense just as we do when we tell a story that has happened to us or to someone we know. The first paragraph from the story is reproduced here. Underline all the verbs. The first one has been done for you.

He <u>came</u> into the room to shut the windows while we were still in bed and I saw he looked ill. He was shivering, his face was white, and he walked slowly as though it ached to move.

Now change all the verbs to the present tense and rewrite the paragraph in the lines below.

_____

_____

_____

Read both paragraphs. Does the meaning seem changed? Which opening paragraph do you prefer?

## Dialogue

Much of this story is a dialogue that occurs between Papa and Schatz. Hemingway does not always tell the reader who is speaking. Examine the first few lines of dialogue.

"What's the matter, Schatz?"  Who is speaking? _____

"I've got a headache."  Who is speaking? _____

"You better go back to bed."  Who is speaking? _____

"No. I'm all right."  Who is speaking? _____

"You go to bed. I'll see you when I'm dressed."  Who is speaking? _____

We can recognize the voice of the speaker in several ways. What clues helped you to know who was speaking?

## Quotation Marks

Read the following excerpt from "A Day's Wait" and underline all the words that are enclosed by quotation marks, including words in this sentence.

Back in the room I wrote the boy's temperature down and made a note of the time to give the various capsules.

"Do you want me to read to you?"

"All right. If you want to," said the boy. His face was very white and there were dark areas under his eyes. He lay still in the bed and seemed very detached from what was going on.

I read aloud from Howard Pyle's *Book of Pirates;* but I could see he was not following what I was reading.

"How do you feel, Schatz?" I asked him.

"Just the same, so far," he said.

Look closely at what you have underlined and then answer the questions below.

1. Do question marks belong inside or outside quotation marks?

   _____

2. If you end a quotation and then identify who said it, does the quotation end with a period or with a comma? _____

3. In what tense are the quotations in the excerpt written?

   _____

4. In what tense is the story written? _____

5. Why are the story and the quotations written in different tenses?

   _____

6. In the directions, there are quotation marks around "A Day's Wait." What do those quotation marks indicate to the reader? Why do the words begin with capital letters? _____

7. One use for quotation marks is for the names of short stories.

   What is another use for quotation marks? _____

**EXERCISES**

1. Imagine that you are in a new city and you are lost. You want to go to the post office. Write a dialogue in which you ask a stranger for directions. Use quotation marks and words such as *I said, she said,* and *he said.*

2. Imagine that you have just received a letter telling you that there is a problem with your school registration. Write a dialogue in which you go to the registrar's office and try to solve your problem. You may want to write this dialogue with a classmate and act it out for the class.

## Sentence Combining

Writers try to use a variety of sentence types so that their writing is interesting to the reader. If there are too many short sentences, the writing sounds choppy and immature. If there are too many long sentences, the writing may be dull and difficult to read. Writers try to maintain a balance.

There are many ways to combine sentences to create longer sentences. One way is to use a comma followed by the word *and.* This method is used to connect sentences that are about similar things. Here is an example from Hemingway's story:

a. He was shivering.

b. His face was white.

c. He walked slowly as though it ached to move.

He was shivering, his face was white, and he walked slowly as though it ached to move.

Try this pattern in the following two examples.

a. He was frightened.

b. His eyes stared at me.

c. He pulled the blanket tightly around him.

_____

a. She was thinking.

b. Her foot tapped on the floor.

c. She absentmindedly drew a small circle in her notebook.

_____

Now create your own sentence using this pattern.

When writers want to show contrast between two ideas, they combine sentences using a comma followed by the word *but.* Here is an example from the story:

a. It would have been natural for him to go to sleep.

b. When I looked up he was looking at the foot of the bed, looking very strangely.

It would have been natural for him to go to sleep, but when I looked up he was looking at the foot of the bed, looking very strangely.

Try this pattern in the following two examples.

{ a. It would have been natural for her to marry the man she loved.

{ b. When he asked her, she refused.

---

{ a. He felt exhausted.

{ b. When he got into bed, he could not sleep.

---

Now create your own sentence using this pattern.

---

# Paragraph Skills

## From Journal to Paragraph to Story

"A Day's Wait" describes a very personal experience between a father and son. Writers often fictionalize experiences in their own lives and make them into stories. You may be able to use some of your journal writing to create fiction. To do this, you take something that is real, add details, characters, and dialogue, and a story begins to emerge. For example, a student's journal contained the following entry: "When I think about the word *fear,* I think about piles of books and a maze of buildings on my first day of school in the United States." This student could not remember all the details of that day, and some of them were too personal to reveal, but she did remember two details—piles of books and a maze of buildings. She used those details to create the following paragraph, which began her story.

The room number on the yellow card was 904E, and the small, dark woman stood on the busy corner staring at the four buildings that made up the college campus. How would she know which one was E? She was afraid to ask a stranger, but finally she approached a tall, thin woman holding a pile of books. She must be a student or a teacher, thought Rosa. "Which building is E?" Rosa asked as clearly as she could. The woman swung a long arm in the air and two heavy books went flying. Rosa bent down to pick them up and the woman did too. All her books tumbled down. Rosa tried to help, but the woman looked at her watch, gathered up her books, and ran off, leaving Rosa standing there just as puzzled as before. Now the buildings seemed more frightening as Rosa looked from one to the other, making herself dizzy with the rush of people, noise, and confusion.

After reading this paragraph, you wonder what happened to Rosa. As an exercise, you may want to complete the story. But the important thing to notice is how a few words from a journal can create the ideas or mood for a paragraph and ultimately for a story or essay.

## Pronouns

When a writer uses pronouns (words like *he, she, it*), the reader should know to which nouns (places or things) the pronouns refer. "In "A Day's Wait," Ernest Hemingway does not do this. Many readers find this very confusing and disorienting. Who is *he*? Who is *we*? Throughout the entire story, Hemingway never tells us who *we* is. Who did you think *we* was?

Rewrite the first paragraph of the story, substituting nouns for the pronouns. The paragraph should begin:

My son, Schatz, came into the room _____

_____

_____

_____

Compare your revised paragraph with Hemingway's original. Which do you prefer? Why?

## Editing Skills

**the apostrophe**

The apostrophe creates an editing problem for many writers. In the following sentences, underline the words that have an apostrophe ('). Then examine the sentences to decide how it is used.

1. "What's the matter, Schatz?"

2. "I've got a headache."

3. When the doctor came, he took the boy's temperature.

4. I read aloud from Howard Pyle's *Book of Pirates*.

> An apostrophe can be used in two ways:
> a. It can be used in contractions to show that part of a word is missing.
> b. It can be used to show possession, that something belongs to someone.

The apostrophe in sentences 1 and 2 is used to show _____.

The apostrophe in sentences 3 and 4 is used to show _____.

**Note:** Contractions are found mostly in dialogue and informal writing. The uncontracted forms are usually used in formal writing and speech. In the Hemingway story, contractions are used in the dialogue, but uncontracted forms are used in the narration and description.

**EXERCISE**

In each of the following sentences, the apostrophe is used to indicate that part of a word is missing. In the blank, fill in the complete word. The first has been done for you.

   _is_    1. "What's the matter, Schatz?"

_____  2. "I've got a headache."

_____  3. "No. I'm all right."

_____  4. "I'd rather stay awake."

_____  5. He'd better not get out of bed today.

_____  6. He's got a high temperature because of the flu.

**EXERCISE**

The second use for the apostrophe is to show possession or that something belongs to someone. Fill in the blanks showing the possessive form.

the bag that belongs to the doctor      the doctor's bag

the father that "belongs" to Schatz      Schatz's father

the dog that belongs to Papa      _____

the car that belongs to Robert      _____

**EXTRA PRACTICE**

In the following paragraph, fill in the nine missing apostrophes and twelve quotation marks. Answers are on p. 343.

Ernest Hemingways story A Days Wait tells about a young boy who is afraid of dying. He hears the doctor say, His temperature is one hundred and two degrees. He remembers his friends at school in France saying, Schatz, you cant live with a temperature over forty four degrees. The boys temperature is very high. You dont have to stay in here with me, he tells his father, if it bothers you. His father doesnt know whats really bothering the boy. When he finds out he says, Schatz, its like miles and kilometers. Schatz believes his father but still he doesnt relax for several days.

## Editing Skills Paragraph

The following paragraph is a first draft that has not yet been edited for surface errors. Correct the errors listed below:

| | |
|---|---|
| 11 capital letters errors | 1 set of quotation marks error |
| 4 *a/an* errors | 4 preposition errors |
| 4 *the* errors | 1 *they're/their/there* error |

My sister, hilda, lives on a apartment in the top of a high hill in san francisco. She works as an computer operator on an big bank their and when she looks out her window, she sees golden gate bridge. She loves heights. She even flew on an private airplane over rocky mountains. Once she said to me, I saw both pacific and atlantic oceans in one day. She would like to travel around the world someday.

Answers are on page 344.

# Essay Skills

## Getting Started

### clustering

Sometimes even though we have ideas about a subject, we cannot seem to write them down. The blank page fills us with fear. One technique that may help you overcome this problem is clustering. It is a simple but effective method to get started writing.

First, begin with a blank notebook page. In the middle of the page, write your nucleus word (the kernel word you will be writing about) and circle the word. (In the example, the nucleus word is *father.*) Then write down any other words that occur to you; circle these words and draw arrows connecting your original word to them.

Write the words down quickly, just as they occur to you. Connect words where you think they belong together. When something new occurs to you, go back to the nucleus and draw a new arrow and circle. You can have as many circles as you have ideas. Don't try to make sense and don't worry if it doesn't seem to be going anywhere. If you temporarily run out of ideas, doodle a little bit by drawing your circles or arrows darker. Keep clustering until you get a sense of what you are going to write. Then stop clustering and start to write.

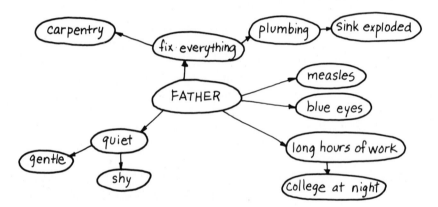

There is no right or wrong way to form the clusters. When you start to write, the words will come and begin to take over; the writing will come easily. Don't stop yourself. Let it happen and see what occurs in your writing.

**EXERCISES**

1. Begin with a clean page. Write the word (fear) in the middle of the page in a circle as shown. Let your mind begin to make connections. You may want to close your eyes. When a word comes to you, write it on the page, circle it, and draw an arrow to it from your nucleus or from its connecting word. Let yourself go and do not judge or even really think about what you are writing. You will know when to stop when you feel a strong urge to write, when you suddenly know what you want to say. Then glance at your word clusters and begin writing on a new page. Write until you feel you have written all your ideas out. You may want to look at your clustering again to see if you had any ideas you did not develop. Then read what you have written and spend a few

minutes making any changes that you think will improve the piece of writing.

2. Do the same with the word *father* or *mother*.

## Suggested Writing Topics

You may want to look at your clustering or at your journal before you begin to write on these topics. Always spend some thinking before you begin to write.

1. Write a narrative (story) about an experience between a child and a parent. Use dialogue. Refer to page 58 to see how your journal can help you with this writing.
2. Have you ever had an experience like Schatz's in which you were confused or afraid? Write about this experience and tell what you learned from it.
3. Parents have to be sensitive to their children. Do you agree or disagree? Write an essay in which you support your point of view with your experiences or observations.
4. Imagine that Schatz is telling the story "A Day's Wait." Rewrite the story from his point of view.
5. Imagine that Schatz is a girl. Rewrite the story and make whatever changes you think should occur.
6. Write a one-act play. There should be two characters. Some situations you might consider are: a first date, a telephone conversation, a job or school interview, asking a parent for permission to get married, a driver's license road test.

Use the following format:

A: I'm not really sure. Where do you want to go?.
B: Uh, I don't know. The movies? Do you like the movies?

Read your dialogue out loud to see if it really sounds like people talking. You may want to act out your play with a classmate.

## Revising

Many writers are not quite sure what to do when they are told to revise their writing. They simply look for misspellings, grammar errors, and other surface problems, then copy the essay over and hand it in. This is not really revising, however; this is editing. Revising means rethinking and restructuring your writing.

One way to become more comfortable with revising is just to go ahead and do it. This chapter suggests a simple and concrete method to get the feel of revising. Although it is not something you would do all the time, it will give you some experience in making decisions about your writing. Follow the steps in the order in which they are listed.

1. Choose an essay you would like to revise.
2. Reread the essay slowly and carefully. Make a copy of the essay. (Save the original essay.)
3. Cross out and remove one sentence from any part of the essay.
4. Move one sentence from one place in a paragraph to a new place.
5. Add one new sentence to any paragraph in your essay.
6. Change one word in the essay to a synonym for that word.
7. Add one transition word or phrase (*therefore, however, but, moreover,* etc.) somewhere in your essay.
8. Rewrite your essay with all the changes you have made.

Compare your original essay with your revised essay. Which do you prefer? Why? Was it difficult to make the suggested changes? Think about how you decided which sentence to remove. Think about how you made the other decisions as well. These are the types of decisions that all writers make when revising their writing.

# Coming of Age and Knowing Ourselves

# CHAPTER FOUR

# Back, But Not Home

*Maria L. Muñiz was born in 1958. She and her family came to the United States in 1963. In 1978 she graduated from New York University. She has written and edited many articles and books. In this essay, "Back, But Not Home," Muñiz describes her feelings about returning to Cuba.*

**W**ith all the talk about resuming diplomatic relations with Cuba, and with the increasing number of Cuban exiles returning to visit friends and relatives, I am constantly being asked, "Would you ever go back?" In turn, I have asked myself, "Is there any reason for me to go?" I have had to think long and hard before finding my answer. Yes. 5

I came to the United States with my parents when I was almost five years old. We left behind grandparents, aunts, uncles and several cousins. I grew up in a very middle-class neighborhood in Brooklyn. With one exception, all my friends were Americans. Out- 10 side of my family, I do not know many Cubans. I often feel awkward visiting relatives in Miami because it is such a different world. The way of life in Cuban Miami seems very strange to me and I am accused of being too "Americanized." Yet, although I am now an American citizen, whenever anyone has asked me my nationality, I 15 have always and unhesitatingly replied, "Cuban."

Outside American, inside Cuban.

I recently had a conversation with a man who generally sympathizes with the Castro regime. We talked of Cuban politics and although the discussion was very casual, I felt an old anger welling° 20 inside. After 16 years of living an "American" life, I am still unable to view the revolution with detachment or objectivity.° I cannot interpret its results in social, political or economic terms. Too many memories stand in my way.

And as I listened to this man talk of the Cuban situation, I began 25 to remember how as a little girl I would wake up crying because I had dreamed of my aunts and grandmothers and I missed them. I remembered my mother's trembling voice and the sad look on her

°filling up

°freedom from personal feelings

face whenever she spoke to her mother over the phone. I thought of the many letters and photographs that somehow were always lost in transit. And as the conversation continued, I began to remember how difficult it often was to grow up Latina in an American world. 30

It meant going to kindergarten knowing little English. I'd been in this country only a few months and although I understood a good deal of what was said to me, I could not express myself very well. 35 On the first day of school I remember one little girl's saying to the teacher: "But how can we play with her? She's so stupid she can't even talk!" I felt so helpless because inside I was crying, "Don't you know I can understand everything you're saying?" But I did not have words for my thoughts and my inability to communicate terrified 40 me.

As I grew a little older, Latina meant being automatically rele-

°assigned

gated° to the slowest reading classes in school. By now my English was fluent, but the teachers would always assume I was somewhat illiterate or slow. I recall one teacher's amazement at discovering I 45 could read and write just as well as her American pupils. Her incre-

°disbelief
°amazed

duity° astounded° me. As a child, I began to realize that Latina would always mean proving I was as good as the others. As I grew older, it became a matter of pride to prove I was better than the others. 50

As an adult I have come to terms with these memories and they don't hurt as much. I don't look or sound very Cuban. I don't speak with an accent and my English is far better than my Spanish. I am beginning my career and look forward to the many possibilities ahead of me. 55

But a persistent little voice is constantly saying, "There's something missing. It's not enough." And this is why when I am now asked, "Do you want to go back?" I say "yes" with conviction.

I do not say to Cubans, "It is time to lay aside the hurt and forgive and forget." It is impossible to forget an event that has altered and 60 scarred all our lives so profoundly. But I find I am beginning to care less and less about politics. And I am beginning to remember and care more about the child (and how many others like her) who left her grandma behind. I have to return to Cuba one day because I want to know that little girl better. 65

When I try to review my life during the past 16 years, I almost feel as if I've walked into a theater right in the middle of a movie. And I'm afraid I won't fully understand or enjoy the rest of the movie unless I can see and understand the beginning. And for me, the beginning is Cuba. I don't want to go "home" again; the life and 70 home we all left behind are long gone. My home is here and I am happy. But I need to talk to my family still in Cuba.

Like all immigrants, my family and I have had to build a new life from almost nothing. It was often difficult, but I believe the struggle made us strong. Most of my memories are good ones.     75

But I want to preserve and renew my cultural heritage. I want to keep "la Cubana" within me alive. I want to return because the journey back will also mean a journey within. Only then will I see the missing piece.

# Vocabulary Development

### word forms

A useful way to increase vocabulary is to learn new word forms of words that you already know. In this way you more than triple the number of words that you can understand and use.

The underlined forms of the following words appear in "Back, But Not Home." They are all words that are commonly used in college-level material.

| *Adjective* | *Adverb* | *Noun* | *Verb* |
|---|---|---|---|
| sympathetic | sympathetically | sympathy | <u>sympathize</u> |
| communicative | communica-tively | communication | <u>communicate</u> |
| <u>persistent</u> | persistently | persistence | persist |
| hesitant | hesitantly | hesitation | hesitate |
| hesitating | <u>(un)hesitatingly</u> | | |

**EXERCISE**

Use the correct word form in each of the following sentences. If the word form is a verb, be sure to use the appropriate ending.

*sympathetic*     *sympathetically*     *sympathy*     *sympathize*

1. The teacher should have treated the small child more _____

   _____ .

2. Because of her experiences, she is _____ to others.

*communicative*     *communicatively*     *communication*     *communicate*

3. In this essay, Maria L. Mūniz _____ her feelings about Cuba.

4. Writing is a ＿＿＿＿＿ process.

*persistent*          *persistently*          *persistence*          *persist*

5. Her ＿＿＿＿＿ in learning English may have helped her to succeed in her career as a journalist.

6. If one does not ＿＿＿＿＿, one will not succeed in this world.

*hesitant*          *hesitantly*          *hesitation*          *hesitate*
*hesitating*          *(un)hesitatingly*

7. Muñiz ＿＿＿＿＿ before she made the difficult decision.

8. Her ＿＿＿＿＿ gave her time to think through all the positives and negatives.

These words will become part of your active vocabulary if you use them. Write sentences using these words in each of their forms. In addition, try to use some of them in your next essay.

# Reading and Thinking Skills

## Comprehension Questions

1. How long has Maria L. Muñiz been in the United States? How old is she now? How old was she when she wrote this essay?
2. What does *its* in line 23 refer to?
3. Has Muñiz forgotten the Cuban political situation that brought her to the United States? Does she think one should? Give evidence from Muñiz's writing to support your point of view.

## Discussion Activities

**Analysis and Conclusions**
1. Why does the author feel awkward visiting her relatives in Miami? What does it mean to be too "Americanized"?
2. Why did the author find it difficult to grow up Latina in an American world?
3. How did she prove that her work was as good as or better than

the work of the other students in her class? What is she doing now that shows that her English is excellent?

4. What is the missing piece to which Muñiz refers in the last sentence of the essay?

**Writing and Point of View**

1. What is this essay about? What is Maria L. Muñiz trying to make you aware of? Does she make you feel what she has been through? If so, how does she do this? Are her examples good ones? Are there enough examples to convince you?

2. In what person is this essay written? Rewrite paragraph 2 in the third person. ("She came to the United States with her parents when she was almost five years old," etc.) Does the meaning of the essay change when it is written in the third person? Which version do you prefer? Why?

3. Which piece of writing seems more personal—the article about Khan Duong or Maria L. Muñiz's essay? Why? How do you decide when your writing should be more personal? more impersonal?

**Personal Response and Evaluation**

1. Compare Maria L. Muñiz's experience with her teachers to your own experiences and those of your classmates. You may want to ask questions like "Who was your best teacher?"

2. Many people experience disappointment when they return to a place they left when they were children. Places change and so do people. What kind of experience do you think the author will have in Cuba? Have you ever returned to a place that you left years before? What was your experience?

3. Is it important to hold on to the customs and cultural patterns of your native country? Is it important to maintain your first language when you are living in a new country?

## Creating Questions

1. Imagine that Maria L. Muñiz is coming to your class to be interviewed. In small groups, create questions that you would ask her. What would you like to know about her that is not contained in the article? One student can play the part of Muñiz and answer the questions.

2. Write a dialogue between yourself and Muñiz in which you ask her questions and she responds to them.

## Role Playing

Imagine that you are returning to your country for a visit. You have to call a travel agent to make your reservations. There are probably many other preparations you will have to make. As a small-group activity, act out your conversations with the people you will have to contact in order to make all your plans. (You may want to tape record or videotape some of these interactions.)

## Journal Writing

The theme of this chapter is going home, returning to a way of life that still lives in memories. The upheaval of moving to a new country, new language, and new way of life is probably one of the most emotionally charged experiences a person can have in life. By this time, you have made many adjustments to your new life; there is probably a part of you, however, that thinks of the past with sadness, with joy, or with a bit of both.

In this journal entry you may want to think about home. A famous American writer, Thomas Wolfe, wrote a book entitled *You Can't Go Home Again.* Do you agree with the title? Do you ever think about returning to your home country? Do you still have friends and family in your country? Where do you feel that your real home is?

If you have difficulty writing about this, you might want to try the clustering technique we explored in chapter 3, using *home* as the nucleus word.

# Word Skills

## Idiomatic Expressions

Each of the following paragraphs contains a context clue that will help you understand some of the idiomatic expressions used in Muñiz's article. Underline these context clues; the first one has been done for you. Then use the expressions when you answer the questions at the end of each paragraph.

***in turn*** (page 67, line 4)

People asked Muñiz if she would go back to Cuba. In turn, she asked herself the same question. When people converse, usually one person speaks and then the other responds in turn, or <u>right after</u> the first person has spoken. When someone asks you a question, are you usually ready to answer in turn or do you have to think for a long time?

***by now*** (page 68, line 43)

By now, you have had experience speaking English. Up to this time, you have also had some experience writing English. Do you feel that your ability to communicate in English has improved by now?

***a good deal of*** (page 68, lines 34–35)

Muñiz has spent a good deal of, or a lot of, time in the United States. She says her English is better than her Spanish since she spent a good deal of her life practicing English. Do you spend a good deal of your time practicing your English?

Now write sentences of your own using these idiomatic expressions.

## Pronouns

In the following sentences, the pronouns have been left out. On the basis of what you know about sentence structure, fill in the appropriate pronouns.

1. I came to the United States with _____ parents. _____ left behind grandparents, aunts, uncles, and several cousins.

2. I had dreamed of my aunts and grandmothers and I missed

   _____.

3. I remembered _____ mother's trembling voice and the sad look

   on _____ face whenever _____ spoke to _____ mother over the phone.

4. In turn, I have asked _____, "Is there any reason for _____ to go?"

Notice that the last sentence is difficult to complete because you do not know what came before it in the reading. In general, a pronoun takes the place of a noun. In order to determine which pronoun to use, you need to know its referent, or the noun to which it refers. For example, in the previous sentence to what noun does *it* refer? _____

Refer to "Back, But Not Home" to check your answers. If you had difficulty, refer to the pronoun chart and then try the next practice exercise.

## PRONOUN CHART

| Subject | Object | Possessive | | Reflexive |
|---------|--------|------------|------|-----------|
| I | me | my* | mine | myself |
| you | you | your* | yours | yourself |
| she | her | her* | hers | herself |
| he | him | his* | his | himself |
| it | it | its* | | itself |
| we | us | our* | ours | ourselves |
| you | you | your* | yours | yourselves |
| they | them | their* | theirs | themselves |

*These words are not used alone. They are followed by nouns or subject words.

**EXTRA PRACTICE**

The following is a famous story told by Akiba Ben Joseph, a great scholar and head of the school for rabbis in Palestine in the first century. Fill in the appropriate pronouns.

Once upon a time there was a smart young man who decided to trick a wise old man. _____ caught a little bird and held _____ in one hand behind _____ back. The boy approached the wise man, and said, "Sir, _____ have a question for _____. _____ want to see how very wise _____ are. _____ am holding a bird in _____ hand. Is _____ alive, or is _____ dead?

The boy thought that if the man said the bird was dead, _____ would open _____ hand to reveal the live bird, but if the man said the bird was alive, _____ would crush the bird, dead. The old man stared into the boy's eyes for a long time. Then _____ said, "The

answer, my friend, is in _____ hands."

Answers are on page 101.

## Quotation Marks

In Chapter 3, we said that quotation marks are used to set off the

_____ words of a speaker or writer. Commas, periods, question

marks, and exclamation marks at the end of the quote go _____

the quotation marks. Quotations usually start with a _____
letter. (Answers: *exact, inside, capital*)

Another use for quotation marks is to set off special words and phrases from the rest of the sentence. We find this four times in the Muñiz article. The first example is:

The way of life in Cuban Miami seems very strange to me and I am accused of being too "Americanized."

Find the other three sentences in the article that use quotation marks in this way. Copy these sentences in the blanks below.

1. _____

2. _____

3. _____

## Commonly Confused Words

**than/then**
Helene called Thomas when she saw that the movie star he liked better than any other was starring in a new movie in their neighborhood. Then they went to see it together. When it ended, they talked in front of the movie theater more than usual. They thought the movie was better than the star's last one. Then they went to get something to drink and then they continued talking. Then it was almost midnight and they both had to rush home.

Examining the use of *than* and *then* in this paragraph should help you complete the following definitions.

_____ means "at that time."

_____ is used to show comparisons.

Fill in the blanks in the following sentences with *than* and *then*.

She lived in Cuba until she was five; _____ she moved to the United States. _____ she started school, where she found it was easier for her to understand _____ to speak. Her teachers thought she knew less _____ she really did because they did not know how to communicate with her _____.

Use these two words in sentences of your own.

# Sentence Skills

## Simple Past Tense

The essay in this chapter uses the simple past tense when the author is describing incidents that occurred in her past. Let's examine some of the sentences from the essay that use this tense. In each of the following sentences, draw a rectangle around the subject and a circle around the verb. The first sentence has been done for you.

1. I came to the United States with my parents when I was almost five years old.

2. I grew up in a very middle-class neighborhood in Brooklyn.

3. All my friends were American.

4. We talked of Cuban politics.

5. I felt an old anger welling inside.

6. I listened to this man talk of the Cuban situation.

In the following spaces, list the subjects and the verbs from the preceding sentences. (The first two have been done for you.)

| Subject | Verb |
|---------|------|
| I | came |
| I | was |
| _____ | _____ |
| _____ | _____ |
| _____ | _____ |
| _____ | _____ |
| _____ | _____ |

Let's examine how the past tense is constructed. From the subjects and verbs you have listed above, you can see that the past tense has a regular form that uses -*ed* at the end of the verb and an irregular form for particular verbs. (See page 349 for a complete list of irregular verbs.) For extra practice, review Muñiz's article and underline all the past tense verbs.

**EXERCISE**   Write a paragraph that tells what you did this morning before you came to school. Use the past tense throughout. Then trade your essay with a classmate, and circle all the past tense verbs your classmate used in the paragraph.

## Comparatives/Superlatives

Comparative and superlative structures are used to describe differences and similarities. Therefore, Muñiz used these structures to describe similarities and differences among languages, cultures, and school experiences. In the exercise below, we will look more closely at comparative and superlative structures by examining several sentences. Some are from Muñiz's article and others deal with the same subject she wrote about.

as _____ as means "to be equal to something or someone"

*line 45:* I recall one teacher's amazement at discovering I could read and write just *as* well *as* her American pupils.

As a child, I began to realize that Latina would always mean proving I was *as* good *as* the others.

She was *as* smart *as* the other children, but she could not communicate with them.

better than
more _____ than  } mean that something or someone is
_____er than  } superior in some way to others

*line 48:* As I grew older, it became a matter of pride to prove I was *better than* the others.

I don't speak with an accent and my English is far *better than* my Spanish.

The little girl understood *more* English *than* the other children realized she did.

She was *more* intelligent *than* her classmates realized she was.

Muñiz was smart*er than* anyone in her school thought she was.

She was often loneli*er than* the other children.

the best
the most _____  } mean that something or someone is superior in
the _____est  } some way to *all* others

Even if she had problems speaking, still she was *the best* writer in her school.

She was able to write *the best* descriptions of her home country.

The teacher who gave her *the most* attention helped her adjust to the school.

*The most* compassionate child became her friend.

*line 42:* As I grew a little older, Latina meant being automatically relegated to *the* slow*est* reading classes in school.

She became *the* bright*est* child in her class.

The following sentences contain some rules about how comparatives and superlatives are formed in English. Refer to the sample sentences above and then fill in the following blanks.

To show that two things are equal, we say that one is _____

good _____ the other.

To show that one thing is superior to the other, we say that it is

better _____ the other.

To show that one thing is superior to all the others, we say that it

is _____ _____.

You may have noticed that there are two ways to form comparatives. Look at the difference between the words in these two columns.

smarter than                more intelligent than

cuter than                  _____ beautiful _____

shorter _____             _____ petite than

prettier _____            more attractive _____

In the left column, the words *smart, cute,* and *short* are _____
<br>one/several

syllables long. The word *pretty* is _____ syllables long, but
<br>one/two

it ends in the letter _____. In the right column, the words *intelli-*

*gent, beautiful, petite,* and *attractive* are _____ syllables long.
<br>one/several

---

When a word is one syllable long or ends in *y*, we form the com-

parative by adding an _____ ending to the word. When the word

is longer than one syllable and does not end in *y*, we form the com-

parative by putting the word _____ before it and *than* after it to

show that it is comparative.

---

The rules for the superlative form are similar. If the word is

_____ syllable long or ends in the letter _____, we put *the* before
the word and add *-est* to the end of the word to create the superlative form:

the    smartest

_____ cute_____

_____ short_____

_____ prett_____

If the word is two or more syllables long and does not end in *y*,
use *the most* in front of the word to create the superlative form:

the        most    intelligent

——————— ——————— beautiful

——————— ——————— petite

——————— ——————— attractive

**EXERCISE**     Answer the following questions, using the comparative and superlative forms.

1. Who is the most beautiful person you have ever seen? Explain why you chose this person.

2. Which world problem is more serious—hunger or lack of education? Explain your answer.

3. Who is the most intelligent person you have ever heard of? Explain why you chose this person.

4. Write three questions using the comparative and superlative structures and ask them of your classmates.

5. Write a paragraph comparing one country you have known with the United States.

## Complex Sentences

**commas with subordinate clauses**

There are several types of sentences that we can use when we write. Most writers try to vary sentence types in order to make their writing more interesting to the reader. If you examine professional writing, you will usually find a combination of short sentences and long sentences. In this chapter we will examine the use of subordination to create longer sentences.

In each of the following sentences, draw a rectangle around the subject and a circle around the verb. The first one has been done for you.

1. I came to the United States with my parents.

2. I was almost five years old.

3. I have lived in the United States for fifteen years.

4. I am still unable to view the revolution with detachment.

Notice that in each sentence there is one subject and one verb. If you were to read an entire essay made up of sentences such as these, you might find it choppy and immature. In order to vary the sentences, it is possible to combine some of these sentences using subordinators. Subordinators are special words that are used to make connections. Some commonly used subordinators are *after, as, because, before, if, since, until, when, where,* and *while.*

Each of the following sentences uses some type of subordination. Analyze these sentences very carefully by performing four operations on each one. (The first sentence has been done for you.)

1. Put a rectangle around each subject.
2. Put a circle around each verb.
3. Put a triangle around each subordinator.
4. If there is a comma in the sentence, underline it.

1. I came to the United States with my parents when I was almost five years old.

2. Although I have lived in the United States for fifteen years, I am still unable to view the revolution with detachment.

3. As I grew a little older, my English began to improve.

4. I have to return to Cuba one day because I want to know myself better.

5. When I try to review my life, I feel both happy and sad.

On the basis of what you have observed in this exercise, complete the following sentences.

When two complete sentences are connected by a subordinator and

the subordinating word is the first word in the sentence, a comma

_____ needed. If the subordinating word occurs in the
      is/is not

middle of the sentence, a comma _____ needed.
                                       is/is not

**EXERCISE**   In each of the sentences in the preceding exercise, the order of the clauses can be reversed. In the following exercise, reverse the sentences. Decide if you need a comma or not. (The first one has been done for you.)

1. When I was almost five years old, I came to the United States with my parents.

2. _____

3. _____

4. _____

5. _____

Do you think the meaning of any of these sentences changes when it is reversed?

**EXERCISE**

In the following paragraph, five commas have been left out between subordinating clauses and main clauses. Put in commas where necessary.

Herman felt relieved when his plane landed at O'Hare Airport in Chicago. Before he had left his country his cousins had sent him a letter. After he read it he felt sure he would recognize his relatives. They promised that they would all carry red roses unless the florist had run out of them. If that happened they would carry daisies instead. Herman looked around until he saw a group of people holding roses. As he ran over to them they put their arms around another man. He felt confused until he saw several people waving daisies at him. Before he knew it they were all laughing and celebrating.

**EXTRA PRACTICE**

1. Change the name in the first sentence of the preceding paragraph to Isabella. Rewrite the paragraph, making all necessary changes so that the paragraph makes sense.
2. Circle all the past tense verbs.
3. Write a paragraph about your own or someone else's arrival in the United States. Use the past tense throughout, and use subordinating words to connect your ideas.

# Paragraph Skills

## Telling a Story: Narration and Time Transitions

In the essay in this chapter, Maria L. Muñiz tells a story or narrative about the last sixteen years of her life. She connects or makes transitions between various paragraphs using phrases that signify time. Some examples of these time phrases are:

when I was almost five years old

as a little girl

as a child

as I grew older

as an adult

The essay begins when Muñiz is almost five years old and arriving in the United States and continues until she is twenty-one years old and writing the essay. Using time phrases to make transitions between ideas is an effective way of connecting ideas. Time transitions are particularly useful for telling a story in which the sequence of events is important.

Time indicators help the audience to follow the story from the beginning to the present or even into the future. Some of the time indicators used by Ms. Muñiz are:

| | |
|---|---|
| I came to the United States when I was almost five years old. | past tense (page 67, lines 7–8) |
| I began to remember how as a little girl . . . | past tense (page 67, lines 25–26) |
| As a child, I began to realize . . . | past tense (page 68, line 47) |
| As I grew older, it became a matter of pride . . . | past tense (page 68, lines 48–49) |
| As an adult I have come to terms . . . | present perfect tense (page 68, line 51) |
| When I try to review my life during the past years, I almost feel as if . . . | present tense (page 68, lines 66–67) |

You can use these time phrases to create your own paragraph. For example:

I came to the United States when I was almost nine years old. I began to remember how as a little boy I had to try extra hard to do well in school. I was left back in the fourth grade because I was shy, and my English was not good. As I grew older, I began to do better in school than a lot of the students who were born in this country. As an adult, I feel proud of my accomplishments. Whey I try to review my life, I realize that there were many difficult moments, but there were also many great times.

Use these time phrases to create a paragraph about yourself or someone you know.

## Editing Skills Paragraph

The following first draft contains seven missing plurals, twenty-six missing capital letters, and four missing commas. Edit this paragraph so that all the errors are corrected. Answers are on p. 344.

i came to the united state when i was fifteen. my homeland is haiti, and i miss all the beautiful beach and the person i knew there. when i arrived in minneapolis, minnesota, on a tuesday in january it was colder than any day i had ever known in my whole life. even my poor suitcase seemed to shiver that day. i remember my first tear froze to my cheek. although i tried very hard to speak english no one seemed to understand me. since i first arrived in this country many thing have changed. because i have a good job now i have a warm down jacket and furry earmuff to protect me from the cold. my mother and father are here too, and we all laugh at those first week and all the problem we had back then.

# Essay Skills

## Narration

**telling a story**

Every day in our lives all of us tell stories. For example, we come home from school and tell our families what happened in our reading class. We might discuss the bus trip and describe one of the people on the bus. We fill our stories with details that will capture the imagination of the listener. We tell stories to give ourselves pleasure and to give our listeners pleasure. Writer Joan Didion said, "We tell ourselves stories in order to live." Stories are a way of making sense of the world.

When we tell stories, we are aware of beginnings and endings. We usually tell a story in the order in which it happened; when we listen to stories, we also like to hear them in the correct order. Have you ever been telling a child an old familiar story and, in trying to rush through it, left out a part? The child will usually stop you and beg you to tell the story "right," with all its parts in the right order. The rules we follow when we tell stories to friends and family are similar to the rules we follow when we write stories that will be shared with our teachers and classmates. Details make the stories rich. And, as we have observed in Muñiz's writing, a sense of time, a chronology that we can follow, makes the story easier to understand.

In the Hemingway story we read in the last chapter, we followed one day in the life of a family. The story began in the morning, continued into the afternoon, and ended later that day. That time framework made the story easy to follow. In the writing exercises for this chapter keep in mind the elements that make a story work for you. You may want to go back to the stories you wrote in the last chapter and revise them, keeping in mind detail and chronology.

**EXERCISES**

1. Compare the writing in the selection in Chapter 1 with the writing in the selection in this chapter. For example, the selection in chapter 1 is written in the third person, using *she, he,* and *they.* The selection in this chapter is written in the first person using *I* and *we.* Which selection do you prefer and why? Is the vocabulary similar? Which one did you find easier to read?

2. What kinds of reading do you do just for your own enjoyment? Share with a classmate the best article, book, or story that you have read in the past few months. What makes a piece of writing appeal to you?

**EXTRA PRACTICE**

These Days

whatever you have to say, leave
the roots on, let them
dangle

And the dirt
      just to make clear
      where they have come from.

CHARLES OLSON (1910–1970)

1. Why do you think this poem has been included in this chapter? What is this poem about?

2. Poems are condensations of emotional feelings into a short, tight form. In a few words, they can say many things. Therefore, each word must be selected very carefully. The words resonate—like the sun, their meaning beams out in many directions. Poems are often symbolic. What might *roots* refer to other than roots of plants in the soil? What might *dirt* symbolize?

3. Do Charles Olson and Maria L. Muñiz have similar ideas? If so, what are these ideas?

## Suggested Writing Topics

Take some time to think about your ideas before you start to write. You may want to look at your journal for ideas or you may want to try clustering to get started.

Choose one of the following topics to write about.

1. "Outside American, inside Cuban." What does Muñiz mean by these words? Have you ever felt this way in relation to your country? If you have, describe your feelings and experiences in a narrative, a story. Keep in mind the order of the events.

2. Write a letter to Maria L. Muñiz telling her how her essay affected you. Offer her advice about whether she should return to Cuba. Explain your reasons.

3. "Like most immigrants, my family and I have had to build a new life from almost nothing. It was often difficult, but I believe the struggle made us strong." How can struggle make someone strong? Tell a story about yourself or about someone you know or have heard of who has grown stronger through struggle.

4. Many people feel confused about how much of their cultural heritage they should keep in America and how much they should give up in order to become more "Americanized." How have you resolved this question? Tell a story describing how you or someone you have heard of dealt with this issue.

5. Do you think that we all have a responsibility to be political? Should we be familiar with what is going on in other countries of the world? Or do you believe our responsibility should be only to ourselves, our families, and our neighborhoods? Explain and give examples supporting your point of view.

## Revising

**getting distance**

When you revise this essay, pretend that you are a stranger. Put away the pen you used to write the essay and use a different pen or pencil. Read your essay out loud and ask yourself questions about it; you may want to write these questions on a separate piece of paper. Some possible questions are:

1. What is the writer trying to say in this essay?
2. Does it make sense?
3. Are there enough examples and are they clear?
4. Are there enough details?
5. Is the essay interesting to read?

Use these questions to help you during the rewriting process. Try to be a helpful critic. Focus on the organization of the essay. Does one idea lead to the next? Are there enough details so that you can form pictures in your mind? How can this piece of writing be made to come alive to its readers?

# CHAPTER FIVE

# The Social Context
# of Identity Formation

*The following excerpt enti-
tled "The Social Context of
Identity Formation" from the
textbook* Human Develop-
ment *examines the effects
of the Depression on a
group of young people
growing up in California.
The authors conclude that
cultural or social changes
have a broad effect on people's daily lives. However,
most people are able to
adapt to such major social
changes by altering but not
losing their sense of identity.*

°ten-year period

°pertaining to Queen Vic-
toria's time, which was
characterized by modest
behavior and manners

°thoroughly

The decade° of the 1920s—the Roaring 20s—was a period of so- 1
cial revolution in the United States. After World War I (and in
some ways because of it), there was a dramatic shift from strict Vic-
torian° prewar standards of behavior to more relaxed standards in
regard to dress, drink, male-female relations, and much more. The 5
20s were also a very prosperous time. After World War I the economic balloon expanded until 1929, when it burst and the Depression began. The stock market crashed; banks and businesses failed;
thousands of men lost their jobs and their life savings. Many families
that had been comfortably middle class in the 20s became poor in 10
the 30s.

In 1931, the Berkeley Institute of Human Development began a
longitudinal study of adolescent development, called the Oakland
(California) Growth Study. The children, 84 boys and 83 girls, were
in fifth grade when the study began, and they and their families 15
were studied intensively° and continuously from 1931 until 1939.
Follow-up surveys of this group were conducted through the 1960s,
by which time many of these Depression adolescents had adolescent
children of their own.

Glenn Elder (1974, 1980), a sociologist, analyzed the data from 20
this study in an effort to determine how the Depression had affected

people who had been adolescents during those hard times. He was particularly interested in families that had suffered a major loss of income and status. Statistics show that average family income in Oakland declined about 40 percent between 1929 and 1933. Small 25 businessmen lost their businesses, and workmen lost their jobs. Most investments became worthless, and savings disappeared. Parents were unable to feed and clothe their families without charity or government assistance—a Depression innovation° that many people found hard to accept. Many men, raised to believe that any man who could 30 not support his family was worthless, suffered a shattering loss of self-esteem.°

°something new

°belief in value of self

In many such families, Elder found, there was a shift of power from the father to the mother. As the father's role declined, the mother's role grew more important. Often the mother both worked 35 at odd jobs to bring income into the household and served as the main decision maker and emotional resource. Because the mother was so busy and the family so poor, the adolescent children were given important adultlike responsibilities. This shift of responsibilities had major effects, which differed greatly for girls and boys.   40

Adolescent girls were given many housekeeping duties. Because they had not even a slight hope of education beyond high school (who could afford it?) and because jobs were so scarce, they concentrated on a domestic future. Middle-class girls whose families had suffered severe losses tended to marry early. In the roaring 20s, the 45 feminist movement had flowered. The great prosperity and liberal social norms of that decade had encouraged young women to think of their future in terms of education and career. The Depression greatly constricted° these possibilities. Young women were forced by social circumstances to adopt a more traditional female identity as 50 homemaker and mother.

°reduced; shrank

The father's loss of status in the family and the mother's extra burdens had a different effect on boys, serving to liberate them from parental controls at an early age. Teen-age boys took jobs, if they could find them, to help keep the family afloat.° In their work or 55 search for work, these young adolescents dealt as one adult to another with many men and women outside the family. The circumstance of the Depression thus accelerated° the development of these boys toward adult roles as breadwinners and achievers. In fact, as adults, men whose families had suffered a drastic° loss of income 60 when they were boys showed higher motivation to achieve than men whose family incomes had not dropped so much.

°on top of things; not sinking under debt

°sped up

°severe

The effects of social circumstances on the identities of the men and women in this study continued to be evident in later life. As adults, the women continued to be family-centered, viewing care of 65 their children as their most significant responsibility. The men did not appear to have suffered from delay or lack of higher education. Their early entrance into the life of work and their need to achieve were enough to make them generally successful in their adult voca- tions. The men were also more family-oriented as adults than were 70 Depression adolescents whose families had not suffered major finan- cial losses. In the 1920s, when these people were born, their parents did not intend to bring them up as they did. Most parents did not plan to place the major burdens of housekeeping on their daughters or to send their sons out to earn money for groceries and rent. But 75 when the Depression came, the parents had to adapt their ways of socializing their children to the unexpected hard times.

Elder's work illustrates two points that had previously been diffi- cult to document. First, the historical context of growing up has im- portant effects on the course of human development, including the 80 personal identity formed in adolescence and early adulthood. Sec- ond, within the identity they choose, most people have the flexibility to adapt to major social changes during their adult years, to modify rather than to lose their sense of identity.

Any great cultural or social changes—in fact, all broad influ- 85 ences—are experienced by individuals through what happens in their daily life. Adolescents learn about life's possibilities—and impossibil- ities—from their relationships with parents and friends and from the adults and books they encounter in high school. These influ- ences all make important contributions to an adolescent's self-image. 90

# Vocabulary Development I

**words relating to research**

As you continue your studies and as you read more newspapers and news magazines, you will encounter various types of research. In this selection, many of the vocabulary words relate to the conduct of research. These words will be useful to you throughout your col- lege career and during your everyday life.

**standards** (page 88, line 4)

After World War I (and in some ways because of it), there was a dramatic shift from strict Victorian prewar standards of behavior to more relaxed standards in regard to dress, drink, male-female relations, and much more.

*standard(s):* anything accepted by general agreement as a basis of comparison; a model.

Are standards in the United States today strict or relaxed? Com- pare the standards in your native country (in relation to dress, smok- ing, drink, and so on) with those in the United States.

**longitudinal study** (page 88, line 13)

In 1931, the Berkeley Institute of Human Development began a longitudinal study of adolescent development, called the Oakland (California) Growth Study. The children, 84 boys and 83 girls, were in fifth grade when the study began, and they and their families were studied intensively and continuously from 1931 until 1939.

*longitudinal study:* a study in which the same group of subjects is repeatedly tested as they grow older or over a long period of time.

Another type of study commonly used is a *cross-sectional study,* in which groups of people of different ages are studied and observed at the same time and measured in the same way. If, for example, the groups are similar in all important respects except age, then differences can be assumed to be due to developmental changes due to aging. In this type of study, people are measured at one time, not over a period of time.

If all the members of your class filled out a questionnaire about their favorite music, would be it a cross-sectional study or a longitudinal study? If class members filled out the questionnaire every two months for two years, would it be a cross-sectional study or a longitudinal study?

**follow-up** (page 88, line 17)

**survey** (page 88, line 17)

Follow-up surveys of this group were conducted through the 1960s, by which time many of these Depression adolescents had adolescent children of their own.

*follow-up:* the recontacting of a person for business or study purposes.

*survey:* a study of the particular facts about some thing in order to determine its condition or character.

A cross-sectional study in which questions are asked of a group, such as the members of your class, is a survey. If you were to return to this group and ask the same questions again, this would be a follow-up survey.

If you could do a survey about one aspect of your class members, what would it be? Would you also do a follow-up survey?

**data** (page 119, line 20)

Glenn Elder (1974, 1980), a sociologist, analyzed the data from this study in an effort to determine how the Depression had affected people who had been adolescents during those hard times.

*data:* facts or information, often in the form of numbers, used in reaching conclusions or in doing studies.

What data would you need in order to know which language is spoken by the majority of students in your class?

**average** (page 119, line 24)

**statistics** (page 119, line 24)

Statistics show that average family income in Oakland declined about 40 percent between 1929 and 1933.

*average:* an arithmetic mean found by adding up all the data on a particular group and then dividing by the number of quantities added. The average of $3,000, $4,000, and $8,000 is $5,000 ($3,000 + $4,000 + $8,000 = $15,000 ÷ 3 = $5,000).

*statistics:* the numerical facts or data that have been collected, classified, and used to explain a certain subject.

As a class project, ask each member of your class how many brothers and sisters he or she has. Add up the numbers and divide by the number of class members who contributed information. You will then have the average number of siblings (brothers and sisters) of the members of your class. What can you determine from these statistics?

# Vocabulary Development II

**synonyms**

Each word in column A means almost the same thing as one of the words in column B. A word that has almost the same meaning as another word is a synonym. Draw a line from each word in column A to its synonym in column B. The first one has been done for you.

| *A* | *B* |
|---|---|
| 1. prosperous | a. growth |
| 2. adolescent(s) | b. modify |
| 3. development | c. teenager(s) |
| 4. liberate | d. rich |
| 5. drastic | e. bring up |
| 6. adapt | f. change |
| 7. shift | g. severe, forceful |
| 8. raise | h. release, free |

Fill in each of the following blanks with a synonym (or its appropriate form) from column B.

1. The postwar period of the 1920s was a _____ time in

   which there was great financial _____.

2. The stock market crash brought about a _____ change in the lives of most Americans.

3. A study was conducted to determine how _____ had to

   _____ their lifestyles because of their family's lack of money.

4. Boys who had been _____ to seek higher education took

   jobs which served to _____ them from their family's control.

Now use these words in sentences of your own.

# Reading and Thinking Skills

## Comprehension Questions

1. According to the excerpt, how was the pre–World War I period different from the Roaring 20s?

2. What event took place in 1929 that radically changed society?

3. What changes occurred as the 1930s began? How did these changes affect the social context of life—the family, educational opportunities, job opportunities, and so on?

4. Describe the longitudinal study begun in 1931 by the Berkeley Institute of Human Development. What was its purpose?

## Discussion Activities

**Analysis and Conclusions**

1. The title of this chapter's excerpt is "The Social Context of Identity Formation." According to what you have read, to what does "social context" refer? What is "identity formation"?

2. According to Glenn Elder's findings, why was there a shift of power from the father to the mother after the Depression began?

3. How did life change for the adolescent girls studied? for the boys studied? Why did these kinds of changes occur?

4. How did the changes affect the lives of these young people as they grew to be men and women? Many of these people became parents in the 1950s. What kind of parents do you think they became? How do you think they brought their children up? On what did you base your answer?

**Writing and Point of View**

1. The authors of this excerpt are trying to convince the reader that "the historical context of growing up has important effects on the course of human development." What evidence do they use to support this point of view? Is there sufficient evidence to persuade you as the reader?

2. In paragraph 1, there are two uses of the word *it*. What does *it* refer to each time it is used?

3. The fifth sentence in paragraph 1 contains two semicolons. Why did the authors use semicolons to connect these sentences? Is there

any other way the sentences could have been connected? Which do you prefer?

4. Is this article more difficult to read than the Muñiz article? How do the styles of the two pieces differ? Which piece did you prefer reading and why?

**Personal Response and Evaluation**

1. Have you had any experience with a historical event or series of events that had a tremendous effect on people's lives? Describe the situation and its effects.

2. Do you know anyone who "suffered a major loss of income and status"? How did that person deal with the situation?

3. The authors claim that "people have the flexibility to adapt to major social changes during their adult years, to modify rather than lose their sense of identity." Do you think adults are more flexible and change more easily than adolescents? Support your opinion with your own observations or experiences.

4. Gail Sheehy in her book *Passages* writes, "The work of adult life is not easy." In what ways is adulthood more difficult than childhood?

## Reading the Textbook

One very important skill for college students is being able to get information from a textbook. When you read a text with a lot of information, like the excerpt that began this chapter, you cannot expect to remember every detail. However, the text itself is constructed in a way that can help you to find and remember the most important ideas. Some students highlight these ideas with specially colored pens, and other students copy them into their notebooks. Copying the main ideas and supporting details into a notebook is a good habit because most people find it easier to remember material they have written down than material they have simply read and underlined.

Paragraph 1 of the excerpt is reproduced here. The main idea has been underlined twice, and the most important details have been underlined once. Notice that not every word is underlined, but only the most important ideas. To make notes from this, you would use the outline form (see page 223).

The decade of the 1920s—the Roaring 20s—was a period of social revolution in the United States. After World War I (and in some ways because of it), there was a dramatic shift from strict Victorian prewar standards of behavior to more relaxed standards in regard to dress, drink, male-female relations, and much more. The 20s were also a very prosperous time. After World War I the economic balloon expanded until 1929, when it burst and the Depression began. The stock market crashed; banks and businesses failed; thousands of men lost their jobs and their life savings. Many families that had been comfortably middle class in the 20s became poor in the 30s.

Reread "The Social Context of Identity Formation." Then, working in small groups, try to determine the main idea of each paragraph. What are the most important supporting details? After you have agreed, copy the main ideas and supporting details into your notebook in outline form. Each group might prepare an outline together and make copies for the rest of the class or put their outlines on the chalkboard. The class can then discuss the choices of main ideas and important details. Each group must be prepared to justify its choices.

## Writing the Survey

The selection in this chapter described a longitudinal study of a large group of people to find out how the Depression had affected their lives. Each part of the study probably included some type of survey in which questions were asked of individual members of the group to determine group response. As a class, prepare a survey containing ten questions that will provide information about your class members. Decide on the questions and then conduct the survey. As a follow-up, you might want to conduct this survey at one-month intervals throughout the semester. If you decide to conduct follow-up surveys, you may want to consider questions whose answers might vary, such as "What is your biggest problem adjusting to life in the United States? What is the easiest part about learning English?" (Questions such as "How tall are you?" will probably not produce any changes in the follow-up surveys.)

## Journal Writing

A student wrote in her journal, "I may look different in five years and I may be living a very different life. I expect I will be married by then or at least I will have found someone to love. But deep down inside I will be the same person. Deep down inside people really don't change very much at all." This journal entry would seem to be in agreement with the article we have read. On the basis of your own experience, do you agree or disagree?

What event in your life has had the greatest influence on you? Is there any event that has made a change in where you live or how you live? Do you feel you are a very different person today from the person you were five years ago?

# Word Skills

## Idiomatic Expressions

Each of the following paragraphs contains a context clue that will help you understand some of the expressions used in "The Social Context of Identity Formation." Underline these context clues; the first one has been done for you. Then use the expressions when you answer the questions at the end of each paragraph.

*in regard to* (page 88, lines 4–5)

After World War I there was a dramatic shift in behavior in regard to dress, drink, and male-female relations. In other words, there was a change in connection with these areas. When each new president is elected in the United States, there are changes in regard to many aspects of American life. During Reagan's presidency, what changes, if any, did you notice in regard to economic policies? Have other presidents had a similar impact in regard to this area?

*by which time* (page 88, line 18)

The follow-up studies were done in the 1960s, by which time many of the children originally studied had children of their own. Some writers are unsure of a subject until they have completed their writing, by which time they know what they think. By that point, their ideas on the subject have taken shape. Were you ever unsure of what you wanted to say until you had started writing, by which time your ideas were clearer?

*in an effort to* (page 88, line 21)

Glenn Elder analyzed the data from the study in an effort to learn more about how the Depression had affected people. In order to try to understand something better, we often analyze or look closely at it. Is there any behavior or situation that you have analyzed closely in an effort to understand it better? How did you go about this?

Now use these idiomatic expressions in sentences of your own.

## Modals

### should

Adolescents hear a lot of advice from well-meaning people who tell them what they "should" and "should not" do. The following is a dialogue between Kim Soon and his uncle.

UNCLE: Kim, now you are nineteen years old and you should behave more like an adult.

KIM: I know. You must mean that I should get home before midnight.

UNCLE: I don't care what time you get home. As far as I am concerned, what is important is that you should finish school.

KIM: I'm a very good student.

UNCLE: You should be careful though. You should not get involved with the wrong people.

KIM: Next you will tell me that I shouldn't have any friends.

UNCLE: When I was your age, I spent more time working than socializing.

KIM: My father tells me the same thing, but I feel that I should have friends too. It should be possible for me to go to school, study hard, and still have time for fun.

UNCLE: You should think about settling down. I was already married when I was your age. Maybe you should get engaged.

KIM: Settled down? Engaged? I'm much too young for that. People are different now. My friends don't think you should get married until you are out of school and on your own for a long time.

UNCLE: You know I only want what is best for you. This culture makes me nervous. I have seen so many young people getting into trouble because they forget old-fashioned traditions and values. Your father told me that he is worried too.

KIM: He should talk to me about it. Uncle, you should tell him that I will never do anything that will hurt the family. Should I tell him that we talked?

UNCLE: No, no, I don't think so. You shouldn't tell him. He may want to talk to you on his own.

KIM: Uncle, you shouldn't worry about me. Maybe I should talk to you more often so you will know that I am serious even though I like to enjoy myself.

UNCLE: Kim, I guess your aunt is right. She said you were very mature and that I shouldn't be so concerned about you.

**EXERCISES**

1. Underline *should,* and the verb that follows it, each time it occurs in the dialogue.

2. Make a list of everything Uncle tells Kim he should do.

3. Make a list of everything Kim thinks he should do.

4. Imagine that a good friend tells you that he or she wants to drop out of school in order to begin making more money. Write a dialogue between you and your friend in which you discuss what he or she should and should not do.

On the basis of what you have observed in the dialogue, fill in the following blanks.

1. The verb that follows the word *should* _____ an -*s* ending.
   has/does not have

2. To make *should* negative, use the word *not* _____ the verb.
   before/after

3. To form a question with *should,* put the subject word _____ the verb.
   before/after

4. Write one sentence with *should.*

   _____

5. Write one negative sentence with *should.*

   _____

6. Write one question with *should.*

   _____

## Pronouns

In Chapter 2, we discussed voice. Writers must decide who the narrator of their piece will be and then write in the first person, the second person, or the third person. Look again at "The Social Context of Identity Formation." In what person is the article written? _____ Is it singular or plural? _____ The last paragraph of the article is reproduced here. Rewrite it in the first-person plural in the blanks provided.

Any great cultural or social changes—in fact, all broad influences—are experienced by individuals through what happens in their daily life. Adolescents learn about life's possibilities—and impossibilities—from their relationships with parents and friends and from the adults and books they encounter in high school. These influences all make important contributions to an adolescent's self-image.

_____

_____

_____

_____

_____

Read the original paragraph and your revised paragraph. Is there a difference in tone? Why do you think the authors wrote the selection in the third-person plural? _____

_____

## Plurals Review

In chapter 1 (pages 16–19) we learned some special rules for plurals. The following sentences have been taken from the selection at the beginning of this chapter. Some of the plural forms have been omitted. Fill in each blank with the appropriate plural form of the word in parentheses.

1. The stock market crashed; banks and _____ failed;
    (business)

   thousands of _____ lost their jobs and life savings.
              (man)

2. Many _____ that had been comfortably middle class in
        (family)
   the 20s became poor in the 30s.

3. Because the mother was so busy and the family so poor, the

adolescent _____ were given important adultlike
    (child)

_____.
    (responsibility)

4. Follow-up _____ of this group were conducted through
    (survey)

the 1960s, by which time many of these _____ had ad-
    (adolescent)

olescent _____ of their own.
    (child)

5. Adolescent girls were given many housekeeping _____.
    (duty)

## Commonly Confused Words

### affect/effect

Glenn Elder analyzed the data from this study in an effort to determine
how the Depression had *affected* people who had been adolescents during
that time period.

Is *affect* used as a verb or as a noun? Does it mean "influence" or
"bring about"?

After the Depression, there was a shift of responsibilities that had major
*effects* on the lives of the boys and girls.

The father's loss of status in the family and the mother's extra burdens
had a different *effect* on boys.

The *effects* of social circumstances on the identities of the men and women
in this study were evident all their lives.

The historical context of growing up has effected changes in the course
of human development.

Is *effect* used as a verb or as a noun in each of the preceding
sentences? If you had to use a synonym for *effect* in these sentences,
what would it be?

Examine how *affect* and *effect* are used in the following paragraph.
Then complete the definitions.

The effects of becoming an adult are varied. Your younger brothers and
sisters can be affected because they can see the positive things you are doing
with your life. The effect may be that they will grow up and try to be like
you. You can effect real changes in their lives.

_____ is a noun that means "result."

_____ is a verb that means "to influence."

_____ is a verb that means "to bring something about."

Fill in the blanks in the following sentences with either _affect_ or _effect_.

1. The birth of her first child had a big _____ on her life.

2. It _____ed the way she related to her own mother.

3. The _____ was very positive. She was able to

_____ some changes in her family relationships.

Now write your own sentences using _affect_ and _effect_.

# Sentence Skills

## Past and Present Tenses Compared

Reread "The Social Context of Identity Formation" and examine its grammatical structure. What tense is most frequently used? _____ In Chapters 3 and 4, we discussed the use of the past tense to describe events that have already taken place. This tense is often used to tell stories. The authors of this selection use the past tense to describe a study that took place in the past and the specific things that occurred at that time. However, when the authors describe and interpret their findings, they use the _____ tense since they are describing what they believe to be general truths.

**EXERCISE**

In the following exercise fill in each blank with either the past tense or the present tense of the verb in parentheses. Check the article for the correct answers.

1. After World War I the economic balloon _____ until
(expand)

1929, when it _____ and the Depression _____ .
(burst)                                          (begin)

2. Statistics _____ that average family income in Oakland
   (show)

   _____ about 40 percent between 1929 and 1933.
   (decline)

3. The effects of social circumstances on the identities of the men
   and women in this study _____ to be evident in later
   (continue)
   life.

4. Adolescents _____ about life's possibilities—and impos-
   (learn)
   sibilities—from their relationships with parents and friends and
   from the adults and books they _____ in high school.
   (encounter)

   What did you look at to help you decide which tense to choose?

## Sentence Decombining

In past chapters we practiced combining short sentences into longer
compound and complex sentences. "The Social Context of Identity
Formation" is a difficult piece to read because many of its sentences
are made up of many ideas and consist of short sentences combined
into long, complicated ones.

In this exercise we will break down long sentences into several
short sentences that may be easier to understand. The first one has
been done for you. After that, fill in the blanks. Then read the shorter
sentences and see if they are easier to understand.

A. In 1931, the Berkeley Institute of Human Development began a
longitudinal study of adolescent development, called the Oakland
(California) Growth Study.
1. The year was 1931.
2. The Berkeley Institute of Human Development began a study.
3. The study was longitudinal.
4. The study dealt with adolescent development.
5. The study was called the Oakland Growth Study.
6. Oakland is in California.

B. Glenn Elder, a sociologist, analyzed the data from this study in
an effort to determine how the Depression had affected people who
had been adolescents during those hard times.
1. Glenn Elder is a sociologist.

2. He analyzed the _____ from the study.

3. He wanted to determine how the _____ had _____ people.

4. He was interested in people who had been _____ during the Depression.

C. Often the mother both worked at odd jobs to bring income into the household and served as the main decision maker and emotional resource.

1. _____ the mother worked at _____

_____ .

2. She did this to bring _____ into the _____ .

3. She also served as the _____ _____ _____ .

4. She also served as an _____ _____ .

D. Because they had not even a slight hope of education beyond high school (who could afford it?) and because jobs were so scarce, they concentrated on a domestic future.

1. Adolescent girls did not have even a _____ _____ _____

education beyond _____ _____ .

2. Few could _____ to go to school beyond high school.

3. Jobs were _____ _____ .

4. Girls concentrated _____ _____ _____

_____ .

E. The father's loss of status in the family and the mother's extra burdens had a different effect on boys, serving to liberate them from parental controls at an early age.

1. The _____ lost _____ in the _____ .

2. The _____ had extra _____ .

3. This had a _____ _____ _____

_____.

4. This served to _____ them.

5. It liberated them _____ _____ _____.

6. This happened to them _____ _____ _____

_____.

F. First, the historical context of growing up has important effects on the course of human development, including the personal identity formed in adolescence and early adulthood.

1. First, the _____ _____ of _____

_____ has important _____.

2. These effects are on the course _____ _____

_____.

3. Human development includes the _____ _____ that is formed.

4. It is formed in _____ and _____ _____.

Choose another sentence from the article and, working with a classmate, decombine it. Remember that there is more than one correct way to do this; your discussion will be very important to your final decision.

# Paragraph Skills

## Cloze Exercise

The first paragraph of the excerpt is reprinted here, with every sixth word removed. Fill in what you think the missing words are, and then compare your answers to the original paragraph. If any of your words differ from the original, show it to a classmate or to your teacher. In most cases, there is more than one possible answer.

The decade of the 1920s—_____ Roaring 20s—was a period _____ social revolution in the United _____. After World War I (and in _____ ways because of it), there _____ a dramatic shift from strict _____ prewar standards of behavior to _____ relaxed standards in regard to _____, drink, male-female relations, and much _____. The 20s were also a _____ prosperous time. After World War I _____ economic balloon expanded until 1929, _____ it burst and the Depression _____. The stock market crashed; banks _____ businesses failed; thousands of men _____ their jobs and their life _____. Many families that had been _____ middle class in the 20s _____ poor in the 30s.

## The Complete Sentence

Sentence fragments sometimes pose a big problem for writers. During editing, it may be hard to find and correct these errors. In the following paragraph, there are several fragments, or incomplete sentences. Read the paragraph and underline the fragments.

In each of our lives. There are certain important passages or steps. Such as: graduating from high school, graduating from college, getting a job, and getting married. People mature. When it is the right time for them. They cannot just follow their friends. Because it is not right for them. Growing into adulthood. Is not an easy process.

The paragraph contains six fragments. Working with a classmate, underline these fragments. If you missed any of them, complete the following exercises.

A complete sentence must:

1. have a subject
2. have a verb
3. express a complete thought

We will examine several sentences to determine how we can know when a sentence is complete and how we can repair a problem sentence. In the checklist in the following table, S means that the sentence has a subject; V means it has a verb; CT means it expresses a complete thought. If a sentence has an *X* in each column, then it is a complete sentence. If it is missing an *X* in any column, then it is a fragment.

|  | *S* | *V* | *CT* |  |
|---|---|---|---|---|
| The baby. <br> (This is a fragment. It has a subject, but it has no verb and it does not express a complete thought. The baby what?) | X |  |  | Fragment |
| The baby laughed. <br> (This is a complete sentence.) | X | X | X | Sentence |
| Jumped. <br> (This is a fragment. It has a verb, but it has no subject and it does not express a complete thought. Who or what jumped?) |  | X |  | Fragment |
| The horse jumped. <br> (This is a complete sentence.) | X | X | X | Sentence |
| When the horse jumped. <br> (This is a fragment. It has a subject and a verb, but it does not express a complete thought. What happened when the horse jumped?) | X | X |  | Fragment |
| When the horse jumped, the baby laughed. <br> (This is a complete sentence.) | X | X | X | Sentence |
| Driving a car. <br> (This is a fragment. It does not have a subject, it has only part of a verb, and it does not express a complete thought.) |  |  |  | Fragment |
| The teenager was driving a car. <br> (This is a complete sentence.) | X | X | X | Sentence |
| To travel to Minneapolis. <br> (This is a fragment. It does not have a subject, it does not have a complete conjugated verb, and it does not express a complete thought.) |  |  |  | Fragment |

|  | S | V | CT |  |
|---|---|---|---|---|
| I want to travel to Minneapolis. (This is a complete sentence.) | X | X | X | Sentence |
| If I want to travel to Minneapolis. (This is not a complete sentence because it does not express a complete thought. What do I do if I want to travel to Minneapolis?) | X | X |  | Fragment |
| If I want to travel to Minneapolis, I will have to take a plane. (This is a complete sentence.) | X | X | X | Sentence |
| Such as chairs, tables, and sofas. ("Such as chairs, tables, and sofas" is a fragment. It does not have a subject or a verb, and it does not express a complete thought.) |  |  |  | Fragment |
| A furniture store has many things, such as chairs, tables, and sofas. (This is a complete sentence.) | X | X | X | Sentence |

Using the criteria of subject, verb, and complete thought, decide whether each of the following is a complete sentence or a fragment.

1. When I finish school.
2. I will look for a job.
3. Got married and moved to Wyoming.
4. Because he wanted to try engineering.
5. Cooking in the kitchen.
6. He cried.
7. Such as going to the movies, dancing at discos, giving parties, and eating out with friends.

Use the space below and at the top of the next page to correct each fragment and make it into a complete sentence.

## Article Review

In the following paragraph taken from the excerpt, all articles *(the, a,* and *an)* have been removed. Insert articles where they are needed in the paragraph, then refer to the original paragraph to check your answers. If your answers differ from the original, show them to your teacher or to a classmate. There is not always only one correct answer.

In 1931, Berkeley Institute of Human Development began longitudinal study of adolescent development, called Oakland (California) Growth Study. Children, 84 boys and 83 girls, were in fifth grade when study began, and they and their families were studied intensively and continuously from 1931 until 1939. Follow-up surveys of this group were conducted through 1960s, by which time many of these Depression adolescents had adolescent children of their own.

## Editing Skills Paragraph

The paragraph below is an unedited first draft that contains many surface errors. The types of errors and the number of times each occurs are listed here. Find and correct the errors.

| | |
|---|---|
| 4 fragment errors | 9 subject/verb agreement errors |
| 1 *they/their/they're* error | 2 plural errors |
| 1 *make/do* error | 1 *in/on* error |
| 2 *to/too/two* errors | 2 possessive errors |

Although getting engaged has changed Samia's life. She doesn't want to marry now. Ahmed, her boyfriend, want to get married right away, but she disagree. She like showing her girlfriend's her diamond ring. She enjoy discussing her future wedding with them. When she is in school. She know that she make her friend's jealous. Such as when her best friends did a real effort not too review there homeworks with her on the cafeteria. As they usually did every afternoon. Samia claim that she like being engaged, but she don't want to get married. Being housewives doesn't sound like two much fun to her.

Answers are on page 344.

# Essay Skills

## What Is an Essay?

Simply put, an essay is a series of paragraphs written on one theme. Traditionally, the main idea for the essay is found in the first paragraph, which is called the introduction. The main idea for an essay is called the thesis statement. The supporting points and details of the essay are found in the body paragraphs that follow the introduction. Each body paragraph has a main idea, called the topic sentence. The essay's final paragraph, which is called the conclusion, restates the thesis and the main points of the essay.

Underline the following words in the preceding paragraph: *introduction, main idea, thesis statement, body paragraphs, topic sentence, conclusion*. Then answer the following questions on the basis of the information in it.

1. What is the first paragraph called? _____

2. What is the main idea for the whole essay called? _____

3. What do the body paragraphs contain? _____

_____

4. What is the main idea for each body paragraph called? _____

_____

5. What is the final paragraph in the essay called? _____

_____

6. What is the purpose of the final paragraph? _____

_____


A diagram of a formal five-paragraph essay follows. (Remember that this is a sample essay form; not all formal essays contain five paragraphs.)

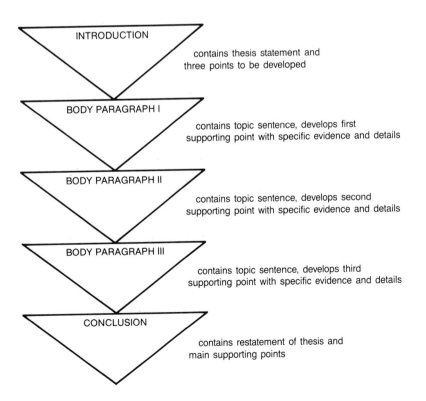

Although this approach to writing is quite formal and traditional, it is the type of writing required in many college first-year writing courses. It is useful to know these terms, and it is also good discipline for the writer to organize his or her ideas to fit this model. However, it should be remembered that this is just one model of writing.

Journal writing, clustering, brainstorming, and other writing exercises help a writer to loosen up and feel more comfortable with the writing process. It is then possible to produce creative and exciting work in any format.

**EXERCISES**

1. Although "The Social Context of Identity Formation" is quite lengthy, it has some of the same characteristics as the shorter essay shown in the diagram. With a classmate or in a small group, reread the article. Underline the main idea or thesis statement for the entire piece. Then underline the topic sentence or main idea for each paragraph. Discuss your choices in your group.

2. Reread the selection for Chapter 2 on page 24. Follow the instructions in the preceding question, and select the thesis statement and the topic sentence for each paragraph.

## Suggested Writing Topics

In past chapters, we have looked at formal and informal ways of organizing your writing. All these techniques can be helpful in any writing task you will ever face. Keep these techniques in mind as you prepare to write. For this assignment, try to write a formal essay based on the above model.

1. The historical events that occur in our country can have profound effects on our lives. Describe a situation in which someone's life was markedly changed because of an event that occurred in his or her country. How did the person cope with the changes?

2. "Adolescents learn about life's possibilities—and impossibilities—from their relationships with parents and friends and from the adults and books they encounter in high school." Do you agree with this statement? Support your point of view with your observations and experiences.

3. Being a high school student differs from being a college student in many ways. Compare your high school experiences with your college experiences in regard to classes, responsibilities, and social life.

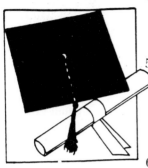

4. Graduating from high school marks the passage from childhood into young adulthood. Describe your high school graduation. Analyze your feelings about leaving childhood behind and moving into adulthood.

5. The authors of the excerpt in this chapter state: "Adolescents tend to follow in their parents' footsteps, taking on values, beliefs and goals that are very much like those of their parents." How do people decide what is right for themselves? Describe how you make these decisions, using examples from your experience or observations.

6. People want to be individual and unique. At the same time, however, they want to be accepted by their peers, so they conform in many ways. Explain how you or someone you know has resolved this conflict.

7. A student writes, "The best part of growing up is freedom. And the worst part of growing up is freedom." What do you think this student meant? How can one deal with the responsibilities and freedoms of adult life? Use your experiences and observations to support your point of view.

8. "Young people should move away from home as soon as they are able to support themselves because it is important for them to be independent and self-sufficient before making a commitment to anyone else." Do you agree or disagree? Support your point of view with your own experience or your observations of others.

## Revising I

1. Analyze an essay you wrote earlier in the semester. First, read just the introduction and the conclusion. Can you determine what the essay is going to be about? Is there a thesis statement? Look at the body paragraphs. Does each one develop a point with supporting evidence and details? Is there enough evidence to support the points? Is there a conclusion?

2. Rewrite the essay so that it follows the model of a formal essay.

3. Following the procedure described in question 1, analyze the essay you wrote for this chapter.

## Revising II

**the patchwork-quilt essay technique**

You may find this exercise interesting and helpful in producing a clear essay. Select an essay you have written, and copy it over line by line. Copy the first sentence, then skip three lines before copying the next sentence. Write on only one side of the page. When you have finished, tear the paper apart so that each sentence is on a separate slip of paper. Then move the sentences around, trying each sentence in several different positions. Keep rereading the essay until you are pleased with the positioning of the sentences. Then copy your newly constructed essay.

You can also do this exercise with a partner or in a small group.

# CHAPTER SIX

# Age and Youth

*"Age and Youth" is an excerpt from* Joys *and* Sorrows, *the autobiography of the great musician Pablo Casals. An autobiography is a nonfiction account of a person's life. This excerpt reveals Casals's feelings about his life at the age of ninety-three.*

**O**n my last birthday I was ninety-three years old. That is not 1
young, of course. In fact, it is older than ninety. But age is a
relative matter. If you continue to work and to absorb the beauty in
the world about you, you find that age does not necessarily mean
getting old. At least, not in the ordinary sense. I feel many things 5
more intensely than ever before, and for me life grows more fasci-
nating.

Not long ago my friend Sasha Schneider brought me a letter addressed to me by a group of musicians in the Caucasus Mountains
in the Soviet Union. This was the text of the letter: 10

°distinguished conductor, composer, or performer of music

Dear Honorable Maestro°—

I have the pleasure on behalf of the Georgian Caucasian Orchestra to invite you to conduct one of our concerts. You will
be the first musician of your age who receives the distinction of
conducting our orchestra. 15

Never in the history of our orchestra have we permitted a
man under one hundred years to conduct. All of the members
of our orchestra are over one hundred years old. But we have
heard of your talents as a conductor, and we feel that, despite
your youthfulness, an exception should be made in your case. 20

We expect a favorable response as soon as possible.

We pay travel expenses and of course shall provide living
accommodations during your stay with us.

Respectfully,
Astan Shlarba 25
President, 123 years old

**115**

°unbelievable

Sasha is a man with a sense of humor; he likes to play a joke. That letter was one of his jokes; he had written it himself. But I must admit I took it seriously at first. And why? Because it did not seem to me implausible° that there should be an orchestra composed of musicians older than a hundred. And, indeed, I was right! That portion of the letter was not a joke. There is such an orchestra in the Caucasus. Sasha had read about it in the *London Sunday Times*. He showed me the article, with photographs of the orchestra. All of its members were more than a hundred years old. There were about thirty of them—they rehearse regularly and give periodic concerts. Most of them are farmers who continue to work in the fields. The oldest of the group, Astan Shlarba, is a tobacco grower who also trains horses. They are splendid-looking men, obviously full of vitality. I should like to hear them play sometime—and, in fact, to conduct them, if the opportunity arose. Of course I am not sure they would permit this, in view of my inadequate age.

°enthusiasm

There is something to be learned from jokes, and it was so in this case. In spite of their age, those musicians have not lost their zest° for life. How does one explain this? I do not think the answer lies simply in their physical constitutions or in something unique about the climate in which they live. It has to do with their attitude toward life; and I believe that their ability to work is due in no small measure to the fact they do work. Work helps prevent one from getting old. I, for one, cannot dream of retiring. Not now or ever. Retire? The word is alien and the idea inconceivable to me. I don't believe in retirement for anyone in my type of work, not while the spirit remains. My work is my life. I cannot think of one without the other. To "retire" means to me to begin to die. The man who works and is never bored is never old. Work and interest in worthwhile things are the best remedy for age. Each day I am reborn. Each day I must begin again.

°opening sections of musical compositions
°type of musical composition
°Johann Sebastian Bach (1685–1750), a great German composer
°blessing

For the past eighty years I have started each day in the same manner. It is not a mechanical routine but something essential to my daily life. I go to the piano, and I play two preludes° and fugues° of Bach.° I cannot think of doing otherwise. It is a sort of benediction° on the house. But that is not its only meaning for me. It is a rediscovery of the world of which I have the job of being a part. It fills me with awareness of the wonder of life, with a feeling of the incredible marvel of being a human being. The music is never the same for me, never. Each day it is something new, fantastic and unbelievable. That is Bach, like nature, a miracle!

I do not think a day passes in my life in which I fail to look with fresh amazement at the miracle of nature. It is there on every side. It can be simply a shadow on a mountainside, or a spider's web gleaming with dew, or sunlight on the leaves of a tree. I have always especially loved the sea. Whenever possible, I have lived by the sea, as for these past twelve years here in Puerto Rico. It has long been a custom of mine to walk along the beach each morning before I start work. True, my walks are shorter than they used to be, but that 75 does not lessen the wonder of the sea. How mysterious and beautiful is the sea! how infinitely variable! It is never the same, never, not from one moment to the next, always in the process of change, always becoming something different and new.

# Vocabulary Development

**prefix *in-***
Knowing prefixes can help broaden your vocabulary. They can increase the number of words you will recognize when you read and the number of words you can comfortably use in your writing. Using these words in sentences will help you remember what they mean.

Placing *in-* before certain words changes their meaning.

All of the members of the orchestra are over one hundred years of age. Still I would like to conduct them. I am not sure they would let me, in view of my inadequate age.

What does *adequate* mean? _____

What does *inadequate* mean? _____

I, for one, cannot dream of retiring. The word is alien and the idea inconceivable to me.

What does *conceivable* mean? _____

What does *inconceivable* mean? _____

The music fills me with awareness of the wonder of life, with a feeling of the incredible marvel of being a human being.

What does *credible* mean? _____

What does *incredible* mean? _____

How mysterious and beautiful is the sea! how infinitely variable! It is never the same, never, not from one moment to the next, always in the process of change, always becoming something different and new.

What does *finite* mean? _____

What does *infinite* mean? _____

Use these eight words in sentences of your own. See if you can find other words like these in your dictionary.

# Reading and Thinking Skills

## Comprehension Questions

1. Was there any truth to the letter Sasha Schneider sent to Casals? Did Casals see it as implausible?

2. What does Casals believe is the best remedy for age?

3. What is Casals's daily routine? Does it ever bore him? Why or why not?

4. In lines 28–33 of the essay, the pronoun *it* is used four times. What does each *it* refer to?

## Discussion Activities

### Analysis and Conclusions

1. What attitude does Casals have toward life? Give examples from the text to support your point of view.

2. What does retirement mean to Casals? Support your answer with examples from the text.

3. Why does Casals live by the sea? What effect does the sea have on him?

### Writing and Point of View

1. How did reading "Age and Youth" affect you? Did you find Casals's style easy to read? Compare this essay with the Muñiz article in Chapter 4. Which did you prefer? Why?

2. Why do you think Casals included the letter in this essay instead of just telling the reader about it? What effect did reading the letter have on you?

3. The excerpt is from an autobiography. What is the difference between an autobiography and a biography? Albert E. Kahn met with Pablo Casals, and Casals told him the story of his life. If you could meet with any famous person to write down that person's autobiography, who would you most want to meet with? Explain why.

4. If this had been a biography, would it be written in the first person or the third person? Why? What biographies or autobiographies have you read that you would recommend to your classmates?

**Personal Response and Evaluation**

1. Have you ever known any older person with a particularly positive attitude toward life? Describe that person.

2. Should people be forced to retire at the age of 65 to give more opportunities to younger people? Give reasons for your answer.

3. Some people believe that Americans do not respect older people enough and do not treat them with enough care and kindness. In your experience, does this seem to be true? Explain.

## Collaborative Story Writing

Form a group of no more than five students. The group should decide on a topic to write a story about. When the group has come to an agreement, the first student chosen should write the first line of the story on a blank sheet of paper. The student should read this line aloud and then pass the paper to the next student. That student should write down the second line of the story and read aloud the first two lines. This process should continue until the group has agreed that the story is complete. Each group could then read its story to the class.

If your group has trouble deciding what to write about, here are some possible first lines:

You are walking down the street and in the gutter you find a big yellow envelope filled with various things.

You wake up in the middle of the night because you hear a strange noise somewhere in the house.

You are in a crowded airplane on a four-hour flight, and suddenly you notice that the person sitting next to you is someone with whom you had a fight several years ago.

It would be useful to tape record the story-writing process in each group. Students might enjoy hearing the tapes of their group, and the whole class could use the tapes as the basis for a discussion of the collaborative writing process.

## Journal Writing

The journal is an excellent tool with which the writer may begin to see his or her experience as unique in the world. Although we may focus on the same aspect of life in our journals, each of our views of the world will be personal and distinctive.

Your representation of the world differs from mine, and this is not only in so far as the world has used us differently—that is to say we have had differing experiences of it. It is also because your way of representing is not the same as mine. We are neither of us cameras. . . . I look at the world in the light of what I have learned to expect from past experiences of the world.

JAMES BRITTON, *Language and Learning*

Let us examine age and the aging process in our journals. Although we are not necessarily old, we are all constantly aging. Casals tells us that age is relative. "If you continue to work and to absorb the beauty in the world about you, you find that age does not necessarily mean getting old." He encourages us to question what it means to be old and what it means to be young. Imagine yourself as an old person. Imagine yourself as a young child. How does this make you feel? Think about this when you write in your journal.

# Word Skills

## Idiomatic Expressions

Each of the following paragraphs contains a context clue that will help you understand some of the idiomatic expressions used in the excerpt from Casals's autobiography. Underline these context clues; the first one has been done for you. Then use the expressions when you answer the questions at the end of each paragraph.

**as soon as possible** (page 115, line 21)

Invitations often request a response as soon as possible; sometimes this is abbreviated as "a.s.a.p." This asks the person being invited to respond <u>as quickly as he or she is able</u>. Is there anything that you would like to be able to do as soon as possible? Why?

**in spite of** (page 116, line 44)

Casals was ninety-three years old when he wrote "Age and Youth." In spite of his age, he remained young in his attitude and feelings for life. Although you may have difficulty learning English, you are still trying and gaining more success each day. In spite of the fact that you face problems in learning a new language, you manage to remain positive. How do you do this?

*in view of* (page 116, line 42)

Casals says that he would like to have the opportunity to conduct the Georgian Caucasian Orchestra. In view of his age, this would probably not be possible. Looking at the fact that he is younger than the other orchestra members, one can see why he would probably not be considered. In view of the fact that you are writing every day, do you think your writing will improve?

## The Phrase *Used To*

Casals tells us that he used to take long walks on the beach, but now his walks on the beach are shorter. Looking back on our lives, we remember many things that we used to do that we no longer do. Write two sentences describing things you used to do that you no longer do.

I used to eat eggs for breakfast every day, but now I eat cereal and whole wheat toast.
I used to live in a houseboat, but now I live in an apartment.

**Note:** In the phrase *used to, used* always ends in *-d. Used to* is always followed by the simple form of the verb with no *-s, -ed,* or *-ing* ending.

**PRACTICE**

1. Underline *used to* and the verb that follows it in each of the preceding sentences.
2. We often follow a *used to* phrase with "but not anymore." Change each of the preceding sentences to read "but not anymore."

I used to eat eggs for breakfast but not anymore.

_____

_____

3. Write a paragraph about yourself and your family describing something you used to do but do not do anymore.

## Prepositions

**in/on/at (time)**

In earlier chapters we looked at the use of _in, on,_ and _at_ in relation to place. These prepositions are also used idiomatically in relation to time. For example, Casals begins, "On my last birthday I was ninety-three years old." It would be incorrect to use _in_ or _at_ in this sentence. We will examine the uses of _in, on,_ and _at_ as they are used to describe time.

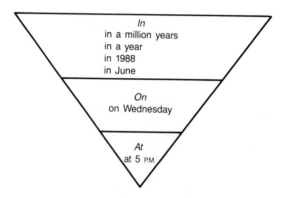

_In_ usually is used for a large block of time:

in a million years

in my lifetime

in 1989

in the spring

in the summer

in the fall

in the winter

in June

in a week

in the second week in April

*On* becomes a little more specific:

on December 27th
on the eighteenth of the month
on weekends
on the weekend
on my birthday
on the Fourth of July
on Thanksgiving
on Tuesday
on that day

*At* is the most specific of all; it is used to pinpoint an exact time:

at midnight
at dawn
at noon
at 6 P.M.
at 10:15
at two o'clock

A birthday would be expressed in one of the following ways:

I was born in 1970, in May, on the tenth of the month at 9:15 P.M.
I was born on May 10 in 1970 at 9:15 P.M.

However, there are some special expressions using *in*. We say, "in a minute" or "in a second" when someone asks how long we will be. If someone asks when he or she will see us again, we say:

"in a minute"
"in a week"
"in a month"
"in a year"

**EXERCISE**

On the basis of what you have learned about prepositions so far, fill in each of the following blanks with *in, on,* or *at.*

1. Pablo Casals was born _____ 1876, _____ Vendrell, Spain,

_____ December 29th.

2. He lived _____ Puerto Rico for many years of his life.

3. _____ a typical day _____ his life, he got up _____ dawn.

4. He made his debut _____ the Concert Lamoureus _____ Paris

   _____ 1898.

5. Casals founded the Barcelona Orchestra _____ 1919.

6. _____ 1950, he organized and played _____ the first of the

   chamber music festivals _____ Prades, France.

7. He also founded the Casals Festival _____ Puerto Rico _____
   the 1950s.

## Commonly Confused Words

### its/it's

Notice how *its* and *it's* are used in the following paragraph. Then, on the basis of what you have observed, complete the definitions that follow.

The Casals reading is remarkable for many reasons. First, *it's* written by a ninety-three-year-old person who is youthful in mind and spirit. *Its* main idea is work and the value of remaining busy and active. Casals writes of an orchestra and tells us that all *its* members are over one hundred years old. *It's* inspiring to know that such a man as Casals and such an orchestra as the Georgian Caucasian Orchestra ever existed.

_____ means "it is."

_____ means "belongs to it."

Fill in each of the following blanks with *it's* or *its*.

1. _____ a rare opportunity to meet someone as positive as Pablo
   Casals.

2. Time goes by very quickly and many people fear _____ pas-

   sage. They think that _____ too late to fulfill their dreams.

3. Casals probably would say that _____ never too late to enjoy

life and all _____ pleasures.

Now write your own sentences using *it's* and *its*.

# Sentence Skills

## Present Perfect Tense

By closely examining the following sentences, we can learn about the present perfect tense and how it is used. Read each sentence, then draw a circle around the verb and a rectangle around the subject. The first one has been done for you.

1. Never in the history of our orchestra (have) we (permitted) a man under one hundred years to conduct.

2. In spite of their age, these musicians have not lost their zest for life.

3. For the past eighty years I have started each day in the same manner.

4. It has long been a custom of mine to walk along the beach each morning before I start to work.

In the space provided, list the subjects and verbs you marked. Then copy any words that appear between the subject and the verb. The first one has been done for you.

| Subject | Auxiliary Verb | Middle Word(s) | Past Participle |
|---------|---------------|----------------|-----------------|
| we | have | | permitted |
| _____ | _____ | _____ | _____ |
| _____ | _____ | _____ | _____ |
| _____ | _____ | _____ | _____ |

After examining the above sentences, fill in the following blanks.

In the present perfect tense, the word _____ follows the
                                              has/have

subject *I* or *we*. The word _____ follows the subject *it*. Since
                                  has/have

we know that *it* is third-person singular, we can assume that *he* is

followed by the word _____ and that *she* is followed by the
                          has/have

word _____.
         has/have

To make the present perfect tense negative, add *not* between *have*
or *has* and the past participle.

You have _____ looked at the mail.

Adverbs such as *always, never,* or *rarely* belong between *have* or *has*

and the _____ _____.

It has never snowed in New Jersey in July.

To form a question, place *have* or *has* in front of the _____.

Have they been to Connecticut?

## Uses for the Present Perfect Tense

The present perfect tense has two uses. The first is to embrace
the past, the present, and the future at once.

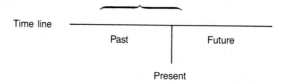

I have started each day in the same manner for the past eighty years.

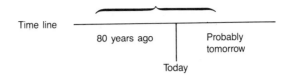

Time line

80 years ago

Today

Probably
tomorrow

The second use is to indicate the indefinite past. The present perfect tense is used in this case when the specific time that something was done is not important; what is important is that it was ever done or ever occurred at all.

We have heard of your talents as a conductor.

It does not matter when we heard this. If when we heard it is important, we use the past tense:

I heard you conduct last week.

Read the following dialogue, observing how the present perfect tense is used.

*An Interview with a World Traveler*

INTERVIEWER: I have heard that you have traveled all over the world. How many countries have you visited?

WORLD TRAVELER: I've lost count. I've gone to at least twenty countries though.

I: That's incredible. Have you been to China?

WT: China, oh yes. I've been there four times already.

I: Have you traveled anywhere else in Asia?

WT: I've gone all over. Let's see, I've visited India, Hong Kong, Thailand, Burma, Korea, and Japan.

I: Which is your favorite country?

WT: That's impossible to say. They're all so spectacular. I've gone shopping in a boat in Thailand. I've climbed mountains to the exquisite pagodas in Burma. I've bicycled in Peking and walked along the Great Wall. I have watched the sun set near the Taj Mahal and I've eaten the greatest curries in India. I've bathed in hot spas in Japan.

I: It sounds wonderful. Have you traveled to any other parts of the world?

WT: I have visited South America and Central America many times. I have studied Spanish for several years. In fact, I have done so much traveling in Brazil that I have begun to learn a little Portuguese.

I: Is there any place you haven't been to that you would like to visit?

WT: Believe it or not, I have never been to Alaska. In fact, I haven't been to the northern part of Canada yet.

I: Is there any reason why you haven't made it there yet?

WT: No particular reason. Just time, I guess. I have always wanted to go to those places, but I have always been on my way somewhere else.

I: Your life sounds like it has been very exciting.

WT: I have tried to keep it that way.

**EXERCISE**    Imagine that you are the person who interviewed the world traveler. Write an article for your newspaper describing the interview. Be sure to use the present perfect tense and tell your readers the places the traveler has visited and what the traveler has experienced.

## Subject/Verb Agreement

**third-person singular**

In the space provided, rewrite the last paragraph of Casals's "Age and Youth," changing *I* to *he*. The paragraph should begin:

He does not think a day passes _____

_____

_____

_____

_____

_____

_____

_____

_____

_____

_____

_____

_____

_____

## The Semicolon

Lines 27–28 of "Age and Youth" contain two semicolons. Underline each of these semicolons, and copy the sentences in which they appear in the space provided.

_____

_____

_____

In each sentence, draw a rectangle around the subject and a circle around the verb. Notice that each sentence contains two subjects and two verbs and that each part of the sentence expresses a complete thought. Each one is therefore a complete sentence. The semicolon connects the two complete sentences and prevents the sentence from being a run-on.

Now write your own sentence in which you use a semicolon.

# Paragraph Skills

## Process Paragraph—Ordering Step-by-Step

In Chapter 3, we discussed the importance of a sense of time or chronology in a narrative. Another type of writing in which order is important is the process or "how to" paragraph or essay. In this type of writing, we describe the order or steps in which we do something.

Process writing enables the reader to understand us better or to do something that we have done before. When we look at Casals's "Age and Youth," we learn something about him from the step-by-step outline of his day-to-day routine.

Casals gets up each morning and goes to the piano. He plays two pre-ludes and fugues of Bach. Then he takes a walk along the beach. He observes the nature that surrounds him.

When we read this, what do we learn about Casals?

There are many uses for the process type of writing, but the most common example is the recipe. The writer attempts to tell the reader, with sufficient detail and in the right order, the way to prepare a dish. The following is a recipe for "Grandma Robbins's Potato Latkes (Pancakes)":

In order to make 18 to 20 potato latkes or pancakes, first peel 6 large potatoes and then grate them into a colander. With your hands, squeeze some of the liquid out and put the potatoes in a bowl. Then grate 1 medium-sized onion into the same bowl and add two beaten eggs and ½ cup flour and ½ teaspoon of salt. Mix this together well. Next, heat oil in a skillet and drop the potato batter by spoonfuls into the hot oil, forming small pancake shapes. Let the latkes fry until they are crisp at the edge and brown. Then turn and cook the other side in the same way. Drain the pancakes on brown paper or paper towels. Then keep them warm in the oven while you cook the others. Finally, serve them to your hungry guests. These are delicious served with sour cream or apple sauce.

Adapted from *Grandma's Pantry Cookbook*

If the recipe is well written, the reader should be able to follow each step and make the dish. In the recipe above, underline all the transition words.

We also use process writing when we want to explain to someone how to do something. If someone asks us how to register for a class or get a passport, for example, we will give the steps that are required to do the activity. In the following example, a student describes the way to eat a slice of pizza:

First, you order the pizza by walking up and looking the counter-person straight in the eye and saying, "A slice, please." The slice comes on a thin, waxy piece of paper. Next, you grab a napkin and quickly slip it under the paper, so you don't spill hot oil all over.

Then you put your index finger in the middle of the crust and try to bend it in half. This way you can hold the slice in one hand without dropping it. At this point, you have to be careful because you can burn your finger on the hot cheese. Slowly, bring the slice close to your mouth. Breathe in as you do this. Then your mouth begins to water in anticipation of the taste. Take a bite at the tip of the triangle and chew carefully because the first taste, believe it or not, is always the best. Eat slowly and enjoy. Always remember to save a little of the cheese and sauce at the end so the crust will not be too dry. Finally, finish it all, even though it is probably cold.

In the description above, underline the transition words.

**EXERCISES**

1. Write a step-by-step explanation of how to get from school to the front door of your home.
2. Write a step-by-step explanation of how to buy a pair of comfortable shoes.
3. Write a step-by-step explanation of how to cook something.
4. Write a step-by-step explanation of how to get a driver's license.

## The Complete Sentence

### run-ons

In Chapter 5, we learned how to find and correct sentence fragments. In this chapter, we will look at run-ons. A run-on occurs when two or more complete sentences are joined with no punctuation or connecting word. Another type of run-on is the comma splice, in which two or more complete sentences are joined only by a comma. Run-ons present editing problems for many writers. In the following paragraph, there are four run-ons. Underline each one.

People in the United States are getting older, today approximately 11% of the population is sixty-five or over. In 1960 only 9% of the population was this old, and it is predicted that 21% of the population will be sixty-five or older by the year 2030. About 75% of these people live on their own another 18% live with an adult child. At least 5 million Americans are caring for a parent on any given day this can create a very stressful situation. Adult children are becoming parents to their parents, however, for some this can be overwhelming. The older parents also often feel the need for some independence and for the right to make decisions about their own lives.

Adapted from *Newsweek*, May 6, 1985

If you had any difficulty identifying the run-ons in the paragraph, read the following explanations.

| | Subject S | Verb V | Complete Thought CT |
|---|---|---|---|
| People in the United States are getting older, | x | x | x |
| today approximately 11% of the population is sixty-five or over. | x | x | x |
| (This is a run-on because two complete sentences are connected only by a comma.) | | | |
| About 75% of these people live on their own | x | x | x |
| another 18% live with an adult child. | x | x | x |
| (This is a run-on because two complete sentences are linked with no sign to connect them.) | | | |
| At least 5 million Americans are caring for a parent on any given day | x | x | x |
| this can create a very stressful situation. | x | x | x |
| (This is a run-on because two complete sentences are linked with no sign to connect them.) | | | |
| Adult children are becoming parents to their parents, | x | x | x |
| however, for some this can be overwhelming. | x | x | x |
| (This is a run-on because two complete sentences are linked by a comma and no coordinating word.) | | | |

There are four basic methods for correcting run-ons:

1. Use a period to end the first sentence and a capital letter to begin the next.

   People in the United States are getting older. Today approximately 11% of the population is sixty-five or over.

2. Use a subordinating word such as *when, while, because, if, although, as,* or *since.* (For a complete list of these words see page 194.)

About 75% of these people live on their own, <u>while</u> another 18% live with an adult child.

3. Use a comma and a coordinating word:

| | |
|---|---|
| , *for* | , *or* |
| , *and* | , *yet* |
| , *nor* | , *so* |
| , *but* | |

At least 5 million Americans are caring for a parent on any given day<u>, and</u> this can create a very stressful situation.

4. Use a semicolon to connect two sentences that are about a similar subject.

Adult children are becoming parents to their parents<u>;</u> however, for some this can be overwhelming.

**EXERCISE**     Correct the following run-ons, using any of the illustrated techniques. Try several approaches since this helps to create variety in your writing.

1. He always loved music Pablo Casals learned to play the cello.
2. His friend Sasha Schneider played a joke on him he sent him a letter inviting Casals to conduct an orchestra.
3. Casals liked to live near the sea he enjoyed early morning walks on the beach.
4. Looking at nature makes Casals very happy he feels connected to life in that way.

## Editing Skills Paragraph

The following paragraph is an unedited first draft that contains many surface errors. The types of errors and the number of times each occurs are listed below. Find and correct the errors.

| | |
|---|---|
| 2 fragment errors | 1 plural spelling error |
| 3 run-on errors | 2 *a/an* errors |
| 3 preposition errors | |

Like Pablo Casals, Marc Chagall was an remarkable man he also lived a long and productive life. He was born on 1887, he died on 1985. Chagall lived for almost a century. He was a great painter. Whose paintings makes people feel happy. They usually show dancing figures. Such as flying cows and pigs, playful lovers and bright colored flowers. Chagall was born in Russia on the Jewish quarter of the town of Vitebsk. He had eight brothers and sisters. Chagall knew he wanted to be a artist when he was a little boy, however, he did not become famous until he was in his fiftys.

Answers are on page 344.

# Essay Skills

## The Introduction

A formal essay usually begins with an introductory paragraph. Generally, the purpose of the introduction is to:

1. capture the readers' interest
2. state the thesis of the essay
3. introduce the major ideas that will be developed in the body of the essay (See diagram in Chapter 5, page 111.)

The introduction is useful to the writer as well as to the reader. It helps the writer plan the rest of the essay. If the introduction is well structured, the writer knows what the rest of the essay will contain. There are several different ways to write an introduction to a formal essay.

**General Statement** One type of introduction starts with a general statement. "Many musicians live long and productive lives." The essay then becomes more specific. "Pablo Casals is a good example. He lived into his nineties, and he continued to play music every day of his life." In this type of introduction, the writer takes the reader from the general (many musicians) to the specific (Pablo Casals).

**Anecdote** Another way to begin an essay is with an anecdote or short story. (See, for example, the Kleiman article in Chapter 1.) This is a very good way to capture your readers' interest. It is a technique that is often used by newspaper and magazine writers.

**Question** The introduction might ask a question that will be answered in the body of the essay. "Why is it that so many famous musicians live healthy and productive lives well into their eighties?" This is another technique that creates a great deal of reader interest.

**Quotation** An introduction can contain a quotation. Be sure to use quotation marks if you are using the exact words spoken or written by someone. "My work is my life. I cannot think of one without the other. To 'retire' means to me to begin to die," writes Pablo Casals in his ninety-third year.

When you write, you can use one of these types of introductions or a combination of several of them. You may create your own method of introduction, but your overall goal is to engage your reader, to make your reader want to continue reading what you have written.

**EXERCISES**

1. What are four ways of writing an introduction? What is the overall goal of the introduction?

2. Review the readings in this book. What kinds of introductions have the various writers used? Is textbook material introduced differently than journalistic writing?

3. As an individual project or in a small group, look at the latest issue of a news magazine. What types of introductions do you find? Why? Discuss this with your group.

4. Using one of the techniques described above, rewrite the introduction to an essay you have written this semester. Then read the original and the rewritten essay. Which do you prefer? Why?

## Suggested Writing Topics

1. Describe an older person who has had an important influence on your life. Include a lot of detail so that the reader can picture the person. Tell a story about the person so that the reader can understand why this person means so much to you.

2. "Work helps prevent one from getting old," Casals writes. Do you agree or disagree? Support your point of view with your experience or observations.

3. Should people be forced to retire at the age of sixty-five to give opportunities to young people? Support your point of view with your experience or observations.

4. Casals says that no day passes in his life in which he fails to look with amazement at the miracle of nature. Analyze his statement and explain whether you have ever felt inspired by the "miracle of nature." Give examples from your own life.

5. "Young people in this country have been accused of not caring for their parents in the way they would have in the old country, in Puerto Rico, in the Old South, or in Italy. And this is true, but it is also true that old people in this country have been influenced by an American ideal of independence and autonomy. The most important thing in the world is to be independent. So we live alone, perhaps on the verge of starvation, in time without friends, but we are independent." Margaret Mead, a famous anthropologist, wrote this statement in an essay on grandparents. Respond to the statement on the basis of your observations and experiences.

6. The *Newsweek* article adapted on pages 131–132 states that there are more people in the United States over the age of sixty-five than there have ever been before in history. What types of problems can this create? What are some ways of dealing with these problems.

## Revising

Revising an essay is a private activity. However, since writing is communication it may be useful to get feedback from fellow students before you begin revising. One technique involves working with a small group of three or four students.

First, make a copy of your essay for each person in the group. The students will take your essay home and read it through. On a separate piece of paper, they will write questions to you about any difficulties they had in reading your essay. You will read the other students' essays and do the same, writing questions that you think will help them in their revising.

When you receive the students' questions, read through them and then revise your essay. You may also want to share the revised essay with your fellow students.

# Relationships and Making Connections

# CHAPTER SEVEN

# Will You Go Out with Me?

*The following article from Newsweek was written by a student at the University of California at Berkeley named Laura Ullman. It is called "Will You Go Out with Me?" and describes the difficulty faced by a woman in deciding whether to ask a man out on a date. This excerpt was chosen because it discusses American dating customs.*

**E**very day I anxiously wait for you to get to class. I can't wait for us to smile at each other and say good morning. Some days, when you arrive only seconds before the lecture begins, I'm incredibly impatient.° Instead of reading the Daily Cal, I anticipate your footsteps from behind and listen for your voice. Today is one of your late days. But I don't mind, because after a month of desperately desiring to ask you out, today I'm going to. Encourage me, because letting you know I like you seems as risky to me as skydiving° into the sea.

°not patient; desirous to do something right away

°sport of jumping from an airplane, by opening a parachute and floating to the ground

I know that dating has changed dramatically in the past few years, and for many women, asking men out is not at all daring. But I was raised in a traditional European household where simply the thought of my asking you out spells naughty. Growing up, I learned that men call, ask and pay for the date. During my three years at Berkeley, I have learned otherwise. Many Berkeley women have brightened their social lives by taking the initiative with men. My girlfriends insist that it's essential for women to participate more in the dating process. "I can't sit around and wait anymore," my former roommate once blurted° out. "Hard as it is, I have to ask guys out—if I want to date at all!" Wonderful. More women are inviting men out, and men say they are delighted, often relieved, that dating no longer solely depends on their willingness and courage to take the first step. Then why am I digging my nails into my hand trying to muster° up courage?

°spoke out abruptly or impulsively

°gather

I keep telling myself to relax since dating is less stereotypical° and more casual today. A college date means anything from studying together to sex. Most of my peers prefer casual dating anyway be-

°conventional or typical; characteristic

**139**

°worrying or bothering
about

cause it's cheaper and more comfortable. Students have fewer anxiety attacks when they ask somebody to play tennis than when they plan a formal dinner date. They enjoy last-minute "let's make dinner together" dates because they not only avoid hassling° with attire and transportation but also don't have time to agonize.

Casual dating also encourages people to form healthy friendships prior to starting relationships. My roommate and her boyfriend were friends for four months before their chemistries clicked. They went to movies and meals and often got together with mutual friends. They alternated paying the dinner check. "He was like a girlfriend," my roommate once laughed—blushing. Men and women relax and get to know each other more easily through such friendships. Another friend of mine believes that casual dating is improving people's social lives. When she wants to let a guy know she is interested, she'll say, "Hey, let's go get a yogurt."°

°thick curded milk sometimes mixed with fruit; popular food in colleges

Who pays for it? My past dates have taught me some things: you don't know if I'll get the wrong idea if you treat me for dinner, and I don't know if I'll deny you pleasure or offend you by insisting on paying for myself. John whipped out his wallet on our first date before I could suggest we go Dutch. During our after-dinner stroll he told me he was interested in dating me on a steady basis. After I explained I was more interested in a friendship, he told me he would have understood had I paid for my dinner. "I've practically stopped treating women on dates," he said defensively. "It's safer and more comfortable when we each pay for ourselves." John had assumed that because I graciously° accepted his treat, I was in love. He was mad at himself for treating me, and I regretted allowing him to.

°kindly or politely

Larry, on the other hand, blushed when I offered to pay for my meal on our first date. I unzipped° my purse and flung out my wallet, and he looked at me as if I had addressed him in a foreign language. Hesitant, I asked politely, "How much do I owe you?" Larry muttered, "Uh, uh, you really don't owe me anything, but if you insist . . ." Insist, I thought, I only offered. To Larry, my gesture was a suggestion of rejection.°

°opened the zipper, a metal fastener with two rows of teeth

°refusal to accept a person or thing

Men and women alike are confused about who should ask whom out and who should pay. While I treasure my femininity, adore gentlemen and delight in a traditional formal date, I also believe in equality. I am grateful for casual dating because it has improved my social life immensely by making me an active participant in the process. Now I can not only receive roses but can also give them. Casual dating is a worthwhile adventure because it works. No magic formula guarantees "he" will say yes. I just have to relax, be Laura and ask him out in an unthreatening manner. If my friends are right, he'll be flattered.

Sliding into his desk, he taps my shoulder and says, "Hi, Laura, what's up?"

"Good morning," I answer with nervous chills. "Hey, how would you like to have lunch after class on Friday?"      75

"You mean after the midterm?" he says encouragingly. "I'd love to go to lunch with you."

"We have a date," I smile.

# Vocabulary Development

### adverbs using -*ly*

One way to enhance your vocabulary is to learn new word forms based on words you already know. A common occurrence in English is for an adverb (a word that modifies a verb but that also sometimes modifies an adjective or another adverb) to be formed by adding -*ly* to an adjective. In the examples below, sentences will be combined to change an adjective to an adverb.

She waits.
She is anxious. }

She anxiously waits.
(We can also use the adverb at the beginning of the sentence.
     Anxiously, she waits.
Notice where the comma is placed.)

She desires to ask him out.
She is desperate. }

She _____ desires to ask him out.

                              or

_____, she desires to ask him out.

She accepted his treat.
She was gracious. }

_____

_____

She asked a question.
She was polite. }

_____

_____

He kissed her.
He was tender. }

_____

_____

He spoke to her about
where they would go.    }    _____
He was quiet.                     _____

She flung her money on
the table.              }         _____
She was careless.                _____


He told her he wished he
hadn't paid for dinner. }        _____
He was angry.                    _____

                                 _____

Now use these adjectives and adverbs in sentences of your own.

_____

# Reading and Thinking Skills

## Comprehension Questions

1. In paragraph 1, how does Ullman let the reader know that she is interested in dating her classmate?
2. According to the article, what is the difference between casual dating and formal dating?
3. What is Ullman going to do that makes her very anxious?
4. How has casual dating improved Ullman's social life?

## Discussion Activities

### Analysis and Conclusions

1. Why does Ullman think that men are pleased that women are asking them out?
2. In paragraph 5, why was John "mad at himself for treating" Ullman to dinner?
3. In paragraph 6, why was Larry upset? Explain Larry's attitude about paying for a date.
4. According to Ullman, how has casual dating changed the dating situation in her college?

**Writing and Point of View**

1. To whom is the first paragraph of the article addressed? Who is "you"?

2. The last paragraph is only one sentence long. Is this an effective conclusion to the article? Would you change it in any way?

3. The style of this article is colloquial, that is, informal and conversational. Contrast Ullman's writing style with Muñiz's (Chapter 4, page 67). Which do you prefer? Why?

4. What is Ullman's main idea? Did she convince you? What examples did she use to support her ideas?

**Personal Response and Evaluation**

1. Do you think it is easier for a woman to ask a man for a casual date or a formal date? Explain, using your observations or experiences.

2. Should women ask men out on dates? Explain, using your observations or experiences.

3. Who should pay for a date? Why? Would you ever "go Dutch" on a date?

## Role Playing

1. Write a dialogue of a woman asking a man out on a date. Try to make your dialogue sound like real people talking. Act out the dialogue in front of the class.

2. Do an improvisation in which two students compose as they go along. One person will ask the other out on a first date. It might be fun to add new variables to the situation. Write these variables on pieces of paper; the students who are performing will pick them out of a bag. (Possible variables include: you used to date the person's brother or sister, you have to babysit for your little brother that night, you cannot stay out after midnight.)

## Journal Writing

It is well to understand as early as possible in one's writing life that there is just one contribution which every one of us can make; we can give into the common pool of experience some comprehension of the world as it looks to each of us.

DOROTHEA BRANDE, *Becoming a Writer*

Each of us has a unique vision of the world. We have all dreamed a personal dream of the person we will love. In addition to that dream, we have had real experiences. In your journal, write about the characteristics that you value in a friend or a date. Describe what it feels like to be in love. How does a person know that he or she is in love? Can men and women be just friends? Should men and women be friends before they get married? Do people who have arranged marriages fall in love? Is love necessary in order for a marriage to survive and be successful? Write about as many of these ideas as you choose.

# Word Skills

## Idiomatic Expressions

Each of the following paragraphs contains a context clue that will help you understand some of the idiomatic expressions used in Ullman's article. Underline these context clues; the first has been done for you. Then use the expressions when you answer the questions at the end of each paragraph.

**go Dutch** (page 140, line 47)

When friends go out together or when women ask men out on dates, they usually go Dutch. In this way, <u>each person pays for himself or herself.</u> Sometimes women prefer to go Dutch on dates. Why might a woman prefer to go Dutch? When would you choose to go Dutch on a date?

**chemistries click(ed)*** (page 140, line 35)

Ullman describes a couple who at first were just friends. Then their chemistries clicked; they felt attracted to each other as lovers. When people's chemistries click, their relationship may become more serious. Have you heard of a friendship that changed when the couple's chemistries suddenly clicked?

*Chemistries clicked* is a very colloquial expression that you would usually not use in formal writing.

**treat (someone) to (something)** (page 140, lines 51, 54)

Ullman writes about a date with John in which he treated her to dinner. If someone pays for you to do something, then that person treats you to it. On dates, the man usually treats the woman to dinner. How would you let someone know that you want to treat him or her to something?

*take the initiative* (page 139, line 16)

Women are beginning to take the initiative with men in relation to dating. In the past, the man was the one who made the first call and showed his interest in a woman. Men always took the initiative. Who do you believe should take the initiative in relation to dating?

## Comparatives/Superlatives

In Chapter 4, we discussed comparatives and superlatives. To review these structures, read the following paragraph.

To indicate that two things are about equal, we use *as [adjective] as*. She is *as tall as* her mother. Comparative forms (*-er than, more beautiful than*) are generally used to compare two things. One thing is *better than* the other. Superlative forms (*the -est, the most beautiful*) are used to compare three or more things, to show which is *the best* of all.

It is also possible to compare in order to show that one thing is not as good as another. The following examples demonstrate how this is done:

**Comparative**
I was not as agile as my brother.
I was worse than he was when it came to dancing.
I was less coordinated than my brother.
I was clumsier than he was.

**Superlative**
I was the worst dancer in the club.
I was the least coordinated person on the dance floor.
I was the clumsiest person in my family.

**EXERCISE**

Write a paragraph in which you describe an awful day in your life. Compare it with better days. You might want to begin: "Last Tuesday was one of the worst days in my life."

## Countables/Uncountables

Examine the following two sentences:

People have fewer anxiety attacks when they ask someone on a casual date than on a formal date.

People have less trouble when they ask someone on a casual date than on a formal date.

In the space provided, copy the words that are different in these two sentences.

_____

_____

One of these is countable and the other is uncountable.

Which is countable? _____

Which is uncountable? _____

If you had any difficulty with the above exercise, read the explanation that follows.

In English, certain nouns are uncountable. This means that they refer to something that cannot easily be counted as a single subject. An article *(the, a, an)* is usually not used with an uncountable noun. Two basic types of uncountable nouns are

*mass nouns* (This includes liquids such as water, milk, soda, coffee, tea, rain; solids that are made up of many small particles such as sand, salt, pepper, snow; gases such as air, hydrogen, oxygen, smoke.)

*abstract nouns* (These words represent ideas and qualities such as love, hate, anger, fear, beauty, ugliness, intelligence, life, freedom, success, truth, peace; categories such as money, furniture, merchandise, food, vocabulary, equipment, luggage.)

Uncountable nouns are treated as singular subjects and take singular verbs. They do not use an *-s* ending to show the plural.

Freedom is basic to life in the United States.

Water is finite and we must conserve it.

Her vocabulary seems excellent.

The new furniture looks beautiful in the living room.

In the above sentences, draw a rectangle around the subject and a circle around the verb. The first one has been done for you.

Write a paragraph using the following five words in any way you choose: *furniture, beauty, water, success, confusion.*

When we compare nouns, we use a different form for countable nouns than for uncountable nouns.

**countable nouns**
I went on *more* dates than my roommate. I had *many more* dates.
I had *fewer* blind dates than my best friend.
I did not have *as many* rejections *as* he did.

**uncountable nouns**
I had *more* fun than he had. I had *much more* fun than he had.
I had *less* excitement in my life than he had.
I did not have *as much* tension *as* he did.

**EXERCISE**

Fill in the blanks in the following dialogue with *much* or *many*, *less* or *fewer*.

ROBERT: How was the party last night?

MAX: Not _____ fun. There were _____ single women than I expected.

ROBERT: About how _____?

MAX: I didn't count. But there were _____ women with their boy-friends.

ROBERT: Was there _____ food to eat?

MAX: There was _____ to drink than to eat.

ROBERT: Was there _____ wine?

MAX: There was _____ more beer than wine.

ROBERT: Was there _____ dancing?

MAX: There were _____ couples on the floor dancing until 3 in the morning.

ROBERT: Did you dance _____?

MAX: I danced _____ than usual because my feet hurt. From now on I'm going to _____ parties and I will have _____ anxiety in my life.
ROBERT: You just feel that way now because you didn't meet anyone.
MAX: You're probably right.

Now write your own sentences using *much, many, less,* and *fewer*.

## The Gerund *(-ing)* Verb Form

When we write, we decide which verb form *(-s, -ed, -ing)* to use on the basis of the tense of the verb. In addition, when we have two verbs together we must decide which form to use for the second verb. Usually the preposition *to* is followed by the simple form of the verb. For example, "I like to sing." There are special rules for the verb form that should follow some verbs. We see several examples of these in the article:

*Paragraph 3*—I *keep telling* myself to relax since dating is less stereotypical and more casual today.
They not only *avoid hassling* with attire and transportation but also don't have time to agonize.

*Paragraph 4*—They *alternated paying* the dinner check.

*Paragraph 5*—"I've practically *stopped treating* women on dates," he said defensively.
He was mad at himself for treating me, and I *regretted allowing* him to.

Below is a list of some of the verbs that require the verb that follows to be in the *-ing* gerund form.

| | | | |
|---|---|---|---|
| alternate | deny | miss | report |
| appreciate | dislike | postpone | resent |
| avoid | enjoy | practice | resume |
| consider | escape | quit | stop** |
| delay | finish | regret* | |

*In a formal letter, regret is followed by the infinitive form of the verb (*to* plus the simple form of the verb): "I regret to tell you. . . ."

**Stop can be followed by either the *-ing* form or the *to* form, but the meaning changes:
  I *stopped talking* to my best friend means "we no longer talk."
  I *stopped to talk* to my best friend means "we spent some time talking."

The verb form that should follow most prepositions *(on, in, off, up, by, about, from, of)* is the *-ing* gerund form. Several examples of this from the Ullman article are reproduced below. Underline the preposition and the verb that follows it. The first one has been done for you.

*Paragraph 1*—Instead <u>of</u> <u>reading</u> the Daily Cal, I anticipate your footsteps from behind.

*Paragraph 2*—Many Berkeley women have brightened their social lives by taking the initiative with men.

*Paragraph 3*—A college date means anything from studying together to sex.

*Paragraph 5*—I don't know if I'll deny you pleasure or offend you by insisting on paying for myself. (There are two examples in this sentence.)
During our after-dinner stroll he told me he was interested in dating me on a steady basis.
He was mad at himself for treating me, and I regretted allowing him to.

There is a special list of expressions after which *to* is followed by the *-ing* gerund form. This is very unusual. *To* is almost always followed by the simple form of the verb with no ending. However, the following expressions are followed by the *-ing* gerund form:

admit to

confess to

look forward to

be used to*

get used to*

Below are examples of how these words are used in sentences:

1. The young man *admitted to asking* his brother's girlfriend out on a date.
2. She *confessed to flirting* with her math teacher.
3. Ullman *looks forward to having* lunch with the man in her class.
4. Ullman is not *used to asking* men out on dates.
5. She says that she will try to *get used to doing* this so she can improve her social life.

*Notice that the meaning of *be used to* and *get used to* is different from *used to,* which we studied in Chapter 6, page 121. *Be used to* and *get used to* mean "to get accustomed to."

## Commonly Confused Words

### though/thought/through
Read the following paragraph, and then complete the definitions that follow.

Even though Ullman's family *thought* it was not proper, she decided to try to ask a man out on a date. She *thought through* exactly what she would say. She asked him *though* she felt sure he would say "no." When she was *through,* he smiled and accepted. She *thought* she had succeeded.

_____ is the past tense of "think."

_____ means "even if" or "and yet."

_____ means "in one side and out the other" or "from the first to the last of."

Fill in each of the following blanks with *though, thought,* or *through.*

1. She _____ he would say "no," even _____ she hadn't even asked him yet.

2. As she watched him walk _____ the door into the class-

   room, she felt afraid, _____ her friends told her that everyone did it.

3. He helped her get _____ the ordeal by smiling at her.

Now write your own sentences using *though, thought,* and *through.*

_____

# Sentence Skills

## Tense Review

**Present Perfect Tense** In paragraph 2 of the Ullman article, we find the present perfect tense (*have/has* plus past participle) three times.

1. In the following spaces, copy the sentences from the paragraph that use the present perfect tense.

   _____

   _____

   _____

2. Draw a rectangle around each subject.
3. Draw a circle around each verb (*have/has* plus past participle).
4. Why did Ullman use the present perfect tense in these sentences?

**Past Tense** In the following sentences, Ullman used the past tense. Complete these sentences by filling in the correct form of the past tense. (Refer to the article or to page 349 if you are not sure of the correct form.)

1. Growing up, I _____ that men call, ask and pay for the
   (learn)
   date.

2. They _____ to movies and meals and often _____ together
   (go)                                    (get)
   with mutual friends.

3. They _____ paying the dinner check.
   (alternate)

4. Larry, on the other hand, _____ when I _____
   (blush)                    (offer)
   to pay for my meal on our first date.

5. I _____ my purse and _____ out my wallet,
   (unzip)                  (fling)

   and he _____ at me as if I had addressed him in a for-
   (look)
   eign language.

   **Present Tense** In the following sentences, decide whether the verb
   needs an *-s* ending.

1. A college date _____ anything from studying together
   (mean/means)
   to sex.

2. Most of my peers _____ casual dating anyway because
   (prefer/prefers)
   it's cheaper and more comfortable.

3. Another friend of mine _____ that casual dating is im-
   (believe/believes)
   proving people's social lives.

4. Who _____ for it?
   (pay/pays)

5. No magic formula _____ "he" will say yes.
   (guarantee/guarantees)

**EXTRA
PRACTICE**

1. Draw a rectangle around the subject in each of the preceding
   sentences.

2. Change *you* to *he* in paragraph 1 of the Ullman article. The first sentence will read "Every day I anxiously wait for him to get to class."

## Sentence Combining

### using *-ing*

As discussed in previous chapters, sentence combining is a method of making sentences longer and more interesting. Writers vary the length of their sentences by combining shorter sentences into a variety of longer sentences. In this exercise, we will practice writing sentences that begin with *-ing* phrases. In order for this to be effective, the subject in the two sentences must be exactly the same.

1a. I grew up.
 b. I learned that men call, ask and pay for the date.

Growing up, I learned that men call, ask and pay for the date.

Waiting for you to get to class, I am _____

_____.

2a. I wait for you to get to class.
 b. I am incredibly impatient.

3a. She treasures her femininity.
 b. She also believes in equality.

_____ing her feminity, she also _____

_____ _____.

4a. He feels shy.
 b. He hasn't asked her on a date yet.

_____ing _____, he _____

_____.

5a. He slides into his desk.
 b. He taps her shoulder and says, "Hi."

_____,

_____

_____.

Now write a sentence of your own using this pattern. Notice where the comma goes in this type of sentence.

# Paragraph Skills

## Cloze Exercise

The sixth paragraph of Ullman's article is reprinted here, with every fifth word removed. Fill in what you think the missing words are; then compare your answers to the original paragraph. If any of your words differs from the original, show it to a classmate or to your teacher.

Larry, on the other _____, blushed when I offered _____ pay for my meal _____ our first date. I _____ my purse and flung _____ my wallet, and he _____ at me as if _____ had addressed him in _____ foreign language. Hesitant, I _____ politely, "How much do _____ owe you?" Larry muttered, "Uh, uh, _____ really don't owe me _____, but if you insist . . ." _____, I thought, I only _____. To Larry, my gesture _____ a suggestion of rejection.

## Special-Feature Paragraph

**tense consistency**

The paragraph you are about to read has something wrong with it. Read the paragraph carefully and discuss with your classmates why it sounds strange.

Ullman wanted to ask a student in her class on a date, but she has a problem. The student is a man and Ullman was a woman. She grew up in a family that has traditional values. They did not believe their daughter should ask a man on a date. They believe the man should ask the woman out. At the same time, Ullman saw her friends asking men on dates. They feel good about it, and they say the men did too. They said it takes some of the pressure off the men. One of her friends meets her boyfriend this way. Women and men in Ullman's college go on casual dates, and often the women ask the men out. The arrangement works well and everyone seemed happy— everyone, that is, except Ullman. At last, she tries it herself. She asks out the man she liked and he tells her he would like to go.

Underline all the verbs in this passage. What tenses are used in the paragraph?

This paragraph is difficult to read because of the unnecessary tense changes. As readers, we do not know when the story is taking place. Try rewriting this paragraph in the past tense. (Note: "Women and men in Ullman's college go on casual dates, and often the women ask the men out" should remain in the present tense since it tells about a general state of being, not a particular event. Are there any other sentences in the paragraph that tell about a general state of being and should remain in the present tense?)

When you write, try not to change tenses unless it is necessary and check for tense consistency. Answers are on p. 345.

## Paragraph Revision

**ordering of ideas**

In the revision process writers reread their work to see if their ordering of ideas is clear and accurate. Sometimes moving sentences around within a paragraph or within an essay can help an essay make more sense to the reader.

Using the rewritten paragraph from the previous section, experiment with moving some of the sentences around within the paragraph.

1. Begin the paragraph with sentence 9, "Women and men in Ullman's college go on casual dates, and often the women ask the men out." If you begin with this sentence, do you have to move any other sentences around in order to make the paragraph logical? Should you add or delete any other sentences?

2. Begin the paragraph with sentence 3, "Ullman grew up in a family that had traditional values." Why should you change *She* to *Ullman* in this case? What sentence should follow this? Should you move any other sentences if you begin this way? Should you add or delete any other sentences?

3. Try moving other sentences around and see if you have to make any other changes to make the paragraph effective.

## Review Editing Exercise

Paragraph 2 of the Ullman article is reproduced here. All capital letters, quotation marks, and apostrophes have been removed. Rewrite the passage, putting them in where appropriate. Check your answers by referring to the original paragraph.

i know that dating has changed dramatically in the past few years, and for many women, asking men out is not at all daring. but i was raised in a traditional european household where simply the thought of my asking you out spells naughty. growing up, i learned that men call, ask and pay for the date. during my three years at berkeley, i have learned otherwise. many berkeley women have brightened their social lives by taking the initiative with men. my girlfriends insist that its essential for women to participate more in the dating process. i cant sit around and wait anymore, my former roommate once blurted out. hard as it is, i have to ask guys out—if i want to date at all! wonderful. more women are inviting men out, and men say they are delighted, often relieved, that dating no longer solely depends on their willingnesss and courage to take the first step. then why am i digging my nails into my hand trying to muster up courage?

For extra practice, change the paragraph to third person—"She knows that dating . . ."

## Editing Skills Paragraph

The following paragraph is a first draft that contains many surface errors. The types of errors and the number of times each error occurs are listed below:

| | |
|---|---|
| 4 fragment errors | 1 article error |
| 1 *your/you're* error | 1 *it's/its* error |
| 1 run-on error | 1 plural error |

Asking someone on a date can be risky. If the person says "no." You may feel rejected and embarrassed. However, it's important to keep in mind that rejection is not always personal there are many reasons why someone cannot accept you're offer. Its not always as simple as it seems. Once someone refused when I asked her to go out the first time. She said she had to take care of her younger brothers and sisters. I felt angry. Until I saw her at the movies. There she was with four little childrens. When she smiled at me. I realized she had been telling a truth. I asked her out again the next week, and she agreed. If her younger sister could come with us.

Answers are on page 345.

# Essay Skills

## The Conclusion

There are several ways to conclude an essay. The most basic conclusion is a summary of the essay that restates the thesis statement and the main supporting points of the essay. The concluding paragraph in this case is about three or four sentences long. For this type of conclusion, it may help to picture the essay as a clock with the introduction starting at twelve o'clock, the body of the essay moving through the hours of the day, and the conclusion arriving back at twelve o'clock to form a complete circle.

What follows is an example of how a writer might conclude Ullman's essay, using a summary conclusion.

Dating has gone through many dramatic changes in the past few years. It is no longer as formal as it once was. Women ask men out, and men accept with pleasure and relief at not always having to make the first move. The age-old problem of who should pay has still not been resolved and probably won't be for some time. Without a doubt, however, the best thing to come out of the entire situation is a healthier and more relaxed attitude on the part of men and women.

Notice that the conclusion begins with the thesis sentence. Then some of the main points of the essay are restated in different words. All the ideas of the essay are brought together in one final summary sentence. The easiest technique for writing this type of conclusion is to reread the essay and look for the thesis sentence and the main points of the essay. Then reword them.

Another type of conclusion is one sentence long. This type of conclusion makes a strong point; it may be humorous and it should be memorable.

"We have a date," I smile.

This is Ullman's conclusion. It is effective because it corresponds so well to the introduction, in which Ullman presents the problem of asking the man for a date. The body of the essay talks about dating in general. The end of the essay returns to the original problem; she asks the man out, and he accepts. This is an example of how a conclusion can take the reader full circle.

"If I miss now, then what?" said Miss Duong, adding that in Vietnam she received high marks.

This is the conclusion to Kleiman's article about Khan Duong in Chapter 1. The conclusion is effective because it leaves the reader with a question. The article describes how difficult Duong finds school in the United States, and the conclusion makes the reader reflect on Duong's problems and their questionable solutions.

**EXERCISES**

1. Reread the conclusions to the articles that we have read so far. Rewrite the conclusions in one of the formats described above. Read the original and your revision. Which do you prefer? Why?

2. Look in newspapers and news magazines, and cut out articles that you find interesting. Examine the conclusions. Bring the articles to class and discuss them with your fellow students. What other types of conclusions do you find?

## Suggested Writing Topics

1. Describe a first date, real or imagined. Use lots of detail to make the experience come alive for the reader. What made this date unique? Why did you choose to write about this particular date?

2. "There is no such thing as love at first sight. In order for love to be real, people must know each other for a long time and have many shared experiences." Do you agree or disagree? Support your point of view with your own experiences or observations.

3. Compare a casual date with a formal date. Consider such things as where people go, what they wear, and who pays for the date.

4. On the basis of your own observations, do you think dating patterns have really changed in recent years? If you are a woman,

would you ask a man out? If you are a man, would you go out with a woman who invited you? Would you go on a Dutch date? Should the man always treat?

5. "When a man wants to show a woman that he cares and respects her, he pays for their date." Do you agree or disagree with this statement? Support your point of view with your own experiences and observations.

6. Many people believe that men and women cannot really be friends. They feel that there is always an attraction between people of the opposite sex. Write an essay analyzing your feelings on this subject. Give examples from your experiences and observations.

## Revising

1. Before you begin to revise, make a list on a separate piece of paper of the points you wanted to cover in your essay. Put a star next to particularly important points. When you reread your essay, look to see that your essay covers those important points. If not, concentrate on including those ideas in your essay when you rewrite. Sometimes concentrating on a small block of information makes it easier to revise your writing effectively than when you look at the entire essay.

2. Earlier in this chapter, we discussed how moving sentences around in an essay can be helpful in the revision process. Doing this can help the writer to rethink a part of the essay or to see that more support is needed to make a point clear. Look at your essay and try to move at least one sentence. Once you have moved this sentence, are there any other changes that need to be made?

# CHAPTER EIGHT

# Love and Marriage

*This selection, which is called "Love and Marriage," is excerpted from Sociology, a textbook by Leonard Broom and Philip Selznick commonly used in colleges. It presents a multicultural perspective on the subject of love and marriage.*

**I**n contemporary America the union of love and marriage is taken    1
for granted as a cultural ideal. Most people understand that the
ideal does not govern all decisions to marry or stay married. But it
strongly influences the expectations people have and therefore what
they experience as success or failure.    5

### Prevalence and Control of Love

Love as a general phenomenon—the experience of warm affection, attachment, and sympathy—is hardly unique to Western society. Furthermore, sex-based love, which combines sexual attraction
with feelings of affection and tenderness, occurs among many peo-    10
ples, although the exact prevalence is in doubt. In some societies,
however, and perhaps in many, the union of sex and love is neither
experienced, nor appreciated.

For the Lepchas of Zongu sexual activity is practically divorced
from emotion; it is a pleasant and amusing experience, and as    15
much a necessity as food and drink; and like food and drink it
does not matter from whom you receive it, as long as you get it;
though you are naturally grateful to the people who provide
you with either regularly.

Whatever its prevalence, sex-based love is not necessarily valued,    20
encouraged, or permitted to determine important decisions. On the
contrary, many societies have fairly elaborate social mechanisms for
the control of love, which is potentially disruptive° of social hierarchies and family alliances. In these societies, the idea of marrying
for love is a social absurdity, an affront° to common sense, and a    25
threat to the fabric° of community life. This is especially true where
kinship dominates social organization, for then the distribution of
property and the protection of social status or group identity may

°producing a break or up-
setting a situation

°insult

°structure

**159**

°prominent °brought about by mental or physical force

be at stake. Under such circumstances a marriage has serious consequences for a network of relatives. To control these consequences, rules and procedures for the selection of mates emerge. Usually these are among the most salient° and coercive° of customs.

Two varieties of patterns controlling marriage are: specification of mates by social norms and external intervention, that is, arrangement of marriages by third parties. Two preliterate cultures are compared with feudal Japan and the present-day United States according to the interplay° of these variables:

°exchange or influence between

1. The Yaruros of Venezuela are a nomadic tribe of fishermen and hunters. Marriage is both arranged and highly specified. The marriage is arranged by a shaman who knows exactly what he must do—find an eligible cross-cousin. A boy's cross-cousin is his mother's brother's daughter or his father's sister's daughter. The daughters of his mother's sister or his father's brother do not qualify. The boy's uncle determines which of the eligible cross-cousins will be selected.

°standard by which a thing is tested
°people who act as agents or intermediaries

2. In eighteenth-century feudal Japan, the patriarchal household was the individual's center of existence. The welfare of the family as a corporate group was accepted as the touchstone° for all decisions. Marriages were carefully arranged, using go-betweens° to avoid humiliating rejections. But the family could range widely in its search for eligible marriage partners. There was no strict specification as among the Yaruros.

3. The Hottentots of southwest Africa resemble the Yaruros in that cross-cousin marriage is required. Hence the field of eligibles is narrowly prescribed. Unlike the Yaruros, however, the Hottentots are free to choose for themselves who to marry so long as a cross-cousin is selected.

4. In American society, individual choice prevails, limited by pressures toward racial, class, and age-group endogamy. Within these limits, a wide range of eligibles is available, and third parties have little control over the matter. They may have a lot to say, but in the end it is the prospective spouses themselves who make the decision.

In addition to the control mechanisms discussed above—arrangement of marriages and specification of eligible spouses—others include (1) child marriage; (2) isolation of potential mates—for example, a system which requires marriage to someone from another village; and (3) close supervision, especially of adolescent girls.

°shut out; exclude

**Caution** Except for close supervision, these mechanisms may not have originated for the purpose of controlling love, but they do have that effect, as well as other effects. Furthermore, the mechanisms do not foreclose° the emergence of love. Indeed, they may encourage it by creating appropriate expectations. Although love may be controlled and channeled, it is not necessarily eliminated.

# Vocabulary Development

**sociology jargon**

Each discipline has its own special language, or jargon. When you study that discipline, you begin to learn its special words. Some of these words can be used and understood as part of your general vocabulary. This article contains several words that relate to sociology and will be useful if you take courses in that field. Some of these words will become part of your college vocabulary and everyday language.

**endogamy** (page 160, line 58)

In American society, individual choice prevails, limited by pressures toward racial, class, and age-group endogamy.

*endogamy* (noun): marriage within the same group, class, tribe, or caste; the opposite is exogamy

How would you define *exogamy*? _____

**hierarchy** (page 159, lines 23–24)

On the contrary, many societies have fairly elaborate social mechanisms for the control of love, which is potentially disruptive of social hierarchies and family alliances.

*hierarchy* (noun): a system of persons or things arranged in a graded order or class

**kinship** (page 159, line 27)

This is especially true where kinship dominates social organization, for then the distribution of property and the protection of social status or group identity may be at stake.

*kinship* (noun): relationship by blood or marriage

In your culture, what is more important—kinship or business relationships? Explain. _____

**nomadic** (page 160, line 38)

The Yaruros of Venezuela are a nomadic tribe of fisherman and hunters.

*nomadic* (adjective): of a group of people (nomads) who habitually move their home to find food, avoid drought, etc.

How would you define *nomad*? _____

**norm** (page 160, line 34)

Two varieties of patterns controlling marriage are specification of mates by social norms and external intervention, that is, arrangement of marriages by third parties.

*norm(s)* (noun): pattern regarded as typical of a specific group
In your culture, what are the norms relating to marriage?

_____

**patriarchal** (page 160, line 45)
   In eighteenth-century feudal Japan, the patriarchal household was the individual's center of existence.
*patriarchal* (adjective): of a system of government (patriarchy) in which the father or male heir rules; the opposite of matriarchal or matriarchy
How would you define *matriarchy*? _____

**shaman** (page 160, line 40)
   The marriage is arranged by a shaman who knows exactly what he must do—find an eligible cross-cousin.
*shaman* (noun): a tribal medicine man or magician
People sometimes go see a shaman when they have had upsetting dreams. What do you think the shaman might do to help them?

_____

# Reading and Thinking Skills

## Comprehension Questions

1. According to the excerpt, love is composed of three parts. What are they?
2. What are two varieties of patterns controlling marriage? What is meant by these terms? Illustrate with examples from the article.
3. What is a cross-cousin?

## Discussion Activities

### Analysis and Conclusions

1. According to Broom and Selznick, the union of love and marriage is taken for granted as a cultural ideal in contemporary America. Do you think this cultural ideal contributes in any way to the high divorce rate in the United States?
2. Is the union of love and marriage a cultural ideal in all societies? Give examples from the excerpt to support your point.
3. In some societies, the idea of marrying for love is viewed negatively. What reasons does the article give for this? What negative consequences can marrying for love have for such a society?

4. Every family has a hierarchy. Certain member(s) of the family make important decisions. In your family, who decided where the family lives? Who decides what the family will eat for dinner? Who makes the decision that a child is mature enough to marry?

## Writing and Point of View

1. "Love and Marriage" is excerpted from the textbook *Sociology*. Was it more difficult to read than the last selection? What made the article hard to understand?

2. Have you read many textbooks in English? What techniques do you use for reading difficult works?

3. What tense do the authors use to present their ideas? Why did they use this tense?

## Personal Response and Evaluation

1. Do you know anyone whose marriage was arranged? Is it a happy marriage? A successful marriage? Researchers say people in such marriages often fall in love eventually. On the basis of your observation, is this true or not?

2. Should people marry for love even if it goes against their families' wishes?

3. Does it matter to children if their parents are in love? Explain your point of view by drawing on your own experience or observations.

4. Draw your own family tree. Who are your cross-cousin(s)? How would you feel if you were told that you had to marry a cross-cousin?

## Role Playing

1. Imagine that you are a sociologist who has come to study the people in your class. You want to know about their customs—how they decide whom to marry, who works to support the family, who cares for the children, and so on. What questions would you ask? What would you like to learn from your interviews? Working in groups, write your questions down.

2. Ask the questions compiled in the preceding activity of a classmate who comes from a different country or culture than your own. Write down or tape the answers.

3. Create a mythical society with its own customs and rules of behavior. This could be done by the class as a whole or in small groups. One group could be responsible for the customs relating

to marriage, another for the customs relating to food, another for those relating to crime, and another for those relating to political decisions. The groups should then share their experiences with the class.

## Journal Writing

We write in our journals to find out who we are and what we think. Many journal writers are surprised by their own writing. When writing essays, we plan; when writing in our journals, we respond spontaneously. It is good to have this balance in our writing experience. Moreover, as many of you have probably already discovered, journal writing can give us ideas that will be useful in the writing of more formal material. We can learn from ourselves.

This chapter is about forming relationships. Relationships are an important part of growing up. When we are younger, we fantasize about our future relationships. We think about the person we will fall in love with and marry someday. Describe your ideal mate.

Think about marriage and its commitments. When is the "right" time to get married? What characteristics are most important in a good relationship? Do you know any couple that seems to have an ideal relationship? What is unique about their relationship?

# Word Skills

## Idiomatic Expressions

Each of the following paragraphs contains a context clue that will help you understand one of the idiomatic expressions used in the article. Underline these context clues; the first one has been done for you. Then use the expressions when you answer the questions at the end of each paragraph.

### *take for granted* (page 159, lines 1–2)

Americans believe that love and marriage naturally belong together. They take this for granted; they accept it without questioning it. There is even a song entitled "Love and Marriage." One line from the song says, "Love and marriage go together like a horse and carriage." Some other beliefs that are taken for granted by this culture are mother love, the happiness of children, and the idea of hard work leading to success. Can you think of other beliefs that you take for granted?

*hardly unique to* (page 159, line 8)

Most families are concerned that their children receive a good education and grow up to be productive human beings. This belief is hardly unique to one family or even to one culture. It is not a belief of only one group or one person; it is shared by many. Are any of your beliefs hardly unique to you but, in fact, the beliefs of most human beings?

*in doubt* (page 159, line 11)

Even though, as a culture, most Americans believe that people should marry for love, it is in doubt how many actually do. The number of people who marry for love is uncertain. Some people marry for money; some marry to please their families. Is there any other widely held notion in American society that you feel is in doubt?

## Countable/Uncountable Nouns

### people/peoples

Paragraph 2 of the article contains the word *peoples*. *People* is a plural form already. What does *peoples* mean? It is a common term in anthropology and sociology.

*People* refers to human beings in general or to human beings living in the same country, with the same history and culture, and usually speaking the same language.

*Peoples* refers to different societies and different cultures around the world. *Peoples* have different languages, histories, and cultures.

Fill in each of the following blanks with either *people* or *peoples*.

1. The French _____ are known for their excellent food.

2. The _____ of Africa speak many different languages and have varying customs and traditions.

3. Many _____ believe that the family is the most important element in human life.

4. Sociologists study the _____ of the world.

## Apostrophe Exercise

Chapter 3 discussed the use of the apostrophe to show possession. "The mother of Helen" is "Helen's mother." In paragraph 6 of the excerpt in this chapter, there are many apostrophes to show family relationships. The paragraph has been reproduced here with the eight apostrophes removed. Fill in the apostrophes where they are needed. Then go back to the original and check your answers.

The Yaruros of Venezuela are a nomadic tribe of fishermen and hunters. Marriage is both arranged and highly specified. The marriage is arranged by a shaman who knows exactly what he must do—find an eligible cross-cousin. A boys cross-cousin is his mothers brothers daughter or his fathers sisters daughter. The daughters of his mothers sister or his fathers brother do not qualify. The boys uncle determines which of the eligible cross-cousins will be selected.

## Articles

### the

Paragraph 8 of the excerpt is reproduced here. All the capital letters have been removed, and the word *the* has been omitted each time it appears. Fill in all the missing capital letters, and add *the* where it is needed. Refer to the original to check your answers. (If you have difficulty with this exercise, review pages 30–32.)

hottentots of southwest africa resemble yaruros in that cross-cousin marriage is required. hence field of eligibles is narrowly prescribed. unlike yaruros, however, hottentots are free to choose for themselves who to marry so long as a cross-cousin is selected.

## Commonly Confused Words

### accept/except

Read the following paragraph, observing the use of *accept* and *except*.

In many parts of the world, people *accept* the fact that the welfare of the family is more important than personal satisfaction. If you *accept* this, then divorce becomes a very serious matter. It is certainly a violation of family. *Except* in the most unusual circumstances, the children of divorce live with their mother. And the father must *accept* the reality that he will not figure in his children's lives as much as he might like. Some fathers say they can *accept* this, *except* that it really hurts them emotionally.

From what you observed in the preceding paragraph, can you determine the difference in meaning between *accept* and *except*? Complete the following definitions.

_____ means "agree to or receive."

_____ means "but" or "aside from the fact that."

Now use these two words in sentences of your own.

# Sentence Skills

## Past and Present Tenses

**Past Tense** Imagine that you are living in the year 2200 and have just discovered an old, weather-beaten pile of papers. You read through the papers and discover the article about love and marriage that began this chapter. Rewrite the first two paragraphs of the article, changing all the verbs to the past tense so that you can tell your world about the people of the past. The first sentence of the rewritten article will read: "In America in the 1980s the union of love and marriage was taken for granted as a cultural ideal."

**Present Tense** Use your imagination and write a paragraph describing your world in the year 2200. Is there still marriage? Are babies born from women's bodies? Do families live together or are children brought up in special areas? Remember that you are describing your world as it is in the year 2200. Use the present tense. For example, your article might begin: "It is the year 2200, and in our world there are many amazing changes from the world of the past."

## Decombining Sentences

As we saw in Chapter 5, sentences that are very long and embedded can be difficult to read. In that chapter we used the technique of decombining, or taking apart, complicated sentences and creating several shorter sentences. In this exercise we will decombine several sentences from the excerpt.

1. Love as a general phenomenon—the experience of warm affection, attachment, and sympathy—is hardly unique to Western society.
   a. As a general phenomenon, love has three parts.

   b. It is the experience of _____ _____.

   c. It is also the experience of _____.

   d. It is also the experience of _____.

   e. It is hardly unique to _____ _____.

   (In these sentences, to what does *it* refer? _____)

2. Furthermore, sex-based love, which combines sexual attraction with feelings of affection and tenderness, occurs among many peoples, although the exact prevalence is in doubt.

   a. Furthermore, sex-based love occurs among _____

   _____.

   b. Sex-based love combines _____ _____ with

   _____ of _____ and _____.

   c. The exact prevalence of _____-_____

   _____ is in doubt.
   (According to this sentence, do sociologists know in how many

   societies there is sex-based love? _____)

3. Whatever its prevalence, sex-based love is not necessarily valued, encouraged, or permitted to determine important decisions.
   a. The prevalence of sex-based love is uncertain.

   b. Sex-based love is not necessarily _____.

   c. It is not necessarily _____.

d. It is not necessarily permitted to _____ _____

_____.

(In the original sentence, to what does *its* refer? _____)

4. Choose two sentences from the article and decombine them.
   [**Note:** There are many ways to decombine sentences, just as there are many ways to combine them. This exercise illustrates one possibility. You may want to experiment with others.]

## Active and Passive Voices

Underline the verbs in the following sentences. The first has been done for you.

1. The union of love and marriage <u>is taken</u> for granted by contemporary Americans.

2. The marriage is arranged by a shaman.

3. Cross-cousin marriage is required by the Hottentots.

4. Sex-based love is not valued by many societies.

**EXERCISE**

1. According to the first sentence, who takes the union of love and marriage for granted?_____

2. According to the second sentence, who arranges the marriage?

_____

3. According to the third sentence, who requires cross-cousin marriage? _____

4. According to the fourth sentence, who does not value sex-based love? _____

The sentences above were written in the passive voice. Fill in the following blanks to change them to the active voice.

1. Contemporary Americans *take* the union of love and marriage for granted.

2. A shaman arranges _____  _____.

3. The Hottentots _____ cross-cousin marriage.

4. Many societies do not _____  _____-_____

_____.

Compare the passive-voice sentences to the active-voice sentences. What differences do you observe?

*Passive:*  The union of love and marriage is taken for granted by contemporary Americans.
*Active:*  Contemporary Americans take the union of love and marriage for granted.
*Passive:*  The marriage is arranged by a shaman.
*Active:*  A shaman arranges the marriage.

In the passive construction, the "to be" verb and the past participle are used. In present passive, we use *am, is,* or *are* plus the past participle. In the past passive, we use *was* or *were* plus the past participle. The preposition *by* is often used in the passive construction.

The passive voice is frequently used when the performer of the activity is unknown or unimportant. This technique emphasizes the receiver of the action rather than the doer of the action.

Both active voice and passive voice are correct forms of English. They offer the writer variety in creating sentences. You may notice that textbooks use the passive voice more frequently than newspapers. It is a more formal style. Many modern writers prefer the active voice.

**EXERCISE**

The following paragraph is written entirely in the passive voice. Add variety to the paragraph by changing some of the sentences to the active voice.

In the past in many European countries, marriages were arranged by a matchmaker hired by the family. This matchmaker was expected to make a lasting match. An unhappy marriage was feared by many young people. However, the parents' wishes were respected by the children. Young people were reminded of their obligations by their family and their community. It was expected by everyone that the marriages would lead to love and mutual respect. Divorce was looked down upon by most of the community and religious leaders. Marriage was regarded as a lifetime commitment by most people in those days. As a result, golden anniversaries were celebrated by many more couples then than at present.

# Paragraph Skills

## Summary Writing

Often, when we read a long text, we want to reduce it to a shorter, more concise form that will be easier to remember. This summary of the longer piece contains the main ideas that we have read. It is useful for studying and for understanding what the writer is trying to express. In the summary, we may paraphrase or restate the writer's original words in our own words. We may use actual quotations in the summary. Whether we use a direct quote or a paraphrase, we identify whose ideas we are using. This helps us when we are reviewing class material or writing a research paper.

Using the article that began this chapter, we can practice summary writing by looking for the main idea in each paragraph. Paragraph 1 is summarized below:

Broom and Selznick state that the union of love and marriage is a cultural ideal that influences people's expectations about their relationships. This ideal may be used in judging their relationships as successes or failures.

**EXERCISES**

1. Write a summary of paragraph 2 of the article that is under 50 words in length.

2. Write a summary for each of the other paragraphs in the article. Try to keep each summary under 50 words.

3. Write a summary of the entire article in fewer than 200 words. Be brief, but be as complete as possible. Try to capture the main ideas.

4. For extra practice, write a summary of the reading from another chapter in this book.

## Parallelism

In each of the following pairs of sentences, put a check next to the sentence that you think sounds better.

1a. In some societies, the union of sex and love is not appreciated, experienced, or enjoying.

 b. In some societies, the union of sex and love is not appreciated, experienced, or enjoyed.

2a. Sex-based love is not necessarily permitted, encouraged, or valuable.

 b. Sex-based love is not necessarily permitted, encouraged, or valued.

3a. Although love may be controlled and channeled, it is not necessarily elimination.

 b. Although love may be controlled and channeled, it is not necessarily eliminated.

You probably chose the second sentence in each of the three pairs. Words in a series usually sound better if they have a parallel structure (all *-ed* words, all *-ing* words, all *to* verbs, and so on). The sentences are thus more balanced and easier to read.

Parallelism is a technique that makes writing smoother and more coherent. The items in a sentence that are being compared should be in the same grammatical form. Any items that are joined by *for, and, nor, but, or,* and *yet* require parallelism.

When people get engaged, they usually feel happy, excited, and nervous. (adjectives)

A traditional American bride wears something old, something new, something borrowed, and something blue. (noun + adjective)

They tell their parents, call their friends, and make plans for their life together. (verbs)

The couple can often be found talking and planning. (gerunds)

**EXERCISE**

Fill in the blanks in the following sentences to create parallel structures.

1. Families with teenagers are sometimes confused, _____,

 and _____.

2. Asking someone for a date can be embarrassing, _____,

 and _____.

3. When couples get married, they want to _____, to

 _____, and to _____.

Now write two sentences of your own containing series with parallel structures.

## Transitions

When we write an essay, we are listing ideas one after another. To help the reader know how the ideas are related, we use certain words that connect one thought to the next. These words are called transition words since they create the transition, or bridge, between sentences. There are many types of transition words. (We studied one group of transition words in Chapter 4; see page 83.)

In this chapter we will look at the following transition words:

on the contrary

hence

in addition to

furthermore

although

**EXERCISE**

1. Whatever its prevalence, sex-based love is not necessarily valued, encouraged, or permitted to determine important decisions. *On the contrary,* many societies have fairly elaborate social mechanisms for the control of love, which is potentially disruptive of social hierarchies and family alliances.

    *On the contrary* means ————————————————.

2. The Hottentots of southwest Africa are similar to the Yaruros because they both require cross-cousin marriage. *Hence* the choice of whom an individual can marry is limited.

    *Hence* means ————————————————.

3. *In addition to* the control mechanisms discussed above—arrangement of marriages and specification of eligible spouses—others include (1) child marriage; (2) isolation of potential mates—for example, a system which requires marriage to someone from another village; and (3) close supervision, especially of adolescent girls.

    *In addition to* means ————————————————.

4. Love as a general phenomenon—the experience of warm affection, attachment, and sympathy—is hardly unique to Western so-

ciety. *Furthermore,* sex-based love, which combines sexual attraction with feelings of affection and tenderness, occurs among many peoples, although the exact prevalence is in doubt.

*Furthermore* means _____.

5. *Although* love may be controlled and channeled, it is not necessarily eliminated.

Can love be controlled and channeled? _____

Can love be eliminated? _____

*Although* means _____.

Now use these five transition words in sentences of your own.

## Editing Skills Paragraph

The following paragraph is a first draft that contains many surface errors. The types of errors and the number of times each type occurs are listed below. Find and correct all the errors.

| | |
|---|---|
| 2 fragments | 2 preposition errors |
| 4 subject/verb agreement errors | 1 possessive error |
| 1 article error | 2 tense consistency errors |
| 2 run-ons | 2 *there/their/they're* errors |

Sociologists examines how people live in groups. They examined phenomena. Such as peoples' behavioral patterns in relation to love and marriage. They want to know if people on France celebrate marriage in the same way as people on Philippines. They're studies show some customs and traditions is similar from place to place. For example. People usually get married with some kind of ceremony they usually get dressed up for there wedding. However, there are some differences. In some places marriages are arranged in other places people meets and falls in love. In general everyone hoped that the marriage will be happy and long-lasting.

Answers are on page 345.

# Essay Skills

## Brainstorming

Whenever possible, you should write about something that interests you. You will then have ideas on the subject and probably be able to come up with something to say. Even if you are writing about a topic that interests you, however, you may have problems writing an essay. Brainstorming is a good technique to use to help you come up with ideas that will develop into your essay.

When you brainstorm, you develop ideas and supporting details by asking questions. The basic questions are: Who? What? Where? When? How? Why? The questions vary, based on the topic. For example, the sample questions below were used to brainstorm for an essay about a special relationship.

Who has the relationship?

My parents, who have been married for thirty-five years, have a special relationship.

What makes them special?

They are best friends no matter how difficult the situation.

Where do they live?

They live in an old house that they have rebuilt themselves.

When did you realize that their relationship was special?

I came to visit them as they were refinishing a floor. They were working on the same area. They bumped heads and kissed. They were in their sixties.

How do they make you feel?

They have always made me feel like they loved me, and they made me believe that I could succeed. Observing their relationship made me believe that relationships can last and grow.

Why do you want to write about them?

I want to show that people can be married for a long time and still be best friends, still be in love.

The writer's next step is reading through the questions and answers and deciding what to emphasize in the writing. As you read through what you have written, this may become obvious. Although brainstorming is a good technique for getting started, you can use it at any time during the writing process. If you are stuck in the middle and need more support or more details, brainstorming can be helpful. It is a useful tool to help a writer create a rich, fully developed essay.

**EXERCISES**

1. Brainstorm about one or more of the following: a special relationship; teenage marriages; the high divorce rate; living together before marriage. Write down your questions and answers. They will be helpful when you begin writing.

2. Brainstorm with a classmate. One of you will ask the questions; the other will write down the answers. Then repeat the activity but reverse roles. At the end of the two sessions, you should have material for two essays.

## Suggested Writing Topics

1. Describe the best relationship you have ever observed. Include details that make clear why this relationship is unique.

2. Despite the fact that people marry for love in the United States, there is a tremendously high divorce rate. Analyze the reasons why so many people in the United States divorce. Use your observations and experiences to support your point of view.

3. Sociologists tell us that the union of love and marriage is not a cultural ideal in all societies. Should it be? Explain. Support your ideas with your observations and experiences.

4. "Parents should have more to say about the person their child marries." Do you agree or disagree? Support your point of view.

5. A student writes, "One of the reasons why so many people get divorced is that they get married too young. Almost all my friends got married straight out of high school and now a lot of them are telling me that it just isn't working." Respond to this statement on the basis of your own experiences or observations.

6. Analyze whether you think living together before marriage would help reduce the divorce rate. Support your ideas with your observations and experiences.

## Revising

Another way to use brainstorming is as a revising technique. Before you begin to revise your paper, take a look at your introduction. Then write the subject matter of your essay at the top of a blank piece of paper. Ask yourself questions about the topic, and answer the questions. Even if you have done this during the writing process, you will probably write several new questions. When you have written about five to ten questions and answers, you are ready to revise. You have had time to reconsider what you were writing about, and your brainstorming may have given you new avenues to explore. Now reread your paper and begin to revise.

This revising technique can be done with a classmate as well. Tell your classmate what your essay is about. The classmate can then write brainstorming questions on the topic. Read your essay, looking to see if your classmate's questions were answered in your essay. These questions may offer suggestions that will help you further develop your essay.

# CHAPTER NINE

# The Story of an Hour

*Kate Chopin (1851–1904) was born and raised in St. Louis. After her husband's death in 1883, she began writing to support herself and her six children. "The Story of an Hour," one of Chopin's most famous short stories, deals with the complexities of love and loss.*

**K**nowing that Mrs. Mallard was afflicted with a heart trouble, 1 great care was taken to break to her as gently as possible the news of her husband's death.

It was her sister Josephine who told her, in broken sentences; veiled hints that revealed in half concealing. Her husband's friend 5 Richards was there, too, near her. It was he who had been in the newspaper office when intelligence of the railroad disaster was received, with Brently Mallard's name leading the list of "killed." He had only taken the time to assure himself of its truth by a second telegram, and had hastened to forestall° any less careful, less tender 10 friend in bearing the sad message.

°prevent

She did not hear the story as many women have heard the same, with a paralyzed inability to accept its significance. She wept at once, with sudden, wild abandonment,° in her sister's arms. When the storm of grief had spent itself she went away to her room alone. She would 15 have no one follow her.

°surrender to feelings

There stood, facing the open window, a comfortable, roomy armchair. Into this she sank, pressed down by a physical exhaustion that haunted her body and seemed to reach into her soul.

She could see in the open square before her house the tops of 20 trees that were all aquiver° with the new spring life. The delicious breath of rain was in the air. In the street below a peddler was crying his wares. The notes of a distant song which some one was singing reached her faintly, and countless sparrows° were twittering° in the eaves.° 25

°shaking; trembling

°small brown birds
°making light, chirping bird sounds
°lower part of the roof that sticks out

There were patches of blue sky showing here and there through the clouds that had met and piled one above the other in the west facing her window.

**178**

She sat with her head thrown back upon the cushion of the chair, quite motionless, except when a sob came up into her throat and 30 shook her, as a child who has cried itself to sleep continues to sob in its dreams.

She was young, with a fair, calm face, whose lines bespoke° repression and even a certain strength. But now there was a dull stare in her eyes, whose gaze was fixed away off yonder on one of 35 those patches of blue sky. It was not a glance of reflection, but rather indicated a suspension of intelligent thought.

There was something coming to her and she was waiting for it, fearfully. What was it? She did not know; it was too subtle and elusive to name. But she felt it, creeping out of the sky, reaching toward 40 her through the sounds, the scents, the color that filled the air.

Now her bosom rose and fell tumultuously.° She was beginning to recognize this thing that was approaching to possess her, and she was striving to beat it back with her will—as powerless as her two white slender hands would have been.                                         45

When she abandoned herself a little whispered word escaped her slightly parted lips. She said it over and over under her breath: "free, free, free!" The vacant stare and the look of terror that had followed it went from her eyes. They stayed keen and bright. Her pulses beat fast, and the coursing° blood warmed and relaxed every inch of her 50 body.

She did not stop to ask if it were or were not a monstrous joy that held her. A clear and exalted perception enabled her to dismiss the suggestion as trivial.

She knew that she would weep again when she saw the kind, tender 55 hands folded in death; the face that had never looked save° with love upon her, fixed and gray and dead. But she saw beyond that bitter moment a long procession of years to come that would belong to her absolutely. And she opened and spread her arms out to them in welcome.                                                                        60

There would be no one to live for her during those coming years; she would live for herself. There would be no powerful will bending hers in that blind persistence with which men and women believe they have a right to impose a private will upon a fellow-creature. A kind intention or a cruel intention made the act seem no less a crime 65 as she looked upon it in that brief moment of illumination.

And yet she had loved him—sometimes. Often she had not. What did it matter? What could love, the unsolved mystery, count for in face of this possession of self-assertion which she suddenly recognized as the strongest impulse of her being!                                       70

"Free! Body and soul free!" she kept whispering.

Josephine was kneeling before the closed door with her lips to the keyhole, imploring for admission. "Louise, open the door! I beg;

°gave evidence of;
showed

°disturbedly

°racing

°except; but

°medicine said to prolong life

°repeated demands
°unknowingly

°calmly
°suitcase; valise

open the door—you will make yourself ill. What are you doing, Louise? For heaven's sake open the door." 75

"Go away. I am not making myself ill." No; she was drinking in a very elixir° of life through that open window.

Her fancy was running riot along those days ahead of her. Spring days, and summer days, and all sorts of days that would be her own. She breathed a quick prayer that life might be long. It was only 80 yesterday she had thought with a shudder that life might be long.

She arose at length and opened the door to her sister's importunities.° There was a feverish triumph in her eyes, and she carried herself unwittingly° like a goddess of Victory. She clasped her sister's waist, and together they descended the stairs. Richards stood 85 waiting for them at the bottom.

Some one was opening the front door with a latchkey. It was Brently Mallard who entered, a little travel-stained, composedly° carrying his gripsack° and umbrella. He had been far from the scene of the accident, and did not even know there had been one. He stood amazed 90 at Josephine's piercing cry; at Richards' quick motion to screen him from the view of his wife.

But Richards was too late.

When the doctors came they said she had died of heart disease—of joy that kills. 95

---

# Vocabulary Development

**suffix -less**

In past chapters, we have discussed ways of increasing your vocabulary using prefixes. We can also increase vocabulary by adding suffixes, or endings, to words. The following sentences have been reproduced from Chopin's story.

The notes of a distant song which some one was singing reached her faintly, and *countless* sparrows were twittering in the eaves.

What does *countless* mean in this sentence? _____

She sat with her head thrown back upon the cushion of the chair, quite *motionless,* except when a sob came up into her throat and shook her, as a child who has cried itself to sleep continues to sob in its dreams.

What does *motionless* mean in this sentence? _____

She was beginning to recognize this thing that was approaching to possess her, and she was striving to beat it back with her will—as *powerless* as her two white slender hands would have been.

What does *powerless* mean in this sentence? _____

When you add *-less* to a word, how does it change the meaning of

that word?_____

Here are some other adjective forms that use this suffix. Can you figure out the meaning of each of these words?

*thoughtless* means _____

*mindless* means _____

*fearless* means _____

*hopeless* means _____

*childless* means _____

*dreamless* means _____

*breathless* means _____

Now try using these words in sentences of your own.

# Reading and Thinking Skills

## Comprehension Questions

1. What do we learn about Mrs. Mallard's health in the beginning of the story? How does this information figure in the ending of the story?

2. Does Louise Mallard's health influence the way she is given the information about her husband's death? Who tells her? In what manner do they tell her?

3. How does Mrs. Mallard respond to her husband's death? What does she do? Support your response with evidence from the story.

4. The next-to-last paragraph of the story is only one sentence long: "But Richards was too late." Explain what this sentence means.

## Discussion Activities

### Analysis and Conclusions

1. "Storm of grief" is a very poetic expression of Mrs. Mallard's feelings. What does this expression mean? How do you picture a "storm of grief"?

2. How does Mrs. Mallard feel as she walks down the stairs with her arms clasped around her sister's waist (lines 84–85)?

3. The last paragraph is only one sentence long: "When the doctors came they said she had died of heart disease—of joy that kills." What does "joy that kills" mean? Do you agree with the doctors' reason for Louise Mallard's death?

### Writing and Point of View

1. In paragraph 5, Chopin begins to create a mood that is very unusual for a story about death. What details in this paragraph make the reader think more about life than about death? Were you surprised at this change of tone?

2. What is Chopin trying to tell us? Does the fact that this story was written in 1894 surprise you? Could this story have been written in the 1980s?

3. Who is telling this story; from what point of view is the story told? Would it have been a very different story if it had been written in the first person? Rewrite the first five paragraphs of the story in the first person. Which version do you prefer? Why?

4. Line 1 in the story does not follow grammatical conventions. It's not clear who "Knowing" refers to. The sentence could be rewritten as "Since Mrs. Mallard was afflicted with a heart trouble, great care was taken. . . ." Which do you prefer?

### Personal Response and Evaluation

1. What is happening to Mrs. Mallard in paragraphs 7 and 8? Have you ever heard bad news and responded in this way?

2. Were Louise and Brently Mallard in love? How do you know?

3. If Brently Mallard had been dead, would Louise have remarried? Discuss this with your classmates.

4. What will happen to Brently? How do you think he will respond to his wife's death? Will he remarry?

5. In the last chapter we read about love and marriage. Do you think Brently and Louise got married because they were in love, or

could it have been an arranged marriage? Do you think attitudes toward love and marriage were the same in 1894 as they are today?

## Reading Skills

**images and symbols**

Reading a story like "The Story of an Hour" makes us feel a certain way; it creates a mood. In Chapter 3, we read "A Day's Wait" by Ernest Hemingway. The mood of that story was lonely and cold. It seemed to be a story about two people who were trying to communicate but could not. The thermometer symbolized a lack of communication; the father and the son were both reading it differently. When we examined that story closer, we saw how Hemingway set the story in the winter, in the ice, in an almost empty house. The images make us feel lonely.

"Age and Youth," the excerpt from Casals's autobiography in Chapter 6, has a very different tone. Casals writes about music and nature. He symbolizes the future when he mentions the sea and a spider's web. These are positive symbols. They are warm and alive, and they tell the reader that life is good.

Chopin gives us mixed symbols. The story is about death, but Chopin includes many details that relate to life. In the space provided, list some of the images that Chopin includes in the story.

_____

_____

Read the list of images. How do these images make you feel? What is the mood in Chopin's story? If paragraph 5 were rewritten to include more negative images, the story might become very depressing.

She could see in the tiny dark square before her house the tops of bare trees all covered with ice and snow and heavy with the coldness of winter. The howling breath of wind was everywhere. In the street a half-naked beggar shook with the cold. The sounds of the screeching wheels of carriages slipping over the ice pierced the air. There were hundreds of freezing sparrows hanging on the icy branches.

Read the story, substituting this paragraph for the present paragraph 5. Does the mood of the story change? Try this with another story. Rewrite a paragraph using the author's style but changing the images to create a different mood.

## Journal Writing

We have been writing in our journals, thinking about our lives and the unique way each of us sees life. Poetry can sometimes be a stimulus for writing because it is so condensed. When you read the poem below, think about Louise Mallard and about the way she viewed her life. She wants "freedom" and she believes that she will get that when her husband is gone. What does "freedom" mean to you? Have you ever felt "locked in a cage" like the Turkish woman who wrote this poem? We can be "locked in a cage" in our jobs, our classes, our relationships, our family, or even in our own minds. Think about these things as you read this short poem.

> I am a bunch of red roses
> You hurt me
> like the helpless nightingale
> you locked in a cage.

> *Bayati, a type of anonymous Turkish poem, translated by*
> *Reza Baraheni and Zahra-Soltan Shokoohtaezeh*

# Word Skills

## Idiomatic Expressions

Each of the following paragraphs contains a context clue that will help you understand one of the idiomatic expressions used in "The Story of an Hour." Underline these context clues; the first one has been done for you. Then use the expressions when you answer the questions at the end of each paragraph.

**break the news** (page 178, lines 2–3)

Because Mrs. Mallard had a bad heart, her sister Josephine and Richards were careful about the way they broke the news of Brently Mallard's death. When we break the news to someone, we are <u>telling them something surprising</u>; the news could be good or bad. Have you ever had to break bad news to anyone? How did you do it?

**at once** (page 178, line 13)

Louise Mallard wept at once; she cried as soon as she heard the news. If someone tells you they need something done at once, they need it done right away or immediately. Have you ever had to do something at once? Does pressure to finish something at once make you nervous, or do you perform well under pressure?

**under (her) breath** (page 179, line 47)

She said the words "free, free, free!" under her breath. She said these words in a quiet voice, in a whisper that only she could hear. When you say something in a low voice that no one else can hear, you say something under your breath. Can you think of a time when you said something under your breath? Why did you do this?

## Adjective Word Order

When we describe, we use adjectives—sometimes lists of adjectives. In English, there is a required order for these adjectives. Below is a chart illustrating adjective word order. After the chart, several sentences from the story are reproduced. Read these sentences, noticing the underlined adjectives and filling in the blanks wherever necessary. Check your answers by referring to the story. This list is meant to help you when you write, but you do not have to memorize it. The more you write, the more familiar you will become with it; it will eventually become natural to you.

| Articles and Possessives | Numbers: Ordinal and Cardinal | *General Description Adjectives and Adjectives Ending in -ed, -ing, -y, -ful, -ous, etc. | Size | Shape | Age | Color | *Adjectives of Nationality and Religion; also Adjectives Ending in -ic, -al, -ed, or -y | Noun Adjuncts | Nouns |
|---|---|---|---|---|---|---|---|---|---|
| the | two | | big | angular | old | green | air-conditioned | convertible | cars |
| her | three | lovely | little | slender | new-born | gray | Burmese | | cats |
| Louise's | | famous | | long | | blue | lacey | evening | gown |
| a | | chipped | huge | square | | blue & white | English | soup | bowl |
| a | | weeping | tiny | round | old | gray-haired | French | | lady |
| a | first | quick | | | | | wild | | scream |

ªThese positions are sometimes interchangeable.

*roomy, comfortable, armchair, a*

There stood, facing the open window, <u>a comfortable, roomy arm-chair</u>.

*spring, the, life, new*

She could see in the open square before her house the tops of

trees that were all aquiver with the new spring _____.

*a, calm, face, fair*

She was young, with a _____ _____ face, whose lines bespoke

repression and even a certain strength.

*two, her, hands, white, slender*

She was beginning to recognize this thing that was approaching

to possess her, and she was striving to beat it back with her will—as

powerless as _____ _____ white slender _____ would have been.

*word, a, whispered, little*

When she abandoned herself a little _____ _____ escaped

*(parted, her, slightly, lips)* _____ _____ _____ _____.

*hands, kind, the, tender*

She knew that she would weep again when she saw _____ _____

_____ _____ folded in death; the face that had never looked
save with love upon her, fixed and gray and dead.

The following sentences are not from the story. Fill in the adjectives in the order required. Refer to the chart if you have difficulty.

1. Louise Mallard climbed the _____ to her

   (winding, staircase, long, dark)

   room.

2. She sat at her _____ and began to write.

   (desk, delicately carved, wooden)

3. Staring at her husband's picture, she held a(n) _____

   (old, fountain,

   _____ in her hand.

   green, pen)

4. She wanted to write, but she suddenly felt tired; she sat on a

_____ and fell asleep.
(flowery, sofa, soft, pink)

**EXERCISE**     Describe a person you saw on the street today, using long strings of descriptive words. After you have finished, refer to the chart to check the order of your adjectives.

## Pronouns

**THIRD-PERSON SINGULAR**

| Subject | Object | Possessive | Possessive Adjective | Reflexive |
|---------|--------|------------|----------------------|-----------|
| she | her | her | hers | herself |

Some sentences from the story have been reproduced below with the pronoun forms missing. Refer to the chart above, and fill in the appropriate pronouns.

1. _____ wept at once, with sudden, wild abandonment, in

_____ sister's arms.

2. When _____ abandoned _____ a little whispered word es-

caped _____ slightly parted lips.

3. There would be no one to live for _____ during those coming

years; _____ would live for _____.

4. There would be no powerful will bending _____ in that blind persistence with which men and women believe they have a right to impose a private will upon a fellow-creature.

5. _____ arose at length and opened the door to _____ sister's importunities.

Now write three sentences describing Louise Mallard and using pronouns such as *she, her, hers,* and *herself.*

## Commonly Confused Words

**where/were**

Read the following paragraph, observing the use of *where* and *were*.

Sometimes our response to bad news is affected by *where* we hear it. If we *were* at home, we might allow ourselves to cry and feel grief. If we *were* out on the street, we might find ourselves trying to hold back our tears and deep feelings until we got to a place *where* we felt safe.

On the basis of what you observed in the paragraph, complete the following definitions.

_____ is the plural past tense of the "to be" verb.

_____ asks in what place something is.

*Wear* and *ware* are also sometimes confused with *where* and *were*. *Wear* means "to have on," as clothing. ("She *wears* a suit to work every day.") *Ware* means "piece of goods to be sold." ("A peddler was selling his *wares*.")

Fill in the blanks in the following sentences with *where, were, wear,* or *ware*.

1. She didn't know what to _____ because she didn't know _____

   they _____ going on their date.

2. The peddler sold his _____(s) on the street corner.

3. They _____ not sure _____ to go after they heard the news.

Now write your own sentences using *where, were, wear,* and *ware*.

# Sentence Skills

## Simple Past and Past Continuous Tenses

**Simple Past** In the sentences that follow the past tense verbs have been omitted. Fill in each blank with the correct form of the verb.

1. She _____ at once, with sudden, wild abandonment, in
       (weep)
   her sister's arms.

2. She _____ with her head thrown back upon the chair,
(sit)

quite motionless, except when a sob _____ up into her
(come)

throat and _____ her, as a child who has cried itself to
(shake)

sleep continues to sob in its dreams.

3. Now her bosom _____ and _____ tumul-
(rise)               (fall)

tuously.

4. Her pulses _____ fast, and the coursing blood
(beat)

_____ and _____ every inch of her body.
(warm)            (relax)

5. And she _____ and _____ her arms out to
(open)              (spread)

them in welcome.

6. "Free! Body and soul free!" she _____ whispering.
(keep)

7. Richards _____ waiting for them at the bottom.
(stand)

**Past Continuous** Underline the verbs in the following sentences.
The first one has been done for you.

1. There <u>was</u> something <u>coming</u> to her and she <u>was</u> <u>waiting</u> for it,
fearfully.

2. She was beginning to recognize this thing that was approaching
to possess her, and she was striving to beat it back with her will.

3. Josephine was kneeling before the closed door.

4. Some one was opening the front door with a latchkey.

5. They were taking care of Louise while Brently was walking in the
door.

Read the sentences above. Then fill in the missing words to describe the past continuous tense.

The past continuous is formed with *was* or _____ and the *-ing*

form of the _____.

The past continuous tense is used to relate actions that took place in the past but that were progressive or continuing actions.

I was thinking about that for a long time.

Louise Mallard was sitting in a comfortable chair in her room.

Her sister was knocking on the door.

Write your own sentences using the past continuous to describe something that took place in the past but that was continuous—for example, taking a bath, eating dinner, or taking a test.

The past continuous tense is also used to relate two actions that happened in the past simultaneously. These actions are often connected with *when* or *while*. *When* and *while* are sometimes used interchangeably.

When I was in Chicago, I saw the Sears Tower.

While I was in Chicago, I saw the Sears Tower.

Usually, however, *when* is used to mean "at that specific time," and *while* is used to indicate something that happened over a period of time.

While Mrs. Mallard was sitting in her room, she was thinking about her husband.

While she was crying, she began to feel happy.

She was coming down the stairs when the door opened.

When Brently came in the house, Richards was bending over Louise.

Complete each of the following sentences with either *when* or *while* on the basis of your observations of the sentences above.

Generally, _____ is used before the simple past tense.

Generally, _____ is used before the continuous past tense.

Fill in the blanks in the following sentences with *when* or *while*.

1. _____ she opened her eyes, he was standing there.

2. She called his name _____ she was dreaming.

3. Ullman was reading the newspaper _____ she was waiting for the student to come in the classroom.

4. _____ they opened the door, she was sleeping.

**EXERCISE**     Write a paragraph describing a dream you once had. Use the simple past tense and the past continuous tense.

## Modals

**unreal conditional:** *if* **and** *would*

A student wrote the following paragraph in response to the question "What would Louise do if she were a widow?"

If Louise were a widow, she would feel free. She would live for herself. She wouldn't have to think about her husband and his feelings. She would travel all over the world and she would also have time to just sit in her room and think. She would meet many men, but she wouldn't get married again. She would value her own life too much.

**EXERCISES**

1. Write a paragraph in response to the following question: "What would Louise do if she were a widow?"

2. Write a paragraph on the following topic: "What I would do if I were an instant millionaire."

3. Write a paragraph beginning with this sentence: "If I were able to travel to any place in the world, I would go to _____."

**Note:** The verb that follows *would* has no ending (no *-s*, *-ed*, or *-ing*). It is in the simple form.

You can also use *could* or *might* in the same way as *would*. In British usage, *should* is used instead of *would*.

If I were rich, I could buy a house for my parents. (*Could* means to have the ability.)

If I were able to travel anywhere, I might go to Sri Lanka. (*Might* means there is a possibility.)

If I were you, I would learn to drive.

If I were you, I should learn to drive. (British usage)

## Sentence Combining

**who/which**

Simple sentences can be combined with the relative pronoun *who* or *which*. *Who* is used to refer to people. *Which* is used to refer to things. Fill in the blanks in the following sentences.

1a. Josephine told her the news.
 b. Josephine was her sister.
Josephine, *who was her sister*, told her the news.

2a. Richards was in the newspaper office.
 b. Richards heard about the railroad disaster.
Richards, *who was in the newspaper office*, heard about the railroad
    disaster.

3a. Richards told Louise the news.
 b. Richards was Brently's best friend.

 Richards, who _____ _____ _____ _____, told Louise the
    news.

4a. Louise began to cry at once.
 b. Louise was Brently's wife.

5a. The armchair faced the window.
 b. The armchair was comfortable.
The armchair, *which faced the window*, was comfortable.

6a. The telegram came at 3 o'clock.
 b. The telegram said Mr. Mallard was dead.

 The telegram, which _____ _____ _____ _____, said Mr.
    Mallard was dead.

7a. The window was wide open.
 b. The window looked out on to the tops of trees.

 Now write your own sentences using *who* and *which*.

# Paragraph Skills

## Special-Feature Self-Test

**the comma**

In the following letter, all the commas have been left out. Fill in commas where you think they belong. Then check your answers on page 346.

March 14 1894

Dear Aunt Millie

I think you should sit down before you read this letter and I think you should have a handkerchief handy. Louise your favorite niece died last night. I hated to come right out and tell you like that but I didn't know how else to say it. All of us who loved her feel terrible. We all knew her heart was bad yet none of us expected this so soon so suddenly. I guess I should tell you what happened shouldn't I? Well it is a strange story. There was a bad railroad accident and we all thought Brently was killed. When Louise got the news she acted very odd. She went up to her room and she locked the door. She wouldn't open it up not even for me. When she finally let me inside she looked peculiar. Even though I knew she had been crying her face was bright shiny and beautiful. As she grabbed me around the waist she stared deep into my eyes. Then we went down the stairs together. Suddenly the door opened. Holding his old suitcase Brently came in. I screamed and Louise fell down. Just like that she was dead. By the way she left a letter saying where she wanted her things to go. She left you her armchair her ivory pen her crocheted shawl and her love.

Always

If you made any mistakes, read the following rules for commas.

## Rules for Commas

1. Commas are used with dates.

   March 14, 1894

2. Commas are used with openings and closings of letters.

   Dear Aunt Millie,
   Always,

3. Commas are used with addresses.

   3433 Madison Avenue, Roseberry, Wisconsin

4. Commas are used with numbers.

    1,000,596

5. Commas are used between complete thoughts that are connected by coordinating words such as

| , *for* | , *or* |
|---------|--------|
| , *and* | , *yet* |
| , *nor* | , *so* |
| , *but* | |

    I think you should sit down before you read this letter, and I think you should have a handkerchief handy. I hated to come right out and tell you like that, but I didn't know how else to say it.
    We all knew her heart was bad, yet none of us expected this.
    There was a bad railroad accident, and we all thought Brently was killed.
    She went up to her room, and she locked the door.

**If the complete thoughts are very short, no comma is necessary.**

I screamed and Louise fell down.

6. Commas are used to separate introductory material from the rest of the sentence.

    Well, it is a strange story.
    Suddenly, the door opened.
    Just like that, she was dead.
    By the way, she left a letter saying where she wanted her things to go.

7. Commas can be used after introductory clauses beginning with *after, although, as, as if, because, before, even, even though, if, since, so that, though, unless, until, when, whenever, where, wherever, whichever, while,* and *whoever.*

    When she got the terrible news, Louise acted very odd.
    When she finally let me inside, she looked strange.
    Even though I knew she had been crying, her face was bright.
    As she grabbed me around the waist, she looked deep into my eyes.

    If these introductory clauses are short, a comma is not necessary.

    As she died she looked at us in amazement.

8. Commas are used after introductory *-ing* phrases.

    Holding his old suitcase, Brently came in.

9. Commas are used to set off words that identify or repeat some-

thing in a sentence; these words could be omitted without changing the meaning of the sentence.

Louise died last night.
Louise, your favorite niece, died last night.

10. Commas are used to set off quotations.

Louise said, "Go away. I am not making myself ill."

11. Commas are used between items in a series.

She left you her armchair, her ivory pen, her crocheted shawl, and her love.

12. Commas are used before tag questions. (A tag question is a short question added to a statement when the speaker seeks confirmation of that statement.)

I guess I should tell you what happened, shouldn't I?

## Comma Practice Exercise

Insert commas where they are necessary in the following paragraph.

Louise Mallard a woman ahead of her time wanted freedom yet she also wanted to be married. She loved Brently Mallard but there were times when she wanted to be on her own. There are many people both men and women who feel this way at times aren't there? Because she had heart problems everyone always worried about her. Inside herself she felt strong and able to face the world. Brently Josephine and Richards felt they had to protect her. When she thought Brently had died she heard a voice inside her saying "free, free, free!" For a few moments only Louise Mallard knew that freedom. Then too soon it was over.

## Paragraphing

The letter on page 193 is all one paragraph. Decide where there should be paragraph breaks. Rewrite the letter, inserting the paragraph indentations and all necessary commas.

## Paragraph Coherence

Each paragraph should contain one basic idea that is developed by the writer. Some writers add ideas that do not belong; when they edit, they are unable to find these unrelated ideas. In the following paragraphs, cross out any sentences that do not belong.

The elderly couple sat together on the park bench. They held hands as they watched the young people pass them. Sometimes they would look at an especially affectionate young couple, and they would smile at each other as if remembering something from their own past. It was a very special day for them. It was their fiftieth anniversary and that night they would celebrate with their children and friends. Fiftieth anniversary parties are often held in expensive restaurants and there is lots of good food. They had looked forward to this event for a long time. They had discovered that as the years went by, they had grown closer together and their love had grown deeper. This love showed in their faces, and it made everyone who saw them that day feel a part of their happiness.

Freedom has a different meaning for each person. For one person, it might be the feeling that comes when he can say whatever he feels whether at home or on the street without fear of arrest. For another it might be "a room of one's own" where no one else can enter without permission. Apartment rents are very high in most major cities right now, and it is hard to find a big apartment that is affordable, so a room of one's own is usually just a dream. For some people, freedom means the ability to love a person regardless of that person's race, sex, or religion. For another, it is the right not to love anyone and still be accepted by the society. For Louise Mallard, freedom seemed to mean the right to be herself and not to be controlled in any way by another. Although she had loved her husband, she still had not felt really free in their relationship. Some people have a hard time meeting the right person. She would never have wished for his death, but when it came, it seemed to offer her the opportunity to explore the one element her life had always lacked, freedom.

Review some of the essays you have written earlier this semester, looking for sentences that do not seem to be connected to the rest of the paragraph. See if they would work better in another part of your essay or if they should be deleted entirely.

## Editing Skills Paragraph

The following is a first draft that contains many surface errors. The numbers and types of errors and the number of times each occurs are listed here. Find and correct the mistakes.

| | |
|---|---|
| 2 fragments | 1 parallel structure error |
| 1 run-on | 2 *where/were/wear* errors |
| 2 preposition errors | 2 missing commas |
| 1 tense consistency error | 2 *their/there* errors |

Because she allowed herself to feel free. Louise Mallard felt guilty. She heard her sister knocking in the door yet she does not answer. She wanted to sit on her room were she felt comfortable Josephine and Richards where waiting for her downstairs. They wanted to see her, to hear her, and knowing that she was all right. There voices bothered her. When she finally opened the door Josephine was their. Louise could not explain the way she felt to her sister. Because she did not think she would understand.

Answers are on page 346.

# Essay Skills

## Freewriting

It is like fishing. But I do not wait very long, for there is always a nibble— and this is where receptivity comes in. To get started, I will accept anything that occurs to me. Something always occurs, of course, to any of us. We can't keep from thinking.

WILLIAM STAFFORD, *A Way of Writing*

This will be one of the simplest yet probably most productive exercises in this book. Freewriting is a way of getting yourself to write. The technique is easy. Take out a pen or pencil and a blank piece of paper. Note the time and start writing. Write for ten minutes. Do not think about spelling, grammar, punctuation, or organization. Just keep writing. Do not stop even if the only thing you can write is "I have nothing to write about." You will not have to hand this paper in. Freewriting is simply for you; it is a way for you to loosen up your hand and your mind.

Many people say that freewriting helps them get over writing blocks, times when they feel they just cannot write. It is a technique that you can use at any time. All you need is paper, pen, and ten minutes. So anytime you want to practice your writing, freewrite. Eventually, you may find that freewriting will help you produce ideas that you can use in your formal writing.

**EXERCISES**

1. Before you begin to freewrite, reread some of your earlier journal entries. These may give you ideas. You also may find it enjoyable to see how much progress you are making in your writing.

2. Reread your favorite reading selection from this book and then freewrite. The reading may stimulate your thinking and give you some interesting ideas.

## Suggested Writing Topics

1. Rewrite "The Story of an Hour" as an entry in Josephine's (Louise Mallard's sister) diary. In your writing, try to see this story through Josephine's eyes. How did she experience her sister's death?

2. Begin your story at the point at which Chopin's ends. Describe what happened to Brently Mallard after his wife's death. In the original story, we know very little about Brently Mallard. What kind of a man is he? Did he love his wife? How did he see their relationship? After her death, did he remarry or did he stay in his house alone and sad? Help the reader really "see" Brently Mallard.

3. Imagine that Louise Mallard had not died and that Brently had not walked in. Describe what Mrs. Mallard's new life would have been like. Louise Mallard was excited about her new-found free-

dom. Was she able to enjoy it? Did she remain free or did she fall in love again? Be descriptive and help your reader see the new Louise.

4. Suzanne Gordon, in her book *Lonely in America,* wrote:

> It is rare to find people who actually like to be single and want to stay that way. What one finds more frequently are men and women who say they adore being single but who spend most of their nonworking time looking for some kind of sexual or romantic attachment.

Do you agree or disagree with this statement? Support your point of view with your experiences or observations.

5. Look at the picture on page 137 and then write the story of this woman. Explain what she did before the picture was drawn and what she did after. What is happening in the picture? Use your writing to bring the picture alive. Use descriptive words and specific details.

6. Is personal freedom overemphasized in the United States? Discuss this issue, using your experiences and observations. You may want to compare the meaning of freedom in the United States with its meaning in another country you have lived in.

## Revising

**reading aloud and developing coherence**

Read the essay or story you have written for this chapter aloud. (You may wish to leave the classroom to do this.) Read in a clear voice and read only the exact words that are on the page. See if your writing "sounds" right to you. Whenever you have to stop, do not correct, just mark that place with your pencil. When you have finished, examine the pencil marks. Why didn't your writing flow? What made you stop? Were words or ideas missing? Were your ideas connected? How can you make the parts you have marked clearer and more natural? Revise and then repeat the same process until you are able to read your essay through without stopping.

You might give a copy of your essay to a classmate to follow the same procedure. It would be interesting to see if you each mark the same places. This would indicate a problem area in your essay to which you should give special attention when you rewrite.

# Working and Finding One's Way

# CHAPTER TEN

# Jobs of the 1990s

*Many interesting possibilities and a few surprises appear in "Jobs of the 1990s," an article by Gwen Kinkead in* Fortune *magazine, which presents the Bureau of Labor Statistics predictions about jobs that will be available in the near future.*

°high technology: computers, robots, etc.
°distant   °unusual

**H**igh tech° alone will not drive the U.S. job market of the 1990s. 1
The far-off° will not be all that far-out.° While technological advances will create new careers and occupations and change the way familiar lines of work are done, the greatest number of jobs in the years ahead will open up for secretaries, nurse's aides, janitors, 5 sales clerks, cashiers, and other such clerical and service employees. That, at least, is the view at the Labor Department's Bureau of Labor Statistics (BLS), the standard source of data on existing and future jobs. The BLS projections,° fairly accurate in the past for major job categories, indicate that data processor mechanics, computer sys- 10 tems analysts, computer operators, and office machine servicers will be in much demand, but so will paralegals, occupational therapists, tax preparers, and people to interview other people for new jobs. As most of the work force beetles° away at tasks not far different from what people do now, others will get jobs that barely exist today, like 15 robotic repair and administering brain scans on nuclear magnetic resonance° units. The list that follows represents a sampling of rapidly growing fields, some huge and others open to a talented and skilled elite.°

°estimates of future possibilities

°beats away at

°quality of resounding or re-echoing

°socially superior group

**Food Services**                                                          20

Feeding the hungry who eat out on the job and on the go will require 6.4 million workers in 1990, according to the Bureau of Labor Statistics, an increase of 32% during the decade. Fast-food restaurants are serving up jobs the fastest, but institutional caterers are expanding too. For example, ARA Services of Philadelphia makes 25 thousands of airline meals daily at Kennedy Airport in New York. Most food service jobs pay low wages, but chefs for caterers start at $20,000 a year.

### Health Care

Of the 17.5 million new jobs the economy is expected to generate 30
by 1990, the largest category° will be the 2.7 million in health care.
Helping the disabled become mobile and productive will take some
12,000 more occupational therapists, a 63% increase. This is but one
example of the many jobs in the expanding health care field.

°division or general class

### Economists
                                                                        35
The number of economists outside academe° will jump 42% to
41,000 in 1990, according to the BLS. It's tempting to suggest more
will be needed because the ones now gainfully employed can't get
their forecasts° right. In a sense that's true. Because forecasts aren't
always accurate, businesses want more reports done to cover various 40
contingencies° in their strategic plans. Peering into the future earned
economists with a master's degree a median° of $40,000 last year.

°schools, universities; the
academic world

°predictions of future hap-
penings

°possible events

°a mathematical value be-
low and above which
there are an equal num-
ber of values; middle
point

### Secretaries

Of all occupations, the decade will provide the greatest number
of jobs for secretaries: an army of 700,000 more will be needed. 45
However, what they do will change. They will still answer phones
but will take shorthand less and do their typing on word processors.
In effect, they will become information processors.

### Waste Management

Getting rid of the 40 million metric tons of hazardous wastes that 50
industries throw off every year will occupy more and more environmental engineers. Quality-control chemists are already scarce. With
liability laws stricter, the chemists check that clients ship the wastes
they said they would, and nothing more—especially nothing illegal.
Starting salaries for this dirty, important work range today between 55
$15,000 and $20,000 a year.

### Lasers

Lasers have many uses in medicine, weaponry, navigation, even
entertainment, and the technology is changing so rapidly that people
who can design, build, and operate laser systems will be chased by 60
many different industries. New uses for lasers are one reason 115,000
more electrical engineers will be sought this decade.

### Real Estate

Baby boomers° have grown up, and like almost everybody else
they want their own homes. They also can afford vacation retreats. 65
Finding them houses will create 34% more jobs for real estate agents
and brokers during the Eighties. This can be a very lucrative° field.
Very successful brokers can gross up to $300,000 in commissions in
a decent year. Most brokers, however, make far less. In 1980, the
national median was $29,000.
                                                                        70

°people born during the
baby boom, the period
between the end of World
War II and the late 1950s,
when the birth rate in-
creased greatly
°profitable; producing
wealth

### Fiber Optics

So that people can talk to one another, computers can exchange
data faster, and families can watch cable TV, telecommunications is

expected to add 125,000 jobs this decade, an 11% increase. Prospects for one transmission technology, fiber optics, are beaming. Phone 75 companies are already rewiring the world with optical cables drawn from glass rods. Physicists and engineers working in fiber optics start at $25,000 a year.

# Vocabulary Development

### words relating to jobs and occupational fields

Many of the words in this article relate to jobs and occupational fields. In Chapter 8, we noted that each discipline or field of study has its own jargon, or special language. This is also true of occupations. Whether you work in a department store or on a nuclear submarine, there is a special vocabulary, a jargon, that is used to communicate effectively. We will examine some of these words as they are used in the article. Some of the questions may require class discussion or outside research.

### Paragraph 1

*janitor:* a person who keeps an apartment or office building clean, maintains its heating system, and makes minor repairs

What does a person have to know to become a janitor? _____

_____

*paralegal:* a person who has some training in law and works as an assistant to a lawyer

What do you think a paramedic is? _____

*robotic repair:* a job that involves the maintenance of robots, which are complex machines that resemble human beings in some ways and perform a variety of tasks

What type of jobs would robots be used for? _____

_____

### Paragraph 2

*caterer:* a supplier of prepared food to restaurants, offices, homes, hospitals, and other institutions

For what occasions might a caterer be used? _____

*chef:* a professional cook

How does someone become a chef? _____

**Paragraph 3**

*disabled:* a person who has a mental or physical problem that makes it difficult to work, walk, talk, etc., or a person who is in need of rehabilitation, which is therapy designed to help restore a person to health

In what kinds of work settings would you expect to find people who work with the disabled? _____

*mobile:* having the ability to more around on one's own

What are some of the devices you have seen that can help a disabled person become more mobile? _____

**Paragraph 4**

*economist:* a person whose job involves analyzing the production, distribution, and consumption of goods and services

How can economists be helpful to big businesses? _____

**Paragraph 5**

*word processor:* a computerized typewriter

What are some of the differences between a typewriter and a word processor? _____

**Paragraph 6**

*quality-control chemists:* people who make sure the wastes that are being discarded are not dangerous to people's health

What kinds of businesses probably hire quality-control chemists?

**Paragraph 7**

*laser:* a device that emits a very intense beam of light. Lasers are used in medicine for diagnosis and surgery and in weaponry to create guns that do not need bullets. Lasers can also help ships and submarines to stay on course.

What types of surgery are lasers especially good for? _____

**Paragraph 8**

*real estate agents and brokers:* people who sell homes, buildings, and land for a percentage of the purchase price

Why would a person sell a house or building through a real estate agent? _____

**Paragraph 9**

*fiber optics:* the technique of using very thin, transparent fibers of glass to transmit light beams and images around bends and corners

What fields will use fiber optics? _____

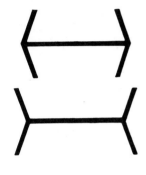

*optical:* having to do with the relation between light and vision; relating to sight

An optical illusion makes something appear different from what it really is. In the figure on the left, the two lines seem to be different lengths. If you measure them, you will find they are the same length.

Describe other optical illusions you have seen. _____

_____

*physicist:* a scientist who deals with matter and energy

What subjects should a person study to become a physicist? _____

_____

**EXERCISE**

Investigate the special vocabulary or jargon of the field in which you are interested in working. You might talk to someone who is already working in that area or consult books and periodicals in your library. Then list five to ten specialized words from the field. Define them and use them in sentences that relate to your intended future job.

# Reading and Thinking Skills

## Comprehension Questions

1. What jobs will open up in the high-tech fields in the 1990s?
2. What occupation will provide the greatest number of jobs? How will this job change?
3. Of all the occupations mentioned in the article, which one has the highest salary?

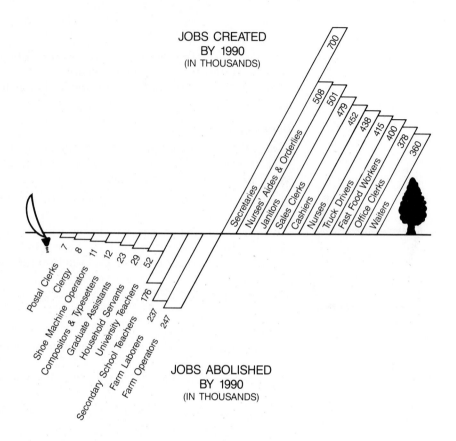

JOBS CREATED
BY 1990
(IN THOUSANDS)

JOBS ABOLISHED
BY 1990
(IN THOUSANDS)

4. See the chart above. According to this chart, how many thousand more nurses will be needed by 1990? How many thousand fewer farm laborers will be needed?

5. According to the article, what do occupational therapists do?

## Discussion Activities

### Analysis and Conclusions

1. This article is about jobs that will be available in the 1990s in the United States. If you were to write a similar article about your country, what jobs do you think would be the most available?

2. Review your answer to question 1. Are there differences between the kinds of jobs that will be available in your country and the kinds of jobs that will be available in the United States? If so, what are the reasons for the differences?

3. In Chapter 6, we read that the proportion of older people in the United States population is increasing. Today approximately 11%

of the population is sixty-five or over, and it is predicted that 21% of the population will be sixty-five or older by the year 2030. Is there a connection between the aging population and the kinds of jobs that will be available? Can you think of jobs that will be needed to service the sixty-five-and-over age group?

4. According to the article, the 1990s will provide the greatest number of jobs for secretaries. Why do you think this need for secretaries will exist? Do you think there will be an increased demand for bilingual secretaries? If so, why?

5. Look at comprehension question 4. Why do you think more nurses will be needed? Why will fewer farm workers be necessary?

### Writing and Point of View

1. What tense is used throughout most of the article? Why does the tense change to present (line 7) or present perfect (line 64)?

2. The article presents a great deal of information in a direct, factual manner. Do you think this style of writing is appropriate for the subject matter, or would you have preferred a less business-like, more personal approach?

3. There are many statistics and facts in this article. Did they make the article seem more convincing? Did you find them hard to read and understand?

### Personal Response and Evaluation

1. Did this article arouse your interest in any occupation that you hadn't thought about before? What made it sound interesting to you?

2. What aspects do you consider when deciding on a field in which to major and work in the future? What factors are most important to you?

3. Do you know anyone who works in any of the jobs mentioned in the article? If you do, describe that person's job to the class.

## Class Presentation

1. Select an occupation that interests you and do research on it in the library. Write one or two pages describing the education needed, the kind of work, the beginning salary, and any other information that you think would be useful to someone interested in that job. Present your findings to the class in a short oral report.

2. Interview someone who works in a job that interests you. Ask

questions to find out about both the positive and the negative aspects of the job. Present your findings to the class in a short oral report.

## Journal Writing

Reading about jobs in the future makes us think about our own future. What will we do with our lives? Is it important to make a lot of money? Is it important to help people? Is it possible to do both? How does one decide on a job for the future?

This journal entry should focus on jobs, decision making, and finding our way in the world. What jobs have you considered for yourself? Why are these jobs attractive or meaningful to you? Did any one person influence you in your ideas about a future occupation? Did any experience in your life influence you in your ideas about a future occupation?

# Word Skills

## Idiomatic Expressions

Each of the following paragraphs contains a context clue that will help you understand one of the idiomatic expressions used in the article. Underline these context clues; the first one has been done for you. Then use the expressions when you answer the questions at the end of each paragraph.

***in a sense*** (page 204, line 39)

The article suggests that there will be an increased demand for economists because the ones who have jobs have not been making accurate predictions about future trends. In a sense, or <u>in a way</u>, that is true. Businesses want more predictions that take into account different possibilities. In a sense, they want to predict the unpredictable. Have you ever tried to accomplish what is in a sense the impossible? Sometimes the very challenge makes it possible. What has been your experience?

***in effect*** (page 204, line 48)

About 700,000 more secretaries will be needed in the 1990s, but the secretary's job will be substantially different. In effect, secretaries will become information processors. Although they will still perform many of the same duties they do today, the computer will in fact have changed their jobs in many ways. Can you think of other jobs that in effect have been changed by the computer?

***get(ting) rid of*** (page 204, line 50)

There is nationwide concern about getting rid of hazardous waste. Dangerous materials have gone into the water in some areas, and people who drink the water in these areas get sick. We have to develop better methods of discarding our waste. Have you ever had to get rid of something and not known what to do with it? How did you solve your problem?

## Verb Forms

### the infinitive

In Chapter 7, we examined a list of verbs that are followed by the *-ing* form of the verb. In this chapter, we will look at a list of verbs that are followed by the infinitive, or *to* plus the simple form of the verb.

Here are some examples taken from the article:

Of the 17.5 million new jobs the economy is *expected to generate* by 1990, the largest category will be the 2.7 million in health care.

It's *tempting to suggest* more will be needed because the ones now gainfully employed can't get their forecasts right.

So that people can talk to one another, computers can exchange data faster, and families can watch cable TV, telecommunications is *expected to add* 125,000 jobs this decade, an 11% increase.

The following list includes the most commonly used verbs that are followed by an infinitive:

| | | | |
|---|---|---|---|
| agree | deserve | learn | refuse |
| appear | expect | manage | seem |
| ask | forget | need | try |
| attempt | have | plan | wait |
| choose | hope | prepare | want |
| decide | know how | promise | would like |

**EXERCISES**

Read the following sentences and underline each verb and the infinitive that follows it. The first one has been done for you.

1. He <u>agreed to work</u> as a secretary during the summer, but he <u>for-got to tell</u> his boss that he was majoring in accounting.
2. There appear to be many job openings in the fast-food industry.
3. The recent college graduate asked to meet the president of the company.
4. He chose to work in a big city because he wanted to meet lots of new people.
5. The advertisement attempted to make the job sound challenging and interesting.
6. The new driver managed to get a job as a taxi driver.
7. The waiter deserved to get a big tip, but his customers refused to give him anything.
8. She planned to go back to school in September even though she expected to keep her job.

In the following sentences, fill in each blank with a verb in the infinitive form. There are many possibilities; no one answer is right. Decide what sounds good to you. The first one has been done for you.

1. The man decided _____*to ask*_____ for an application.

2. He knew he needed _____ a high school diploma, and

   he was prepared _____ the interviewer about the other job qualifications.

3. His friend promised _____ a copy of the records from his country.

4. He had _____ his birth certificate, his green card, and his passport for the interview.

5. Even though he knew how _____ many machines, he

   hoped _____ some training on the job.

6. In his country he had learned _____ a computer, and

   that knowledge seemed _____ important to the company.

7. As he waited _____ called for the interview, he tried

   _____ his nervousness.

8. The first thing he said to the interviewer was, "Good afternoon.

I would like _____ for your company."

Fill in each of the following blanks with a verb that fits meaningfully in the sentence. Choose either the infinitive or the *-ing* form of the verb.

1. The woman learned _____ the phone right away.

2. She enjoyed _____ to new people every day.

3. Still she missed _____ her own language.

4. She needed _____ with old friends at night.

5. She tried _____ together with them but some nights she

had _____ the date.

6. She always appreciated _____ friends for lunch though.

Write a paragraph describing a job. Include both verbs that are followed by the infinitive and verbs that are followed by the *-ing* form of the verb.

## Pronouns

**THIRD-PERSON PLURAL**

| Subject | Object | Possessive | Possessive Adjective | Reflexive |
|---------|--------|-----------|---------------------|-----------|
| they | them | their | theirs | them-selves* |

*Themselves* always ends in an *s*. It is always plural; there is no singular form.

Refer to the chart above, and fill in the appropriate pronoun form in each of the following blanks.

Baby boomers have grown up, and like almost everybody else

_____ want _____ own homes. _____ also can afford vacation

retreats. Finding _____ homes will create 34% more jobs for real estate agents and brokers. _____ buying of new homes creates jobs

for bankers too. _____ have to negotiate loans and mortgages. In

desiring all these things for _____, the baby boomers are trying to

fulfill the American Dream. _____ believe it should be _____ if

_____ work hard enough to achieve it.

## Commonly Confused Words

**past/passed**

Read the following paragraph, observing the use of *past* and *passed*.

In the *past,* men *passed* up being with their families so they could succeed in their jobs. Often their children grew up and their childhoods had *passed* their fathers by. A man once told me, "I got off the bus and a boy drove *past* me on his bicycle. He waved and I didn't recognize him. He was my son." Those days have *passed* for most men and they will stay in the *past.* Nowadays fathers are as involved as mothers in their children's lives, and they are enjoying it too.

On the basis of what you observed in the paragraph, complete the following definitions.

_____ means "went by," "handed to," or "succeeded in."

_____ means "a time before the present" or "by."

Now write sentences of your own using *past* and *passed.*

# Sentence Skills

## Future Tense

**will**

One of the most common ways of expressing the future and making predictions is to use *will* followed by the simple form of the verb.

I will meet you after class.

There will be a tremendous need for secretaries in the 1990s.

The article we have just read makes predictions about the 1990s; therefore, it uses *will* and the future tense throughout. Paragraph 5 of the article has been reproduced below. Underline *will* each time it appears and the verb that follows it.

Of all occupations, the decade will provide the greatest number of jobs for secretaries: an army of 700,000 more will be needed. However, what they do will change. They will still answer phones but will take shorthand less and do their typing on word processors. In effect, they will become information processors.

**EXERCISES**

1. Notice that the verb that follows *will* has no ending. Rewrite the above paragraph to describe what one secretary will do. The revised paragraph has been started for you below:

Of all occupations, the decade will provide the greatest number of jobs for secretaries: an army of 700,000 more will be needed. Each secretary will have a very different job than in the office of the

1980s. She will still answer phones ————————————————

————————————————————————————

————————————————————————————

————————————————————————————

2. In the following paragraph, notice the patterns for creating negatives and questions with *will*.

The secretary will not use a typewriter. The secretary will not take shorthand. However, high tech will not totally control the office of the 1990s. The personal touch will be important. In the 1980s most secretaries are women, but in the 1990s this will not be as common. Men and women will compete for the demanding, high-paying secretarial positions. "Will you come into my office, Mr. ——?" will be heard in offices throughout the country.

a. When you create a negative with *will*, where does *not* belong?

————————————————————————————

b. When you ask a question with *will*, where does the subject belong?

————————————————————————————

3. Write a statement with *will* answering the following question: When will this class end today?

_____

Write a negative statement with *will* answering the following question: Will you ever be any younger than you are today?

_____

**Note:** The contraction *won't* is often used in writing and conversation instead of the full form *will not*.

Write two questions using *will* that you will ask of a classmate—for example, "What will you do this weekend?" Ask your questions of the person sitting to your right. (If there is no one to your right, ask the questions of anyone you choose.)

**be going to**

When we speak about the future, we often use the *be going to* form. This form is sometimes used in writing, but it is used more commonly in speech. When you hear it spoken, it may sound like "gonna" or "gunna." However, it means the same thing as *will* and can be used almost interchangeably. However, there are some special uses for each. *Going to* is often used to express specific future plans or intentions, while *will* is almost always used to express promises, requests, offers, and predictions. *Will* is more often used in formal writing than *be going to*.

going to:  I am going to go to the movies tomorrow night.
They are going to get married next month.

will:  He promises that he will return the car tonight.
Will you lend me five dollars?
Will anyone trade a ticket to the football game for fifty dollars?
It will snow tomorrow morning.

**EXERCISES**

1. Write a paragraph telling what you are going to do next weekend. (If you do not have any plans, you may want to write about what you are going to do next month or next summer.)

2. Rewrite the paragraph from exercise 1 in the third-person singular (she or he).

3. Imagine that you are a fortune teller who can make predictions about the future. Write a paragraph telling what you believe will happen in your family, your city, or your country in the next year. Or write a paragraph telling what will happen to some of the characters in a television program you have seen.

## Present and Present Continuous Tenses

In addition to using *will* and *be going to* to express the future, we sometimes use the simple present tense and the present continuous tense. The time context and the time expression indicate that the event is taking place in the future. Verbs such as *arrive, come, go,* and *leave* are often used in the present tenses even when they have a future meaning.

The plane arrives at six o'clock.
The babysitter comes at seven tonight.
We go on vacation after the children finish school.
They leave for Hawaii in June.
They are arriving late tonight.
She is coming over when she finishes her homework.
We are going out tonight.
They are leaving after the third of the month.

**EXERCISES**

1. Write sentences using the present and present continuous tenses of *arrive, come, go,* and *leave* to express future time.

2. Where will you be five years from now? What will your life be like? Write a paragraph describing your future, using *will* and *be going to.*

## Subject/Verb Agreement Review

In the following sentences from the article, the present tense verbs have been omitted. Decide whether each verb should have an *s* ending. Draw a rectangle around the subject if you have difficulty choosing the correct form.

1. The list that follows _____ a sampling of rapidly grow-
   (represent/represents)
   ing fields.

2. ARA Services of Philadelphia _____ thousands of meals
   (make/makes)
   daily at Kennedy Airport in New York.

3. Most food service jobs _____ low wages, but chefs
   (pay/pays)

   _____ at $20,000 a year.
   (start/starts)

4. The chemists _____ that clients _____ the
   (check/checks)                    (ship/ships)
   wastes they said they would and nothing more.

## Sentence Combining

Using what we have learned in past chapters, combine the following sentences using coordinating words like *and, but,* and *so* or subordinating words like *because, as, when,* or *while.* (For a more complete list of coordinating and subordinating words, see page 194.)
Refer to the article to check your answers. If your sentences differ
from the sentences in the article, show them to your teacher or a
classmate. There is more than one right answer in each case.

1a. Fast-food restaurants are serving up jobs the fastest.
 b. Institutional caterers are expanding too.

2a. Most food service jobs pay low wages.
 b. Chefs for caterers start at $20,000 a year.

3a. Forecasts aren't always accurate.
 b. Businesses want more reports done.

4a. Secretaries will still answer phones.
 b. They will take shorthand less.
 c. They will do their typing on word processors.

# Paragraph Skills

## Paragraph Coherence

Each paragraph should have an inner coherence; the ideas should
be connected so that they flow one to the next. The sentences from
paragraph 2 of the article are reproduced here out of order. Try to
arrange them in the correct order. The first sentence has been marked
for you. Then refer to the original article to check your answers.

**food services**

_____ Fast-food restaurants are serving up jobs the fastest, but institutional caterers are expanding too.

_____ Most food service jobs pay low wages, but chefs for caterers start at $20,000 a year.

___1___ Feeding the hungry who eat out on the job and on the go will require 6.4 million workers in 1990, according to the Bureau of Labor Statistics, an increase of 32% during the decade.

_____ For example, ARA Services of Philadelphia makes thousands of airline meals daily at Kennedy Airport in New York.

Discuss with your classmates how you decided on the order in which to put these sentences.

The following is a paragraph describing a person's first day in a new job. Arrange these sentences in the order that makes the most sense to you. The first sentence has been marked for you.

_____ "Mr. Western's office," I said meekly and then pushed the wrong button and lost the call.

___1___ When I began working for the Smith Western Company as a secretary, I was nervous.

_____ He told me that we should get acquainted and that I should begin to learn the office routine.

_____ I agreed with him and listened as he began a long series of explanations about how everything worked.

_____ I opened the glass door and stared in amazement; the office seemed enormous and there were so many people whose names I would have to learn.

_____ There was a large computerized typewriter and a telephone with about thirty buttons.

_____ Little by little though it began to fall into place, and at the end of the first week I had actually begun to like the place.

_____ My boss, Mr. Western, called me into his room right away.

———— After he finished his introduction, I went to my desk.

———— It rang as I sat down.

Compare your order with a classmate's. Discuss how you each decided on the order in which to place these sentences. As readers and writers, we discover that there are many indications that help us follow a story. They help the writing to flow from one idea to the next. When you write, keep in mind the kinds of clues you looked for to help you order this paragraph.

## Special-Feature Self-Test

**pronoun agreement, reference, point of view**
Pronoun agreement is a common error made in writing. In paragraph 1, there is at least one pronoun error in each sentence. Find each error and underline it.

1. When she graduated from high school, they wanted her to go to college, but she thought she should get a job. On the other hand, you know how important it is to get an education. We want you to get that degree and have an easier life than we've had. She listened to it and in the end I applied to college and got a job at night.

In paragraph 2, the errors have been corrected. Compare paragraphs 1 and 2 and refer to the explanations that follow.

2. When Lily graduated from high school, her parents wanted her to go to college, but she thought she should get a job. On the other hand, she knew how important it was to get an education. Her parents wanted her to get a degree and have an easier life than they had. She listened to their advice and in the end, she applied to college and got a job at night.

## Pronoun Rules

1. *Pronouns take the place of nouns. Pronouns must refer clearly to the nouns they replace.*

When she graduated from high school, they wanted her to go to college, but she thought she should get a job.

Who is "she"? You should make clear who the subject of your story or essay is before you use a pronoun.

Who is "they"? Did the writer make a mistake or does "they" refer to Lily's parents? The reader is unsure.
Rewrite this sentence and make it clearer.

_____

We want you to get that degree and have an easier life than we've had.

Who is "we"? Lily's parents? This should be made clearer to the reader.
Rewrite this sentence and make it clearer.

_____

2. *Pronouns should not shift point of view unnecessarily.*

On the other hand, you know how important it is to get an education.

Who is "you"? The reader, the writer, a friend of the reader's? Unless there is a clear reason to use *you*, it can be confusing to the reader.
Rewrite this sentence and make it clearer.

_____

She listened to it and in the end I applied to college and got a job at night.

Who is "I"? The paragraph is written in the third person. Why does the writer suddenly shift the point of view?
Rewrite this sentence and make it clearer.

_____

3. *Pronouns must agree in number with the word or words they replace.*

We want you to get that degree and have an easier life than we've had. She listened to it and in the end I applied to college and got a job at night.

What is "it"? Her parents are two people, and they said several things.
Rewrite this sentence and make it clearer.

_____

## Practice Paragraph

The following paragraph contains many pronoun errors. Rewrite the paragraph in the space provided, correcting all the errors.

Don found out that when people work for their family, often you have to work harder than when you get a job from someone else. Don didn't want a job as a bookkeeper, but it was the only job his uncle could give us. The bills would arrive every day and Don would pay it. Many times, however, he lost them. His uncle talked to him about how they could help him organize better, but it never worked. Working as a bookkeeper was only temporary, but for Don it felt like forever. When his uncle's bookkeeper came back from vacation, Don said that I was glad to see him go.

_____

_____

_____

_____

_____

Answers are on p. 346.

## Editing Skills Paragraph

The following paragraph is a first draft that contains many surface errors. The types of errors and the number of times each occurs are listed below. Find and correct the errors.

| | |
|---|---|
| 2 fragments | 1 *their/there/they're* error |
| 2 run-ons | inconsistent pronoun use |

Looking for a job can be difficult their are many different types of problems. For one thing, the interviewee is never sure what to bring on the first interview. I usually bring too much this can be confusing to the interviewer. From now on, I will bring only the necessary documents. Such as your résumé, your birth certificate, and your high school diploma. In addition, I try to impress the interviewer by dressing very neatly and never chewing gum. I always look directly into the interviewer's eyes. I want the interviewer to

believe that I can be trusted. If I remember to follow my own advice.
I believe I will get a job very soon.

Answers are on page 346.

---

# Essay Skills

## Outlining

Many writers find outlining helpful in their prewriting organization, and some books teach very formal outlining techniques. However, writers can spend so much time outlining that they don't have enough time to write. The outlining technique presented here is simple and effective; it will help you to think your essay through before you actually begin to write.

The outline is a guide that you will refer to as you are writing. It can be changed as you go along. Its purpose is only to help you organize and to give you the confidence that you will have something to say throughout your essay.

An outline does not have to be written in complete sentences. It is a list of ideas that you will develop more fully. The basic shape of an outline follows:

I. Main Idea or Topic Sentence
  A. Supporting detail #1
    1. Development 1
    2. Development 2
  B. Supporting detail #2
    etc.

To see the outline in action, let's examine the first paragraph of the article that began this chapter.

I. High tech will not be only job market in 1990s.
  A. Technology will advance but there will be many jobs in non-tech fields.
    1. tremendous need for secretaries
    2.    "    "  "  nurse's aides
    3.    "    "  "  janitors
    4.    "    "  "  sales clerks
    5.    "    "  "  cashiers
    6.    "    "  "  clerical and service employees

B. Information comes from Labor Department's Bureau of Labor Statistics (BLS).
1. need for some technical workers
   a. data processor mechanics
   b. computer systems analysts
   c. computer operators
   d. office machine servicers
2. but also a need for nontechnical workers
   a. paralegals
   b. occupational therapists
   c. tax preparers
   d. job interviewers

II. Sampling shows that there will be jobs in both technical and nontechnical fields.

This outline is probably more technical than the author's outline. You have the option of making your outline more detailed or very brief, with just a few key words to help you remember what you wanted to write about. Keep in mind that all writers are different. Some writers find outlines essential to orderly writing; others say they do all their outlining in their head. In the next exercises, you will have the opportunity to try outlining and see if it works for you.

**EXERCISES**

1. Prepare an outline for one of the other paragraphs in the article.

2. Prepare a brief outline for the entire article.

3. Before you write your next essay, prepare a brief outline using the techniques you have just learned. See if the outline helps you to organize your essay.

## Suggested Writing Topics

1. There is no conclusion to "Jobs of the 1990s." Write your own conclusion to the article. Refer to Chapter 7 for guidelines.

2. Study the chart on page 208. Write an essay analyzing the material in the chart. Most of the new jobs seem to be in the low-tech area. What does this mean for people who are planning for their future occupations? What advice would you give to someone in college who is not sure what to major in?

3. The following comes from a recent issue of *U.S. News and World Report.*

   While many people equate success with money, power and position, others define the word as helping their communities, the needy or the sick. In a word: Service.

For these individuals, money is not the motivator, although many earn a respectable living. Instead, the contacts with people, the joy of aiding others and the learning that comes with the job are the big rewards.

In short, success becomes a matter of personal fulfillment.

Responding to what you have just read, explain how you define success. Use examples and specific details to support your point of view.

4. Some people say that workers should be paid according to how much they contribute to society, how much they help people. These people say it is wrong that a teacher or a nurse is paid less than a lawyer or an accountant. Do you agree or disagree? Support your point of view with your own experience or your observations of others.

5. Describe a person who is very satisfied in his or her job. Explain what it is about the job that the person finds so fulfilling. Include enough details so the reader will see the person you are describing and understand why the job is so rewarding.

## Revising

Revising is critical to the production of fine writing, writing that really speaks to the reader. The great French philosopher Jean Paul Sartre stopped writing when he went blind because he felt that in order to write, one had to see. Revising was a very important aspect of his writing.

I think there is an enormous difference between speaking and writing. One rereads what one rewrites. But one can read slowly or quickly: in other words, you do not know how long you will have to take deliberating over a sentence. It's possible that what is not right in the sentence will not be clear to you at the first reading. Perhaps there is something inherently wrong with it, perhaps there is a poor connection between it and the preceding sentence or the following sentence or the paragraph as a whole or the chapter, etc.

All this assures you that you approach your text somewhat as if it were a magical puzzle, that you change words here and there one by one, and go back over these changes and then modify something farther along. . . .

When you revise your essay, look most carefully at the connections between sentences and paragraphs. View your essay as "a magical puzzle" that you can keep changing. You can reread and rewrite as many times as are necessary until its pieces fall into place and you have writing that makes you pleased and proud.

# CHAPTER ELEVEN

# The Work Itself:
# A Social Psychologist Looks
# at Job Satisfaction

*The following excerpt, entitled "The Work Itself," is from a textbook called Applied Social Psychology by Stuart Oskamp. It presents research exploring the variables that influence whether people feel satisfied in their jobs.*

## The Work Itself

**R**esearch has shown many work attributes to be related to job satisfaction. Locke (1976) concluded that most of them have in common the element of mental challenge.

Probably the most basic attitude here is that the work must be personally interesting and meaningful to the individual in question (Herzberg, Mausner, & Snyderman, 1959; Nord, 1977). Obviously, this specification makes work satisfaction subject to a wide range of individual differences, for individuals with one set of values, abilities, and backgrounds may find a particular kind of work personally interesting, while people with different values, abilities, and backgrounds may find the same work completely unmeaningful. A more objective aspect of meaningfulness is task significance—the impact of the work on the lives of other people (Hackman, Oldham, Janson & Purdy, 1975). For example, a worker riveting° aircraft wings has a more significant job than one riveting trash containers, and is likely to feel more satisfaction with it.

Application of skill is another job attribute that contributes to work satisfaction (Gruneberg, 1979). On assembly lines and other jobs that involve much repetitive° work, the amount of variety in the job has frequently been found to be positively related to job satisfaction (Walker & Guest, 1952; Hackman & Lawler, 1971; Kremen, 1973). "Utility workers" and others who rotate from job to job usually show higher satisfaction than workers who perform only one operation all day long, and this finding has been the basis of many "job enrich-

°fastening together with a bolt of metal

°doing the same thing over and over again

°improvement; expansion

°mechanical; without thought

°deal with

°return response

°involving relations between people

°having no reference or connection to any particular person

°motivation; the more work produced, the higher the salary

°something that contradicts itself but still may be true

ment"° schemes. Again, individual differences are important, for not all workers value more varied or challenging jobs (Hulin, 1971). 25

Another job aspect related to skill is job autonomy—the worker having a say in when and how to perform the job. A somewhat similar work attribute is task identity—doing a "whole" job, or at least a portion where one's personal contribution is clear and visible. Both of these factors have been found to be positively related to job satisfaction (Hackman & Lawler, 1971). 30

Too little challenge in the work, as in completely automated° tasks, generally leads to boredom and lowered satisfaction. However, so much challenge that the worker cannot cope° with it may lead to 35 failure and frustration, also an unsatisfying state of affairs. Thus success or achievement in reaching an accepted standard of competence on the job is an important factor in satisfaction (Locke, 1965; Ivancevich, 1976), though again individual differences make this a less important factor for individuals with a low need of achievement 40 (Steers, 1975). Although success can generally be judged by workers themselves, external recognition confirms the worker's success and also provides feedback° about the level of achievement. Of course, recognition, in the form of awards, promotion, or praise, is also part of the general working conditions and of the interpersonal° aspects 45 of the job, and so it has multiple implications for satisfaction.

A final task attribute that contributes to satisfaction is the relative absence of physical strain (Chadwick-Jones, 1960). This is one major advantage of automation in heavy industrial jobs; for some jobs and some individual workers it can offset automation's disadvantage of 50 promoting boredom.

### Working Conditions (Impersonal°)

**Pay.** Pay is one of the most important working conditions for almost all occupational groups (Smith, Kendall, & Hulin, 1969; Lawler, 1981). Yet even here there is conflicting evidence, for some studies have found pay to be relatively unimportant in determining job 55 satisfaction for certain groups of workers (Opsahl & Dunnette, 1966). Gruneberg (1970) concluded:

> It appears that money means different things to different groups, and is likely to have greater importance for individuals who can- 60 not gain other satisfactions from their job. . . .

Another aspect of pay is the system by which wages are determined. Most studies have found that hourly pay is preferred to piecework systems by most workers, and straight salaries are preferred to incentive° schemes (Opsahl & Dunnette, 1966; Schwab & Wallace, 65 1974). One reason for this is that piecework systems tend to disrupt social relationships on the job, which are another major source of worker satisfactions. However, there is an interesting paradox° here, for wage incentive schemes generally result in greater productivity than does hourly pay (Warr & Wall, 1975). 70

# Vocabulary Development

**context clues**

When people speak to us, we have clues to help us understand what they are saying. We can watch their faces, listen to their tone of voice, notice their body language. In a similar way, written material often contains useful clues to help the reader understand words and special phrases. These are called context clues, clues that provide the meanings of words used in the piece of writing. The following sentences from the article contain examples of such context clues.

*Paragraph 2*

A more objective aspect of meaningfulness is task significance—the impact of the work on the lives of other people.

According to this sentence, what does "task significance" mean?

*Paragraph 4*

Another job aspect related to skill is job autonomy—the worker having a say in when and how to perform the job.

According to this sentence, what does "job autonomy" mean?

A somewhat similar work attribute is task identity—doing a "whole" job, or at least a portion where one's personal contribution is clear and visible.

According to this sentence, what does "task identity" mean?

As you read other texts, look for context clues to help you determine the meanings of difficult words without having to use the dictionary.

# Reading and Thinking Skills

## Comprehension Questions

1. According to the excerpt, what factor is most basic to work satisfaction?

2. What types of external recognition does the author mention?

3. According to the excerpt, too little challenge in work may lead to some problems. What are some of the problems caused by too few challenges? On the other hand, problems are also created when the work offers too many challenges. What are these problems?

4. The final paragraph mentions four systems of determining pay. What is hourly pay? What is a piecework system? What is a straight salary? What is an incentive scheme? How do these systems compare?

## Discussion Activities

### Analysis and Conclusions

1. Why is variety in the job an important factor in work satisfaction? Can there ever be too much variety?

2. What does it mean to rotate from job to job all day long?

3. Do you agree with the author that riveting aircraft wings is a more significant job than riveting trash containers? What makes one job more significant than another?

3. The author states that piecework tends to interfere with friendships on the job. Do you think this is true? Have you ever had any experiences or have you known anyone who has had experiences doing piecework? Did they have a similar experience to the one the author describes?

### Writing and Point of View

1. Compare the style of writing in this excerpt with the style in "Jobs of the 1990s." Which did you prefer? Why?

2. Do you find the textbook entries in this book to be more challenging reading than the other entries? What is it about the textbook entries that differs from the other readings?

3. For what audience was this selection written? How do you know? What indications are there that this excerpt was not written for a general audience?

### Personal Response and Evaluation

1. Of all the factors that the author mentions as contributing to job satisfaction, which is the most important to you?

2. What is the most satisfying job you have ever had? Discuss why this job was so satisfying. Do your reasons for liking the job correspond to the excerpt's analysis of job satisfaction?

3. Have you ever had a job that you did not like? If you have, describe the job to the class or to your group and explain in detail why this job was not satisfactory to you.

4. The author states that "success can generally be judged by workers themselves." If workers know they are doing a good job, why is external recognition so important?

## Questionnaire

This textbook article is based on the findings of many different researchers (the names in parentheses). The researchers named attempted to find out what factors were most important in determining job satisfaction. It is important for you as students to examine and question such research. Most of us have had jobs or know people who have jobs. If we were to develop our own questionnaire dealing with job satisfaction, some of us might give responses similar to those given by the people surveyed for this article. Some of us, however, might have different expectations. Working is a very individual experience.

As a group, make a list of questions that you would ask in order to determine what factors people think are important for job satisfaction. Then make enough copies of the questionnaire to distribute at least five copies to everyone in the class.

To indicate which respondents are members of the class, each student should put a *C* in the top right-hand corner of his or her questionnaire. Each student should then fill out the questionnaire and ask four other people outside of class to answer the questionnaire.

As a class, add up the responses and compare the results of your survey with the findings in the excerpt. Did you find that most people thought mental challenge was the most important factor in job satisfaction? Did most people favor straight salaries? Were the responses from the class members, the *C* group, different from the other responses to the questionnaire? If so, what might explain this?

You will learn many things from doing this activity. You will learn how to create a questionnaire. You will learn how research is conducted, and you will be able to compare your results with the results of other researchers. You may then realize how interesting and often unpredictable research is.

## Journal Writing

A student once wrote that the worst job she ever had was stuffing feathers into pillows in an un–airconditioned factory in the summertime. The feathers got stuck in her mouth and her lungs, and she coughed all the time. The workers couldn't turn on a fan because the feathers would blow all over the factory. The student couldn't quit the job because she spoke very little English and needed the money. So she stayed and coughed.

The story is unforgettable. Every detail of it—the feathers, the pillows, the heat, and the coughing—remain in the mind of the reader. In your journal entry, think about the best or worst job experience you have ever had. (If you have never worked, write about an imaginary experience.) Close your eyes and recall every detail—the smells, tastes, colors, voices. When you can see a picture of the job clearly in your mind, start to write. Write everything down, not stopping to worry about grammar, spelling, or organization. Concentrate on making the experience vivid and alive.

# Word Skills

## Idiomatic Expressions

Each of the following paragraphs contains a context clue that will help you understand one of the idiomatic expressions used in the excerpt. Underline these context clues; the first one has been done for you. Then use the expressions when you answer the questions at the end of each paragraph.

***in common*** (page 226, lines 2–3)

Research shows that there are many factors that relate to job satisfaction, but most of these factors share one element that is the same. Most of them have in common the element of mental challenge. Although each of us is unique, we also have many characteristics in common with other human beings. What characteristics can you think of that most humans have in common?

***in question*** (page 226, line 5)

The most basic attitude seems to be that the work should be interesting and meaningful to the person in question. When something is in question, it is not simply accepted but is under consideration or is being looked into in some way. Can you think of some issue that is in question in the world today?

*have a say* (page 227, line 28)

Most people want to have a say in what they do in their jobs. They want to have some control over what they do and they want to be listened to in relation to their work experience. Do you think employees should have more of a say in their workplace?

## Comparatives

The excerpt discusses research studies conducted to determine factors relating to job satisfaction. The author compares one factor to another. In the following sentences, the comparatives have been deleted. Fill in the missing comparative form in each sentence. If you have difficulty, review comparatives on page 77. The first one has been done for you.

1. According to the author, mental challenge is *more* _____ *important than* _____ high pay.
   (important)

2. A worker riveting aircraft wings may feel his job is _____ _____ the job of a worker riveting trash containers.
   (significant)

3. A job that has a variety of tasks makes a worker feel _____ _____ a repetitive job does.
   (happy)

4. External recognition makes many workers feel _____ _____ just knowing they have done a good job.
   (satisfied)

5. Physical strain can be _____ mental challenge.
   (tiring)

## Cloze Exercise

**prepositions**

Paragraph 3 of the excerpt is reproduced here, with all the prepositions removed. Fill in each blank with a preposition that sounds correct. Then refer to the original paragraph to check your answers. There may be more than one correct answer in each case. If your answer varies from the original, check with a classmate or your teacher.

Application _____ skill is another job attribute that contributes _____ work satisfaction. _____ assembly lines and other jobs that involve much repetitive work, the amount _____ variety _____ the job has frequently been found to be positively related _____ job satisfaction. "Utility workers" and others who rotate _____ job _____ job usually show higher satisfaction than workers who perform only one operation all day long, and this finding has been the basis _____ many "job enrichment" schemes. Again, individual differences are important, _____ not all workers value more varied or challenging jobs.

---

## Countables/Uncountables

Fill in each of the following blanks with the word *countable* or *uncountable*.

*Much* is used before _____ nouns such as *love. Many* is used before _____ nouns such as *individuals. Fewer* is used before _____ nouns. *Less* is used before _____ nouns.

Fill in each of the blanks in the following sentences with *much* or *many*.

1. _____ research has shown that _____ people need job satisfaction.

2. _____ work satisfaction is subject to _____ individual differences.

3. _____ people may find _____ work meaningless.

4. Human beings bring to their jobs _____ abilities and _____ backgrounds that influence their response to their work.

Fill in each of the blanks in the following sentences with *fewer* or *less*.

1. A job riveting trash containers has _____ significance than a job riveting aircraft wings.

2. _____ challenge in the work leads to _____ employees feeling satisfaction in their work.

3. There are _____ accidents when there is _____ physical strain.

4. _____ people prefer piecework systems of pay over straight salaries.

---

## Collective Nouns

Another category of nouns is collective nouns. A collective noun is a word for a group of people, animals, or objects that are considered as a single unit. The following are examples of collective nouns: *family, class, committee, factory, government, group, majority, minority, nation, public, team.*

A collective noun used as a subject usually takes a singular verb in American English.

The public is ruled by a system of laws.

The committee is meeting on Thursday.

However, if one is trying to emphasize the individual members of the unit, then the plural verb is used.

The team have argued among themselves about who should be called best player.

In British English, the plural verb is used with collective nouns. Collective nouns are countable nouns; they can be used in the plural.

In each of the following sentences, choose the correct form of a present tense verb that fits meaningfully in the sentence.

1. The class _____ to know when a test will be given.

2. That group _____ to go out together on the weekends.

3. The family that _____ together _____ together.

4. The audience _____ the performers to concentrate on the play each night.

5. The crowd _____ among themselves about who should get in the crowded train first.

---

## Commonly Confused Words

**whole/hole/all**

Read the following paragraph, observing the use of *whole, hole,* and *all.*

In general, *all* workers prefer to do a *whole* job and not just a little piece of a big job. When they do little pieces of a job and never see the final product, whether it is a car or a report, they may feel that they have taken a shovel and dug a *hole* in the ground. They are lost and feel that their jobs are meaningless.

From what you observed in the paragraph, complete the following definitions.

_____ means "an empty spot."

_____ and _____ mean "the entire quantity."

Although *all* and *whole* mean the same thing, they are used differently. We refer to "*all* the workers," yet "the *whole* work force." *All* is generally used with a plural noun or with an uncountable noun.

*All* of the workers received a promotion.
*All* of the recognition went to the president.

*Whole* is usually used with singular countable nouns, including collective nouns.

The *whole* factory is on strike.
The *whole* car was destroyed in the accident.

In the following sentences, fill in each blank with *all* or *whole.*

1. _____ people want to be satisfied in their jobs.

2. The _____ system of advancement in the job should be made

   clear to _____ the employees.

3. Not _____ workers want to be involved in the _____ operation of the company in which they work.

Now use these words in sentences of your own.

# Sentence Skills

## Present Perfect Tense, Active Voice

The present perfect tense (*have/has* plus the past participle) can be used to describe an event that happened at an unknown or unspecified time in the past. The excerpt in this chapter uses this tense to describe the results of research. The verbs in the present perfect tense have been omitted from the following paragraph. In each blank, fill in either *has* or *have* and the past participle of the verb.

One important function of research is to question and perhaps validate common sense or what most people would believe to be true about a subject. The research discussed in the excerpt _____ (show) many things about job satisfaction that many of us might have guessed would be true. It _____ (indicate), for example, that most people _____ (select) mental challenge as the most important factor in job satisfaction. Researchers _____ (find) that individual differences play a big part, but they still agree that an interesting and meaningful job is better than a repetitive and boring one. People _____ (say) that they prefer to have a say in when and how they perform their jobs. They _____ (express) a preference for jobs in which they can feel a sense of achievement. In addition, workers _____ (indicate) that they like to receive external recognition for their achievements. As might be expected, they _____ (tell) research-

ers that pay is one of the most important working conditions. This research _____ what most of us would expect in relation
(validate)

to job satisfaction.

---

## Present Perfect Tense, Passive Voice

In Chapter 8, we compared the active voice and the passive voice. In this chapter, we will examine how the passive voice is used in the present perfect tense.

On assembly lines and other jobs that involve much repetitive work, the amount of variety in the job has frequently been found to be positively related to job satisfaction.

In this sentence, it is not important who has found the amount of variety in the job to be related to job satisfaction. In passive voice, the doer of the action is usually not important, only that the action has been done.

Both of these factors (job autonomy and task identity) have been found to be positively related to job satisfaction.

Again, in this sentence *who* is not as important as *what* was found. The form for present perfect tense in the passive voice is:

*have/has* plus *been* plus the past participle

In each of the following sentences, complete the verb in the present perfect tense in the passive voice. Then use your own ideas to finish the sentence.

1. Many discoveries that _____ made in the last ten years have really shocked me. One of them is _____

   _____ .

2. One medical procedure that _____ tried in the past five years that really interests me is _____ .

3. A problem in the world that _____ unsolved for many years is _____ .

## Modals

**may/can**

Reread "The Work Itself" and underline *may* or *can* each time it appears and the verb that follows it. Make a list of the words in the space below.

*may*          *can*

Fill in the following blank based on what you have discovered.

The verb that follows *may* or *can* _____ an *(-s,-ed,-ing)* end-
                                      (has/does not have)
ing.

Read the paragraph that follows. Underline *can* and *may* and the verbs that follow these words. Then fill in the blanks in the sentences below.

If you look in the help-wanted section of your local newspaper, you can see that there are many jobs available requiring different kinds of skills. People try to get jobs that they can do with confidence. Even though occasionally a person may find a job that involves a lot of training, this is not usually a job hunter's goal. According to the excerpt, this is a personal decision. Some people can cope with a lot of challenge in their work, but many workers want predictability. They do not feel confident thinking that their job may change from day to day. Moreover, the type of work that people want to do varies greatly. Some people may find one type of job interesting, and to someone else that job may seem boring.

Choose *may* or *can* to complete the following sentences.

_____ means "to be able to."

_____ is used to express possibility.

Now use these words in sentences of your own.

**EXERCISES**

1. Write a paragraph describing something you believe may happen in the near future to you, to someone else, or to the world in general.

2. Write a paragraph describing something you are able to do now that you could not do in the past. Use the word *can* in your paragraph.

## Substitution Words

Writers do not want to repeat the same words over and over. They often substitute words such as *one, this, that, these,* and *those.* In order for these words to be effective, the reader must know what they are replacing.

The following paragraphs from the excerpt illustrate the use of substitution words. In each paragraph, underline the substitution and the word or words to which it refers. The first one has been done for you.

Probably the most basic attitude here is that <u>the work must be personally interesting and meaningful to the individual</u> in question. Obviously, <u>this specification</u> makes work satisfaction subject to a wide range of individual differences. . . .

"Utility workers" and others who rotate from job to job usually show higher satisfaction than workers who perform only one operation all day long, and this finding has been the basis of many "job enrichment" schemes.

Underline "this finding" and the word or words to which it refers.

Thus success or achievement in reaching an accepted standard of competence on the job is an important factor in satisfaction, though again individual differences make this a less important factor for individuals with a low need of achievement.

Underline "this" and the word or words to which it refers.

A final task attribute that contributes to satisfaction is the relative absence of physical strain. This is one major advantage of automation in heavy industrial jobs. . . .

Underline "this" and the word or words to which it refers.

Most studies have found that hourly pay is preferred to piecework systems by most workers, and straight salaries are preferred to incentive schemes. One reason for this is that piecework systems tend to disrupt social relations on the job, which are another major source of worker satisfactions.

Underline "this" and the word or words to which it refers.

**EXERCISE**     The following paragraph is very repetitious. Edit the paragraph, substituting some of the words mentioned above. Keep in mind that the reader must know what the substitute word is referring to. There are many possibilities for editing this paragraph. Be creative.

It is not always easy to predict the job variables that will satisfy workers. Workers have different values, abilities, and backgrounds. The different values, abilities, and backgrounds of workers influence the way they view their work. A young woman with a baby might think that a day-care center is the most important variable in her workplace. The idea of having a day-care center may not mean very much to a single person who would like to have a job in which meeting other single people is encouraged. Meeting other single people could be encouraged by having time to socialize and a comfortable place to socialize. Having the time and place to socialize may be totally unimportant to a person who is newly married and looking for career advancement and promotions. Career advancement and promotions would probably be less important to a person who is getting ready to retire and is trying to make sure that the place of business has a retirement plan that will ensure the person's future comfort. A place of business must take into account the needs of the people who work for the place of business and try to satisfy the needs of as many of the people who work for the place of business as possible.

# Paragraph Skills

## Note Taking—Paragraph Construction

Many textbook writers try to create material from which students will be able to take notes easily. The excerpt in this chapter is a good example. Each paragraph contains a topic sentence and several supporting or explanatory details. If a student were taking notes from this text, it would be easy to decide what facts should be highlighted. Some students do this with specially colored pens, and some copy these main ideas into a notebook. Copying the main ideas into a notebook is a particularly good habit because people tend to remember material better if they have written it down than if they have simply read and underlined it.

**EXERCISES**

1. A paragraph from the excerpt has been reproduced below. The important ideas have been underlined in the first two sentences. Read the rest of the paragraph and underline the other important ideas or explanatory details that you would copy into your notebook if you were studying for a course on this subject.

   Another <u>aspect of pay</u> is the <u>system</u> by which <u>wages are determined.</u> <u>Most studies have found</u> that <u>pay is preferred to piecework systems</u> by most workers, and <u>straight salaries are preferred to incentive schemes</u> (Opsahl & Dunnette, 1966; Schwab & Wallace, 1974). One reason for this is that piecework systems tend to disrupt social relationships on the job, which are another major source of worker satisfactions. However, there is an interesting paradox here, for wage incentive schemes generally result in greater productivity than does hourly pay (Warr & Wall, 1975).

   When you have completed this exercise, compare your underlines with a classmate's. How did you decide what to underline? If you have different words underlined than your classmate has, discuss your reasons for your decisions.

2. With a classmate, choose another paragraph from the selection and together underline the main idea and the supporting or explanatory details.

## Special-Feature Paragraph

**contrast transition words**

In the following paragraph, underline all the contrast transition words or phrases.

John accepted a job working as a bus driver even though he often got carsick. The first few days of training were difficult, but finally he passed his road test. That first Monday morning he was beginning to feel queasy. Still, he started up the engine and backed out of the garage. A senior bus driver sat near the front of the bus and said, "Step on it, John. We have to make time. Otherwise, we'll be late." John wanted to drive slowly; however, he wanted to keep his job, so he stepped on it and the bus lurched forward. Instead of thinking about how sick he felt, John stared out the front window and counted to ten, then twenty. When he was up to one hundred, he told the older bus driver that he had a problem with car sickness. "I used to have it too. Just relax. You're doing fine," the experienced driver responded. John believed the reassuring words; on the other hand, he worried that he wouldn't make it through the next hour, although he was trying to forget about his stomach. Yet he made it through the day and through the next two weeks. In contrast to his early fears, five years later John found himself sitting near the front of a big old bus telling a new bus driver to "just relax."

Check your answers on page 347. If you missed any, continue reading.

Contrast transition words guide the reader to expect a change of direction or something unexpected to happen. Here is a list of some of the more common contrast transition words:

instead of

but

however

yet

even though

although

still

otherwise

in contrast with

on the contrary

on the other hand

**EXERCISES**

1. Rewrite the paragraph above in the present tense. The first sentence will read: "John accepts a job working as a bus driver even though he often gets carsick."

2. Reread the excerpt at the beginning of this chapter, and circle all the contrast transition words. Then read the sentence that precedes the circled word or words and the sentence that follows. Do you find a contrast in meaning?

3. Write a paragraph in which you use three of these contrast transition words. Possible topics include the following: the first day on a new job, learning how to do something new, problems with first impressions.

## Pronouns

**the indefinite pronoun**

The following is a list of indefinite pronouns. Each of these words is treated as a singular.

| | | |
|---|---|---|
| one | anybody | anyone |
| each | everybody | everyone |
| either | nobody | no one |
| neither | somebody | someone |

If a pronoun is used to refer to one of these words, the pronoun must be in the singular form.

*Each of the women* who applied for the job handed in *her* résumé.
\**Someone* left *his* notebook on the teacher's desk.
\**Everybody* should be in *her* seat when the movie begins.

\*In such cases, *his* or *her* is correct. You should not use *their* in written English, although you may hear it in spoken English.

***EXERCISE***    In each of the following sentences, choose the correct pronoun.

1. One of the girls put _____ essay on the teacher's desk.
   (her/their)

2. Everyone wants _____ ticket to win the lottery prize.
   (her/his/their)

3. Hardly anyone passes _____ road test the first time.
   (her/his/their)

4. Neither of the passengers paid for _____ share.
   (her/his/their)

5. Somebody gets _____ name in the newspaper every day.
   (her/his/their)

## Editing Skills Paragraph

The following paragraph is a first draft that contains many surface errors. The types of errors and the number of times each occurs are listed below. Find and correct the mistakes.

| | |
|---|---|
| 1 fragment | 1 pronoun agreement error |
| 2 run-ons | 1 subject/verb agreement error |
| 3 *there/their* errors | 1 *though/through* error |
| 2 *who/which* errors | |

According to Oskamp there are many factors involved in job satisfaction. People have to feel there jobs are meaningful and interesting it has to offer the workers a mental challenge. Even through their is individual differences in what people think is important. Most people agree that the jobs should offer some challenge. Pay has greater importance for individuals which cannot gain other satisfactions from there jobs. Jobs who offer external recognition, good pay, and a mental challenge are sought by most people, each person wants a feeling of fulfillment.

Answers are on page 347.

# Essay Skills

## Summary Writing

In Chapter 8, we began to examine the summary. The summary condenses a piece of writing into its essential points. What is the purpose of a summary?

A summary can be used to include another writer's ideas in your own writing. A summary can be used to take notes from library material when doing research for term papers. The techniques for summary writing can be helpful when you take notes in class, by training you to listen for the essential points in a lecture.

What are the techniques for writing a summary? First, use your own words. In this way, the words remain in your memory and are more useful to you when you study. Occasionally you may want to copy a few words or phrases from the original piece of writing, but, in general, the most effective summary is written in your own words. Look for the main ideas in the writing and include them in your summary. Then look for the important supporting or explanatory details. You are examining what is essential to the piece of writing.

Second, the summary should be organized in your own way so that you will best remember the material. You do not have to follow the exact organizational pattern of the original author. The summary is yours, and it should reflect your way of thinking and writing.

Third, even though the summary is organized by you and is written in your own words, it should not contain your ideas. You are summarizing another writer's ideas for your own use.

Finally, use your own style of writing. Do not copy the original author's writing style.

Reread the excerpt at the beginning of this chapter, then read the following summaries. Although their styles are quite different, each is a good summary. Summary writing is individual.

The author presents many work attributes that relate to job satisfaction. The main factors about the work is that it should: (1) offer a mental challenge; (2) be interesting and meaningful; (3) seem significant; (4) offer variety and autonomy. There should be little physical strain, and external recognition should be available. Pay is a factor, especially if there are not many other satisfactions from the job. In relation to pay, most people prefer a straight salary rather than hourly pay or piecework systems.

What makes people like their jobs? This article asks this question. People like jobs where they have some challenge but not too much. They want variety, yet they don't want to feel overtaxed. People like to feel that they have a say in their jobs and, at the same time, have the ability to see a job from start to finish. They don't want to have to work too hard; if they do, they want some recognition for what they have done. Higher pay helps, and most people would rather get a straight salary than hourly pay.

Which summary do you prefer? One is more informal and uses fewer of the author's original words. Which would you find it easier to study from? Just as in any other form of writing, you have to begin to develop your own style.

**EXERCISES**

1. Write a summary of the text selection in Chapter 2 (page 24) and/or the text selection in Chapter 5 (page 88).

2. In a small group, read your summaries or make copies for each member of the group. Compare your summaries with those of your classmates. Discuss what makes a good summary. Which summary in your group do you like best? Why?

3. Choose an article from a newspaper or news magazine, and write a summary of its contents.

## Suggested Writing Topics

Before you begin to write on the topic of your choosing, you may want to try one of the prewriting techniques presented earlier. You may want to cluster (page 61), brainstorm (page 175), freewrite (page 197), or consult your journal for ideas (page 58).

1. In essay form, write about your experiences creating the questionnaire and discuss the results you obtained from it. How did your results compare with the findings in the article? What were the differences? How do you explain these differences?

2. Choose the three factors that are most important to you in determining job satisfaction, and write an essay explaining your choices. Support your choices with details of your own experiences and your observations.

3. Describe in detail the worst job you have ever had. Close your eyes and try to imagine how it felt to work in that place. When you begin to write, concentrate on trying to make your reader really feel what it was like to work there. Use descriptive words and dialogue if appropriate.

4. Following the same procedure as in question 3, write about the best job you have ever had.

5. Use your imagination and write an essay describing your dream job. Begin your essay with the sentence "If I could have any job in the world, I would work as a _____." Make your writing rich with details.

6. Imagine that you run a small company and have only enough money to offer your workers three of the benefits listed below. Which would you choose? In essay form, explain the reasons for your choices.

   comprehensive retirement plan

   good health plan

   bright, cheerful cafeteria with nutritious and inexpensive food

   day-care center for children of employees

   end-of-year bonuses based on work output

   stock in the company

   employee social events such as Christmas parties and summer picnics

7. "People should be forced to change jobs every ten years. If they work at the same place for any longer than that, they begin to fall into dull routines, and their work is no longer as good as it was when the job was new and exciting." Do you agree or disagree? Write an essay supporting your point of view with your own experiences or your observations of others.

## Revising

**the interview approach**

   Choose a partner and make a copy of your essay for that person. Each of you will have a turn being interviewer and interviewee. The interviewer will read your essay aloud. Then, the interviewer will ask the interviewee the following questions about his or her essay, writing down the answers as they are spoken:

1. What is the main idea of your essay? What are you really trying to say?

2. If you had to leave out one line or one part, what would it be?

3. If you had to add something to one part of the essay, where would you add it and what would you add?

4. What part(s) of your essay do you like best?

5. What part(s) would you like to rewrite completely?

6. Do you think your essay says what you wanted it to say? How could you have said it better?

When you have finished the interview, give a copy to the interviewee. Then change roles and follow the same procedure. When both interviews are completely finished, read your own interview and make any changes in your essay that you feel are necessary to improve your writing.

# CHAPTER TWELVE

# A Mortal Flower

*Han Suyin, whose real name is Rosalie Chou, was born and raised in Peking. Eventually she became a doctor and the author of many novels, one of which,* A Many Splendored Thing, *was made into a movie. "A Mortal Flower," an excerpt from one of the volumes of her autobiography, describes her experience of looking for her first job.*

**T**he day after meeting Hilda I wrote a letter to the Rockefeller   1
Foundation, applying for a job.

Neither Father nor Mother thought I would get in. "You have to have pull. It's an American thing, Rockefeller Foundation. You must have pull."   5

°important people

Mother said: "That's where they do all those experiments on dogs and people. All the Big Shots° of the Nanking government also came here to have medical treatment, and sometimes took away a nurse to become 'a new wife.' "

It made sense to me, typing in a hospital; I would learn about   10
medicine, since I wanted to study medicine. And as there was no money at home for me to study, I would earn money, and prepare myself to enter medical school. I had already discovered that a convent-school education was not at all adequate, and that it would take me at least three more years of hard study before being able to enter   15
any college at all. Science, mathematics, Chinese literature and the classics . . . with the poor schooling given to me, it would take me years to get ready for a university.

°lower intestines

"I will do it." But clenched teeth, decision tearing my bowels,° were not enough; there was no money, no money, my mother said   20
it, said it until I felt as if every morsel of food I ate was wrenched off my father's body.

"No one is going to feed you doing nothing at home." Of course, one who does not work must not eat unless one can get married, which is called: "being settled at last." But with my looks I would   25
never get married, I was too thin, too sharp, too ugly. Mother said

it, Elder Brother had said it. Everyone agreed that I should work, because marriage would be difficult for me.

Within a week a reply came. The morning postman brought it, and I choked over my milk and coffee. "I'm to go for an interview. At the Peking Union Medical College. To the Comptroller's° office." °director's; controller's

Father and Mother were pleased. Mother put the coffee pot down and took the letter. "What good paper, so thick." But how could we disguise the fact that I was not fifteen years old? I had claimed to be sixteen in the letter. In fact, said Papa, it was not a lie since Chinese are a year old when born, and if one added the New Year as an extra year, as do the Cantonese and the Hakkas, who became two years old when they reach their first New Year (so that a baby born on December 31st would be reckoned° two years old on the following January 2nd), I could claim to being sixteen. °counted; calculated

"You look sixteen," said Mama, "all you have to do is to stop hopping and picking your pimples. And lengthen your skirt."

What dress should I wear? I had two school uniforms, a green dress, a brown dress, and one dress with three rows of frills° for Sunday, too dressy for an interview. I had no shoes except flat-heeled school shoes, and tennis shoes. There was no time to make a dress and in those years no ready-made clothes existed. Mother lengthened the green dress, and added her voile° scarf. I squeezed two pimples on my forehead, then went to the East market and bought some face powder, Butterfly brand, pink, made in Shanghai by a Japanese firm. °ruffles; lace °sheer fabric

The next morning, straw-hatted, with powder on my nose, I went with my father to the gates of the hospital.

"It's not this gate, this is for the sick. It's the other gate, round the corner," said the porter.

The Yu Wang Fu Palace occupied a whole city block. We walked along its high grey outer wall, hearing the dogs scream in the kennels, and came to its other gate which was the Administration building gate. It had two large stone lions, one male, one female. We crossed the marble courtyard, walked up the steps with their carved dragons coiling in the middle, into an entrance hall, with painted beams and intricate° painted ceiling, red lacquered° pillars, huge lamps. There was cork matting° on the stone floor. °complicated °covered with shiny varnish or paint °woven floor covering

"I'll leave you," said Papa. "Try to make a good impression." And he was gone.

I found the Comptroller's office easily, there was a messenger in the hall directing visitors. An open door, a room, two typewriters clattering and two women making them clatter.

I stood at the door and one of the women came to me. She had the new style of hair, all upstanding curls, which I admired, a dress with a print round the hem; she was very pregnant, so that her belly seemed to be coming at me first. She smiled. "Hello, what can I do for you?"

"I have an interview."

She took the letter from my hand. "Glad you could come. Now, 75 just sit you down. No, sit down there. I'll tell Mr. Harned you've come."

The office had two other doors besides the one to the corridor, on one was "Comptroller." That was the one she went through and returned from. 80

"Mr. Harned will see you now."

°sacred temple

Mr. Harned was very tall, thin, a small bald head, a long chin, enormous glasses. I immediately began to quiver with fright. His head was like a temple on top of a mountain, like the white pagoda° on the hill in the North Sea Park. I could not hear a word of what 85 he said. A paper and a pencil were in my hand, however, and Mr. Harned was dictating to me, giving me a speed test in shorthand.

I went out of his office and the pregnant secretary sat me in front of her own typewriter. I turned a stricken face to her, "I couldn't hear. I couldn't hear what he said. . ." 90

"Wait, I'll tell him." She bustled off. At the other desk was a blonde, thin girl, who had thrown one look at me and then gone back to clattering. The pregnant one reappeared, a pink sheet in hand: "Now just copy this on the typewriter, best you can."

I hit the keys, swiftly; the typewriter was the same make as mine, 95 a Royal.

"My, you are fast. I'll tell Mr. Harned."

°kindly, gentle
°large glasses that make eyes bulge

And Mr. Harned came out, benign° behind those enormous goggle glasses.° "Well, Miss Chou, we've decided to take you on as a typist, at thirty-five local dollars a month. To start Monday. Is that 100 all right?"

I nodded, unable to speak. Had he said ten dollars I would have accepted.

The kind secretary said: "Now take your time, and wipe your face. How old are you, by the way?" 105

"Sixteen, nearly."

"Is that all? Why my eldest is bigger than you, and she isn't through school yet. I told Mr. Harned you were shy and upset, and that's why you couldn't take dictation. He's all right, just takes getting used to, that's all." 110

"I couldn't understand his English."

"Oh, you'll get used to it. Now, I won't be around on Monday, I'm going to have a baby. It's your letter that got them interested in you, you wrote such good English, better than all the other letters we've had. Mr. Harned will give you a try." She whispered. "I put in 115 a good word for you."

°good-bye

"Thanks, thanks a lot . . . I need the money, I . . . ."

"Yes, dear, we know." Obviously she wanted her typewriter back, and her chair. I was still sitting on it. "Well, toodle-doo° for now, hope you enjoy yourself in this job. I've been here six months and I've enjoyed every minute. Don't let Mr. Harned worry you, he's really great, once you get used to him." 120

I had a job, had a job, had a job.

# Vocabulary Development

**a reading program**

The best way to develop your vocabulary is to read. In reading, you will encounter words as they are really used and become accustomed to seeing them and reading them. They will become part of your stored memory. You will begin to use these words in your own speaking and writing and begin to recognize them when you hear them.

Eudora Welty, a famous American writer, described her experiences as a reader in her book *One Writer's Beginnings:*

I learned from the age of two or three that any room in our house, at any time of day, was there to be read in, or to be read to. My mother read to me. . . . It had been startling and disappointing to me to find that story books had been written by people, that books were not natural wonders, coming up of themselves like grass. Yet regardless of where they came from, I cannot remember a time when I was not in love with them—with the books themselves, cover and binding and the paper they were printed on, with their smell and their weight and with their possession in my arms.

Begin a reading program. Every day for thirty minutes read something in English. The newspaper is a good beginning. Then you might subscribe to a news magazine like *Newsweek, Time,* or *U.S. News and World Report.* Read one article a day. Try not to use your dictionary for every word you do not know. Use context clues (see Chapter 11). If you like the way an article is written, copy the entire article or at least a paragraph into your notebook. Your mind and hand will work together and help you to remember words and sentence patterns.

Visit your school or public library often. It is not hard to obtain a library card in most areas of the United States. Become a borrower. Take books home and read them. If you see a movie you enjoy, find out if there is a book on which the movie was based. Then read the book. Ask your teachers and friends to recommend books. You never can read too much. All of the exercises you can do to increase your vocabulary will never give you as much real vocabulary growth and pleasure as becoming a reader will.

# Reading and Thinking Skills

## Comprehension Questions

1. Why don't the author's parents think she will be called for an interview at the Rockefeller Foundation? What is "pull"?
2. Why does the author want to get a job in a hospital?
3. Why does her family think she will never get married?
4. The girl is surrounded by her family and by strangers. Who actually helps her?

## Discussion Activities

### Analysis and Conclusions

1. What happens during the interview with Mr. Harned? Why does she get the job after all?
2. Why isn't the girl's family more helpful and supportive? Is there anything in the story that makes you believe they care for her despite their behavior?
3. Do you think the young girl has confidence in herself when she goes for the interview? Support your point of view with evidence from the story.
4. What do you think the title "A Mortal Flower" means in relation to the story that is being told?

### Writing and Point of View

1. Compare this story with "The Story of an Hour." Which story did you find easier to read? Which story did you prefer? Why?
2. Using evidence from "A Mortal Flower," show how Han Suyin made you aware of how she felt during the job interview. What descriptive words did she use?
3. "A Mortal Flower" is excerpted from an autobiography, as is "Age and Youth" by Pablo Casals (page 115). What is similar about these two pieces of writing? What is different? Which did you prefer? Why?

**Personal Response and Evaluation**

1. If you were going on a job interview, what would you do that was similar to what the girl in this story did? What would you do that was different? Why?

2. What should you do on an interview so that you make a good impression? What shouldn't you do?

3. What steps should a person take in order to find a job?

## Role Playing

In a small group, write a dialogue of an interview. It can be a job interview, a school interview, an interview with a landlord, or an interview with a loan official. Two people should be talking. Read the dialogue out loud in your group to make sure that it sounds natural. Each group should act out its dialogue in front of the class.

## Résumé Writing

Write your résumé as though you were preparing to go for a job interview. What should employers know about you that will make them want to hire you? What special talents do you have? What education do you have? What job experience have you had? Your résumé may take the following form, or your teacher may suggest another style to you.

**Name**
**Address**
**City, State, Zip Code**

**Telephone Number**

**Date of Birth** (This is optional.)

**Educational Background:**
(List the schools you have attended in reverse chronological order, the most recent one first. If you majored in something special or have any unique educational experience, mention it here.)

**Work Experience:**
(List the jobs you had in reverse chronological order, the most recent one first. You may want to explain the duties of your jobs if you think it will help you get the job you are applying for.)

**Special Abilities:**
(List the languages you speak and any other unique abilities you have that may help you get the job.)

**References:**
(List the names and addresses of two or three people who know you well enough to recommend you for a job. You should contact these people before using their names. A former employer and a teacher would be good choices.)

Type your résumé, single-spaced, making sure there are no typing or spelling errors. Use 8½″ × 11″ white or off-white typing paper. Make sure your original is neat and clean; have copies duplicated and keep your original for future reference. See the sample résumé.

---

RÉSUMÉ


Carmen Perozo
116 Broadway, Apt. 4B
Madison, New Jersey 07940
(201)377-7802
Date of birth: 10/15/66


EDUCATIONAL BACKGROUND

| | |
|---|---|
| September 1985–present | New Jersey State College, second year<br>Major undecided; probably accounting or business<br>Grade point average: 2.8 |
| April–July 1985 | Riverside Learning Center, New York, New York—<br>studied English as a Second Language |
| 1980–1984 | San Sebastian High School, Bogota, Colombia<br>Average: B + |


WORK EXPERIENCE

| | |
|---|---|
| August 1985–May 1986 | Part-time bookkeeper and salesclerk<br>Winston Gift Shop, Madison, N.J. |
| June 1985–August 1985 | Waitress, Three Brothers Restaurant,<br>Madison, N.J. |


SPECIAL ABILITIES

I speak fluent Spanish and French. I have studied English for five years (three in Colombia and two in the United States). I type 50 words a minute on an electric typewriter, and I can operate a word processor and a calculator.


REFERENCES

| | |
|---|---|
| Kaye Winston, owner | Professor James Manley |
| Winston Gift Shop | Accounting Department |
| 331 Main Street | New Jersey State College |
| Madison, New Jersey 07940 | Madison, New Jersey 07940 |

## Journal Writing

Han Suyin's story is about success. A young girl many had seen as a failure goes off on her own to a strange place, meets a kind, supportive person, and has a successful experience. She gets a job. In your journal, write about your experience with success. Have you ever had an experience like this nervous young girl's in which you were afraid of failure but, in the end, succeeded? If you have had this kind of experience, write about it.

The following quotation is taken from an article in *Self* magazine entitled "5 Ways to Cash in on Your Mistakes":

Failure intimidates most people, but to the successful it is a challenge to try again. Look behind most successes and you'll find a solid foundation of failures they have learned from. Success is not something we are born to—we achieve it.

Think about this quote. What is failure? Can we learn from it? Has a failure ever led to a success in your life? For this journal entry, think about failure and success. What is the relationship between the two?

# Word Skills

## Idiomatic Expressions

Each of the following paragraphs contains a context clue that will help you understand one of the idiomatic expressions used in "A Mortal Flower." Underline these context clues; the first one has been done for you. Then use the expressions when you answer the questions at the end of each paragraph.

*to have pull* (page 249, lines 3–4)

The girl's family thinks she has to have pull before her letter of application will be considered. They think she has to have influence from someone who is important in order to get a job. Have you ever needed to have pull in order to do something in your life?

*ready-made clothes* (page 250, line 47)

At the time Han Suyin writes of, no ready-made clothes existed.

People could not just walk into a department store and buy clothes off the racks. All clothes were made by hand, usually at home. In today's world it is rarer to find homemade clothes than ready-made clothes. Have you or has anyone in your family ever made your clothes, or are all of your clothes ready-made?

***make a (good) impression on*** (page 250, line 64)

The girl's father hopes that she will make a good impression on her future boss. He wants the comptroller to think good things about her when he meets her. It is also possible to make a bad impression on someone. Often our first impression of someone remains with us. Has anyone ever made one type of impression on you, and you later found that person to be very different from what you had first thought?

***to get used to*** (*someone/something*) (page 252, line 122)

The secretary promises the girl that she will like Mr. Harned once she gets used to him. She has to grow accustomed to the kind of person he is. When we meet someone for the first time, we do not know how to behave. We have to get used to the person. Can you think of any person in your life that it took you a long time to get used to? Can you think of anything else in your life that took you a long time to get used to (speaking English, perhaps)?

## Articles

**the**

The word *the* has been omitted throughout the following paragraph. Rewrite the paragraph, adding *the* where it is necessary.

Trying to get a job at Rockefeller Foundation is difficult for a girl who does not have pull. Finally, morning postman brings letter. She is to go for an interview at Peking Medical College, to Comptroller's office. She prepares her clothes and goes to East Market to buy face powder to cover her pimples. Next morning, she goes with her father to Yu Wang Fu Palace to Administration Building. They cross marble courtyard and go into entrance hall. Her father leaves. She finds office and meets her future employer, Mr. Harned. His bald head reminds her of temple on hill in North Sea Park. She takes typing test and gets job.

Check your answers on page 347.

## Adjective Word Order

In Chapter 9, we examined the typical adjective word order used in English. In order to review this, the following sentences have been taken from "A Mortal Flower," but the order of the adjectives has been mixed up. In the blanks, arrange the adjectives in the correct order. If you have difficulty, see the chart on page 185.

1. I had _____, a green dress, a brown
   (two, uniforms, school)
   dress, and one dress with three rows of frills for Sunday, too dressy for an interview.

2. I had no shoes except _____ and tennis
   (shoes, flat-heeled, school)
   shoes.

3. We walked along its _____, hearing the
   (outer, high, wall, grey)
   dogs scream in the kennels, and came to its other gate which was

   the _____.
   (gate, Administration, building)

4. It had _____, one male, one female.
   (two, stone, large, lions)

5. Mr. Harned was very tall, thin, _____,
   (bald, small, head, a)
   a long chin, enormous glasses.

## Commonly Confused Words

### bought/brought
Read the following paragraph, observing the use of *bought* and *brought*.

The postman *brought* the letter to the girl, and she *brought* it to show to her parents. They thought the paper was thick and they were surprised that she had gotten such a fast response to her letter. Everyone worried because she looked very young, so she went to the market and *bought* some face powder to cover the pimples on her face.

On the basis of what you observed in the paragraph, complete the following definitions.

_____ is the past tense of *bring*.

_____ is the past tense of *buy*.

Now use these two words in sentences of your own.

# Sentence Skills

## Past Perfect Tense

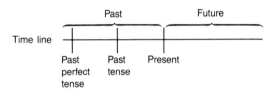

The chart above shows how the past perfect tense works. As you can see, the past perfect tense is a way of expressing something that has occurred in the past, before something else that happened in the past. If we are writing about two things that happened in the past and we want to show that one happened before the other, we use the past perfect tense for the thing that happened first.

For example:

1. In 1978 my father moved to California.
   In 1983 my mother and I moved to California to be with him.
   My father had lived in California for five years before my mother and I moved there to be with him.
2. I went to the movies at 8 o'clock in the evening.
   I saw you at midnight in the ice-cream store.
   I had gone to the movies before I saw you in the ice-cream store.
3. She ordered the book in September.
   It was delivered in November.
   She had ordered the book two months before it was delivered.

> The past perfect tense is formed with *had* plus the past participle of the verb.

Let's examine how the past perfect tense is used in the story.

*Paragraph 4 (lines 10–14):*

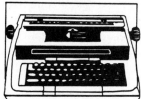

It made sense to me, typing in a hospital. . . . I would earn money, and prepare myself to enter medical school. I *had* already *discovered* that a convent-school education was not at all adequate . . .

Which came first, the realization about convent-school education or starting the job in the hospital?

*Paragraph 8 (lines 32–35):*

Father and Mother were pleased (with the letter about the job interview). Mother put the coffee pot down and took the letter. "What good paper, so thick." But how could we disguise the fact that I was not fifteen years old? I *had claimed* to be sixteen in the letter.

Which occurred first, the letter about the job interview or the letter in which she claimed to be sixteen?

*Paragraph 23 (lines 91–93):*

At the other desk was a blonde, thin girl, who *had thrown* one look at me and then gone back to clattering (on the typewriter).

Which happened first, the clattering on the typewriter or the throwing of the look? (This one may be confusing since the girl goes back to typing again.)

**EXERCISE**

Answer the following questions using the past perfect tense. You may want to do this in pairs, one student asking another the questions.

1. When did you come to this country? What had you heard about the United States? How much of it turned out to be true? How much turned out not to be true? Give examples from your experience.

2. What did you do on your last vacation? Had you ever done that before?

3. Tell about something that happened in your life that changed your way of living and/or your way of thinking. What had your life been like before this took place? What was it like afterwards?

## Modals

### *would* **plus the simple form of the verb**

In Chapter 6, we discussed the use of *used to* plus the simple form of the verb to describe actions in the past. In a similar way, we use *would* plus the simple form of the verb to describe actions that occurred repeatedly in the past.

**EXERCISES**

1. In the following paragraph, underline *would* each time it occurs and the verb that follows it.

When I was a little girl in school, I would visit my grandmother for lunch. I would climb the heavy wooden stairs to her apartment, and she would be waiting for me. She would make cold sandwiches in the warm months and hot food in the winter. Her apartment would smell, not of her cooking, but of her perfumes, filled with the flowers of summertime all year round. We would sit at a square table with a lace tablecloth that faced the street, and we would watch the people getting on and off the bus as we ate our lunch. We would play games trying to guess who they were and where they were going. I was probably the only child who wouldn't miss a day of school because it meant not seeing my grandmother for lunch.

2. Write a paragraph describing something in your past that occurred repeatedly. Use sentences like "I would talk to my father about . . ." or "I would visit my relatives . . ." or "I would eat candy and not think about getting cavities."
   *Would* plus the simple form of the verb can also be used to express future wishes or ideas that occurred in the past: "When I was a little boy, I would imagine myself grown up as an airline pilot." Han Suyin uses this construction in "A Mortal Flower."

3. Paragraph 4 of the story is reproduced below. Underline *would* each time it occurs and the verb that follows it.

It made sense to me, typing in a hospital; I would learn about medicine, since I wanted to study medicine. And as there was no money at home for me to study, I would earn money, and prepare myself to enter medical school. I had already discovered that a convent-school education was not at all adequate, and that it would take me at least three more years of hard study before being able to enter any college at all. Science, mathematics, Chinese literature and the classics . . . with the poor schooling given to me, it would take me years to get ready for a university.

4. *Would* plus the simple form of the verb can also be used to express ideas or wishes from the past that were not realized. Write a paragraph in which you describe future wishes or ideas you had in the past. For example, "I thought I would live in Tokyo when I was an adult" or "I believed I would marry my next-door neighbor" or "I used to think that I would look like my mother, but instead I grew up to look like my father."

## Third-Person Singular Exercise

1. Change paragraph 4 of the story (reproduced above) from the first person (I) to the third person. The first sentence will begin: "It made sense to her, typing in a hospital; she would learn about medicine. . . ."

2. Read the original paragraph and the altered paragraph. Is there any difference in meaning? Why do you think Han Suyin wrote in the first person? Go to the library and ask the librarian to direct you to the autobiography section. Are most of these books written in the first person? Why?

3. As an extra exercise, while in the library borrow the autobiography of someone whose life you find interesting. Read the autobiography and use the third person to take some notes about the person's life. Share your findings about that person with the class.

# Paragraph Skills

## Special-Feature Paragraph

**transition words**

The following paragraphs, which describe how to prepare yourself for a job interview, contain many transition words. There are transitions that indicate importance or emphasis as well as transitions that indicate time. Underline all the transition words in the paragraphs.

The first thing you have to do to prepare for a job interview is to write your résumé. Most of all, the résumé should emphasize all the related experience you have had. The résumé should be clear and should keep in mind that the person reading it will probably be reading many other résumés. The best thing you can do is to make it obvious why you can do the job better than anybody else. Your résumé should be neat and, if possible, typed. The biggest advantage of a typed résumé is that it is easy to read.

Once you have organized your résumé, check your closet. Special attention should be paid to what you will wear for the interview. You don't want to be dressed up as if you were going to a party, but you also don't want to be under-dressed. You should consider getting your hair trimmed before the interview. Remember that neatness counts. You should be neat in your appearance as well as in your résumé.

Finally, you must keep in mind that employers do not like people to smoke or chew gum during an interview. The basic reason for this may be that you appear too relaxed. Remember you are not visiting a friend; you are trying to get a job. If you follow all of the above advice, you have a good chance of getting the job you desire.

Check your answers on page 347. If you had any difficulty, refer to the lists below. Transition words add a flow to your writing.

*Time transitions:* first, next, then, before, after, during, now, while, finally

*Emphasis transitions:* keep in mind, remember that, most of all, the most important, the best thing, the basic reason, the chief reason, the chief factor, special attention should be paid to

**EXERCISES**

1. Rewrite the above paragraphs, changing them from the second person (you) to the third person (he or she). The first sentence should read "The first thing a person has to do to prepare for a job interview is to write his [or her] résumé."

2. The following paragraphs give directions for writing a business letter. All the transition words and phrases have been removed. Refer to the above lists or any others that you prefer, and fill in the appropriate transitions. You can delete or add words and phrases in order to make the paragraphs more coherent.

People write business letters to request information, to complain about a product they have bought, to explain why they haven't paid a bill on time. They write to request job interviews, to introduce their résumés. Business letters generally consist of an introduction, a body, and a conclusion. Formal essays consist of these same parts. The introduction to a business letter is usually found in the first paragraph. It is what makes the reader want to read more. It introduces the main idea that the letter will be about. The body of the letter offers specific details or examples to support the main idea that has been presented in the introduction. The letter ends with the conclusion, in which the ideas from the rest of the letter are summarized and/or restated.

The form of a business letter is important. On the upper right-hand side of the page, the writer types his or her address, including the zip code. Under the address is the date the letter is written. One line below this on the left-hand side of the page is the address to which the letter is being sent. The writer skips a line and types "Dear ——:" and skips two more lines, indents five spaces, and begins the introductory paragraph. The entire letter is typed, indenting for each new paragraph. The letter is concluded. The writer skips two lines and types "Sincerely," or "Yours truly," in line with the address and date on the right-hand side of the page. The writer signs his or her name. The letter is folded into thirds and placed in a long, rectangular business envelope that is addressed, stamped, and mailed.

3. Compare your rewritten paragraphs with a classmate's. You will probably have very different paragraphs. Discuss how you decided where to put transitions.

4. As individuals or in small groups, write business letters following the above directions. Your letter may introduce your résumé and request a job interview; it may request information or complain about a product you have bought. Try to use transition words and phrases in your letter.

## Editing Skills Paragraph

The following paragraph is a first draft that contains many surface errors. The types of errors are listed below. Find the mistakes and edit the paragraph. Answers are on p. 347.

| fragments | tense inconsistencies | *bought/brought* errors |
|-----------|----------------------|-------------------------|
| run-ons | point-of-view changes | *though/through* errors |

One thing Bob always has trouble with. Whenever he gets a new job he gets nervous and he was late. This time through he brought a noisy alarm clock and set it the night before. Then, of course, there was a power failure in my building and the time was wrong. I jumped out of bed when the alarm sounded I ran into the shower and I was ready to leave on time. He thought he had a lot of time so he walked slowly down the street looking in all the store windows. When he walked into the job his boss was looking at her watch shaking her head. I couldn't figure it out until I got home that afternoon and realized his clock was wrong.

# Essay Skills

## Description

In "A Mortal Flower," Han Suyin describes Mr. Harned:

Mr. Harned was very tall, thin, a small bald head, a long chin, enormous glasses.* I immediately began to quiver with fright. His head was like a temple on top of a mountain, like the white pagoda on the hill in the North Sea Park. I could not hear a word of what he said. A paper and a pencil were in my hand, however, and Mr. Harned was dictating to me, giving me a speed test in shorthand.

*Han Suyin did not use parallel structure in this sentence. It could be rewritten: "Mr. Harned was very tall, thin, and bald. He had a long chin and wore enormous glasses." Which version do you prefer?

This description helps the reader to see Mr. Harned and to feel the terror the young girl feels during her job interview. "Mr. Harned was very tall, thin . . ." We picture a person who is cold and unfriendly. If she had wanted him to appear warm and cuddly, she could have described him as "short and chubby." Then we read that he wears "enormous glasses." His glasses probably magnify his eyes and make him seem even more frightening and forbidding. She continues, "His head was like a temple on top of a mountain, like the white pagoda on the hill in the North Sea Park." A temple on top of a mountain is something far away and not easily approached, and a pagoda is a holy temple that in some cases women are not even allowed to visit. Han Suyin uses similes, comparisons that use the word *like* or *as*, to create a mood of distance and fear.

"I could not hear a word of what he said." Once again, the girl is removed from Mr. Harned. They cannot communicate. "A paper and a pencil were in my hand, however, and Mr. Harned was dictating to me, giving me a speed test in shorthand." Han Suyin does not tell us that Mr. Harned handed her the paper. He does not even smile at her. There is no connection between the two of them. He dictates to her; he does not speak to her or talk with her. Throughout the paragraph, Han Suyin creates a mood of aloofness on the part of Mr. Harned and perceived isolation on the part of the girl. She is alone and frightened during the interview. In fact, we find out later in the story that Mr. Harned is benign (kindly or gentle), but we do not get this feeling in our first impression of him. Han Suyin has used description to create a mood and a feeling about a character.

The following excerpt from *Sleepless Nights* by Elizabeth Hardwick illustrates how description can make us feel about a character.

For a time she had a lover, Bernie. He was terrible to look at. Very short, and if not fat, with too many muscles and bulges. Bernie was put together like a pumpkin, or two pumpkins, one placed on top of the other. The top was his merry, jack-o'-lantern face with its broken teeth.

The reader is told that Bernie is terrible to look at. In the next lines, however, Hardwick tells us that he looks "like a pumpkin, or two pumpkins, one placed on top of the other." A pumpkin is a big, round, orange fruit that makes us think of Halloween. Moreover, Hardwick goes on to say, "The top was his merry, jack-o'-lantern face with its broken teeth." A jack-o'-lantern is a pumpkin that is cut into a face; sometimes a candle is put inside it as a decoration. It has a holiday mood and feeling. Hardwick tells us that Bernie's face is "merry." Santa Claus is "merry." Overall Hardwick has written a short description that creates a fun, holiday mood and that makes us feel that Bernie is a likable fellow even if he is "terrible to look at."

In one of her letters, the New Zealand writer Katherine Mansfield says:

The old woman who looks after me is about 106, nimble and small, with the loveliest skin—pink rubbed over cream—and she has blue eyes and white hair and one tooth, a sort of family monument to all the 31 departed ones.

The images are soft and gentle. Words like "nimble" and "small" begin to suggest a picture of a child. Mansfield describes the woman's skin as "pink rubbed over cream," a very poetic but also lovely image. The one tooth, which could have made the woman frightening and witchlike, is described in a humorous way. The reader likes the old woman and feels she is beautiful in a very special way.

Description makes us feel something about a person or a place. By our choice of words, we can make a person or a place seem inviting or forbidding, kindly or hostile. It is up to us as writers to choose the words that best convey what it is we are trying to express.

**EXERCISES**

1. Write a description in which you make the person being described seem frightening and forbidding. Use similes (comparisons that use the words *like* and *as*).

2. Write a description in which you make the person being described seem friendly and gentle. Use similes to create your image.

3. Rewrite Han Suyin's description of Mr. Harned so that he seems to be a warm and friendly man.

4. Write a description of someone in your class and read it aloud to the class. See if anyone can recognize the individual you have written about.

## Suggested Writing Topics

Before you begin to write, you may want to use some of the prewriting techniques discussed throughout the book. You also may want to refer to your journal for ideas.

1. Describe a job interview you have been on. Create a mood so that your reader can feel what your experience was like. Use descriptive words.

2. First impressions do not always reveal the total person. Have you ever had an experience in which a first impression of a person turned out to be wrong? Describe what happened and what you learned from it.

3. Write a letter of recommendation to Mr. Harned telling him why he should hire Miss Chou. (See page 264 for the correct form for a business letter.)

4. Write a dialogue that takes place between the girl and her parents when she returns home to tell them that she has gotten the job. (You may want to act out your dialogue in front of the class with two other classmates.)

5. Looking for a job can be very difficult. Use this as your thesis, then give examples and experiences to support your point of view.

6. "Success is not something we are born to—we achieve it." Explain the steps you think someone has to go through in order to achieve success. What does success mean to you?

7. Many people learn more from their failures than they do from their successes. Give examples from your own life or from your observations of others to support this point of view.

8. Imagine that you are an employer who is interviewing someone for a job. In a well-developed essay, describe what you would expect in an employee. What are the characteristics you value and why are they important?

## Revising

One great aim of revision is to cut out. In the exuberance of composition it is natural to throw in—as one does in speaking—a number of small words that add nothing to meaning but keep up the flow and rhythm of thought. In writing, not only does this surplusage not add to meaning, it subtracts from it. Read and revise, reread and revise, keeping reading and revising until your text seems adequate to your thought.

JACQUES BARZUN

Jacques Barzun's paragraph may seem confusing to you when this chapter has been about adding detail to your writing, making your descriptions come alive. However, there is a difference between rich, exciting language and repetitive writing. Look at what you have written, and every time you see the words *in my opinion,* cross them out. It is obvious that your writing is in your opinion because you have written it. Every time you see the words *you know,* cross them out. If your reader knows, why bother to say it again? Every time you find yourself repeating something you have already said a few sentences before, cross it out. In place of those excess bits of writing, add some new and exciting ideas. Keep reading and revising until "your text seems adequate to your thought."

# Sex Roles and Establishing Self

# CHAPTER THIRTEEN

# The American Male

*This article from* U.S. News & World Report *was written by a group of editors at the magazine and focuses on the ways the American male has changed in response to the women's movement and economic pressures. Macho is no longer enough; men are becoming more sensitive, open, and caring. This is creating new problems as well as new pleasures.*

L ittle more than a generation ago, life was far simpler for the American male. More often than not, he was family patriarch and breadwinner. His wife catered to his needs and raised his children. His word around the home was law.

Not any more. As a result of the women's revolution and economic pressures, men today face a world in which macho no longer is enough. The new and improved model of the male is expected to share in breadwinning and child rearing and be both tender and tough.

°sacred figures

Where once independence and aloofness were desirable, now openness, sensitivity and intimacy are prized. The shift in society's cultural icons° tells the story. John Wayne and Humphrey Bogart have been replaced by Dustin Hoffman and Robert Redford. Even the modern tough guy Clint Eastwood displays a new sensitivity on the screen in "Tightrope" as the divorced father of two.

°evidence of something
no longer in existence

But change in real life is far more complicated than in the movies, especially when men have few clear role models to follow. Many struggle to blend vestiges° of traditional masculinity with what are regarded as softer, or feminine traits. "Men are confused and searching for their identity," says Mathilda Canter, a psychologist in Phoenix. Experts point to signs of the confusion: The wave of androgyny in popular culture in the persons of Boy George and Michael Jackson and the trend toward young males' wearing earrings.

°capable of being hurt

Forget the stereotypes of the vulnerable° female and the confident man. Some psychologists report that today more men seek help than do women. "By and large, women are more sure of where they are and where they are going," says New York psychologist Herbert Freudenberger.

**Changing rules.** Males in their 30s and 40s—"the transitional generation"—have suffered the most. "Many of them married with 30 one set of rules and now feel that the rules have changed," says Graham Spanier, a sociologist at the State University of New York at Stony Brook. Some of their marriages end up in shambles.° Even those whose marriages are intact struggle with the shift in values.

°great destruction

Men in their 50s and 60s also have a hard time coping on occa- 35 sion. Some reach the verge of retirement only to find that their wives have decided they want to go to work. Psychologist Canter tells of a 57-year-old man who initially supported his wife's desire to get a job. But when she was promoted from office worker to a management post and began to travel, his world started to crumble.     40

Only men in their 20s, who came of age after society began to assimilate° a decade of social upheaval,° seem to take matters in stride. But they have other problems in an era when the rules of courting are unclear. They often are unsure of how to treat single women and are more cautious about marriage. Result: A bachelor boom. 45 The proportion of men between ages 25 and 29 who are single soared from 23 to 38 percent between 1960 and 1984.

°absorb; take into itself
°disturbance; turmoil

Psychologists say some men respond to the current confusion by fleeing commitment and rejecting pressure from women to be more open. Others take refuge in what has been dubbed° "the new macho," 50 convinced that women still want a traditional man, even though they say otherwise. Fearful of being branded "wimps," they contend that real men don't eat quiche or change diapers but instead swig° beer and smoke cigars. Recent films such as "Cloak and Dagger," in which boys learn to be men by shooting to kill, are indicative of macho's 55 return, says Peter Biskind, editor of *American Film* magazine.

°named or called

°drink deeply

**Reagan's role.** Sociologist Michael Kimmel of Rutgers University links the popularity of macho to Ronald Reagan, who talks of "strength rather than compassion."° Kimmel draws a parallel with the late 19th century when there was also "tremendous concern about men be- 60 coming soft." That crisis of masculinity, says Kimmel, was resolved by the entry of Roughrider Teddy Roosevelt into the White House and the founding of the Boy Scouts.

°pity for the suffering of others

But experts agree that macho's rise is really only a blip° in a long-term trend toward change. They say it is impossible for men to re- 65 turn to the old ways in a society in which more than half of all married women and about 65 percent of younger wives are in the labor force.

°a short-lived signal

Studies show that, slowly and sometimes painfully, men are adjusting. The Institute for Social Research at the University of Mich- 70

igan found that between 1965 and 1981 men in. the 24-to-44-year
age group increased the amount of time they devoted to housework
by 20 percent. Many now take a major role in their children's lives
from the day of birth. A survey by Levi Strauss & Company found
that 4 out of 5 fathers are present in the delivery room as compared 75
with only 27 percent a decade earlier. The study also found that
most fathers now change diapers. Anxious to excel in their new roles,
°flourishing; growing   some are enrolling in fathering courses that are burgeoning° nationally.

Divorced men get involved, too. Boston University psychologist 80
Ron Levant, who teaches a course for fathers of school-age children,
says about half the men enrolled are separated or divorced fathers,
many with joint custody.

All of these changes have caught the eyes of advertisers. "They
recognize that men are involved in the home in ways that were un- 85
heard of 10 years ago," says Alice Goldberg, director of research
services for Benton & Bowles, a New York advertising agency. Now,
diaper ads show men holding the baby, and a toothpaste ad has the
father brushing the child's teeth.

In some ways, says Tufts University historian Donald Bell, the 90
°farming   current shift marks a return to America's agrarian° past, when "there
was much sharing of work, emotional roles and child rearing."

Just as many working women strive to be "Supermom," more fathers also try to be "Superdad" in seeking to balance the often conflicting demands of home and job. But that's harder to do than in 95
preindustrial America because job and home are in different places.
Samuel Osherson, a Harvard University psychologist, cites a financial analyst who was on the verge of becoming a partner in his firm.
His boss wanted him to work 60 hours a week, while his wife wanted
more family time. "He tried to satisfy both without great success,"100
says Osherson.

Many men complain that, like women, they are trapped by soci-
°things that bind tightly   ety's strictures.° To loosen their bonds, they band together in orga-
°closely related to   nizations that are male counterparts° of the women's movement. Some
each other   provide men with emotional support in times of stress, a develop-105
ment that psychologists applaud. Others such as Fathers United for
Equal Rights are politically oriented and push for changes in divorce
and custody statutes. Many organizations also advocate paternity leave
for new fathers—as women have maternity leave—and more flexible
work hours to give men freedom to meet family responsibilities. What110
all these groups share is a desire to have society accept men in a
wider range of roles. "The motto of the movement is be yourself,"
says Dan Logan, who heads a Washington, D.C., organization called
Free Men.

°disturbance

°knocks about

Other signs of men's growing self-awareness: Courses in men's 115 studies are springing up in universities, and the *New York Times Magazine* now has a regular column called "About Men."

Out of all the turmoil,° say experts, ultimately will emerge a less rigid definition of masculinity that allows men to be comfortable with whatever paths they select. That switch is already under way. Over 120 time, much of the conflict that now buffets° relations between the sexes will diminish. "The problems will gradually iron themselves out," says University of Vermont psychologist Phyllis Bronstein. "We're at the awkward stage right now."

# Vocabulary Development I

**words relating to relationships and sex roles**

Many of the words in this article relate to relationships and sex roles. We will examine some of these words as they are used in the article.

**Paragraph 1**

*patriarch:* the male leader of the family; the father or male heir who rules the family

Based on the above description, what is the female leader of a family

called? _____

*breadwinner:* a person who supports himself and others by his earnings

How do you think the term "breadwinner" came about?_____

_____

**Paragraph 2**

*macho:* tough and strong, rather than caring and compassionate

Is it still important in some cultures for a man to be macho?_____

_____

*child rearing:* the bringing up or raising to adulthood of a child

The following are additional idioms connected with child rearing:

*bring up:* I was brought up by my Aunt Tillie and my Uncle Harry.

*raise:* They raised me on a farm in Kansas after my parents died.

*rear:* I was reared to believe that a child should respect adults.

Who brought you up? _____

Where were you raised? _____

What were you reared to believe? _____

**Paragraph 3**

*intimacy:* close involvement
Can a father have the same intimacy with a young child as a mother?

_____

*sensitivity:* having strong feelings and caring for others' feelings
In your culture, are men allowed to express sensitivity as much as

women are? _____

**Paragraph 4**

*androgyny:* having the characteristics of both sexes, being both feminine and masculine at the same time
Do you think that modern clothing expresses androgyny, or are dif-

ferences between the sexes apparent? _____

**Paragraph 9**

*wimp:* a weak, helpless person (This is a very colloquial expression that has a negative meaning; calling someone a "wimp" is very insulting.)
Have you ever known someone you thought to be a wimp who turned

out to be a very different type of person? _____

_____

*quiche:* a cheese pie (There is a popular book entitled *Real Men Don't Eat Quiche,* which made fun of the stereotype of what a real man is. Quiche [pronounced kēesh] is a light food and, according to the book, macho or tough men would order steak.)
Quiche has been used to stereotype masculinity. What is another ex-

ample of a stereotype? _____

**Paragraph 13**

*joint custody:* arrangement by which care of the children is shared by the father and mother after a divorce. In one arrangement the father takes care of the children for four days and the mother takes care of the children for the next four days. The children take turns living with each of the parents.
What are some of the effects joint custody might have on children?

_____

Reread "The American Male" and underline these words. Read the sentences in which they appear and the sentences that come before and after in order to understand the context in which the words are used.

# Vocabulary Development II

**antonyms**

Each of the words in column A means almost the exact opposite of one of the words in column B. A word that means the opposite of another is called an antonym. Draw a line from each word in column A to its antonym in column B. The first one has been done for you.

| **A** | **B** |
|---|---|
| 1. patriarch | a. femininity |
| 2. agrarian | b. intimacy |
| 3. independence | c. tough |
| 4. masculinity | d. maternity |
| 5. aloofness | e. matriarch |
| 6. indifference | f. compassion |
| 7. tender, vulnerable | g. industrial |
| 8. paternity | h. involvement |

Now use these words in sentences of your own.

# Reading and Thinking Skills

## Comprehension Questions

1. "The American Male" describes changes in men's roles in our society. According to the article, what are some of the changes?
2. According to the article, why is there a bachelor boom?
3. What are some of the studies that show that men are adjusting to their role changes?

## Discussion Activities

### Analysis and Conclusions

1. How has advertising responded to the fact that men are more involved in the home? Which advertisements have you seen that reflect this trend?

2. According to the article, "even the modern tough guy" in the movies "displays a new sensitivity." Do the movies that you have seen recently seem to support this statement?

3. Do the people that we see on television and in movies affect our own behavior? Explain, using examples from your experiences.

### Writing and Point of View

1. This article refers to statements made by many authorities in order to support its point of view. What are some examples of this? Did these quotes make this article seem more convincing to you?

2. This article presents facts and ideas objectively, yet each of the authors probably has opinions about this very controversial issue. How do you think the authors of the article feel about this issue? Support your answer with evidence from the article.

3. What would you have liked to know that was not in the article?

### Personal Response and Evaluation

1. The article outlines many changes in the relationships between men and women. Do you think these changes are positive or negative? Support your opinions with evidence.

2. Are these changes being felt in other cultures and other parts of the world too? Explain your answer.

3. Should men have a role in child rearing? What should it be?

4. Will these changes in sex roles affect children? What do you think the result will be?

5. Can fathers care for children as effectively as mothers can?

## Role Playing

Imagine that you are the interviewer who prepared this article. What questions did you ask to get the information in the article? Write ten questions and then interview your classmates to see if the changes described in the article also apply to members of your class.

Possible questions include the following:

1. Who does the cleaning in your home?
2. Who do you think should take care of the children?
3. Which male movie star would you like to be like (if asking a man), or which male movie star would you like to be married to (if asking a woman)?

## Journal Writing

In this chapter, we have read and discussed sex roles, especially the male roles. We all have to make decisions about what the right roles are for ourselves. We have to decide how we will behave in our families, with our children, our spouses, our dates. There is no one right way for all people. In addition, we are always changing, responding to the society or culture in which we live.

In this journal entry, write about the ideal man and the ideal woman. Write about how changes in sexual roles have affected you. Would you like to make changes in how you treat the opposite sex or in how they treat you? As you write, you may discover some things about yourself that will surprise you.

# Word Skills

## Idiomatic Expressions

Each of the following paragraphs contains a context clue that will help you understand one of the idiomatic expressions used in "The American Male." Underline these context clues; the first one has been done for you. Then use the expressions when you answer the questions at the end of each paragraph.

***more often than not*** (page 271, line 2)

In the past, men's and women's roles were very clear-cut. More often than not, the woman stayed home and cared for the children. Usually the man went off to work. Today, more often than not, both men and women work. They share the responsibility for the home and for their children. In your family, who does the dishes more often than not? Who does the laundry more often than not?

***by and large*** (page 271, line 26)

By and large, people are adjusting well to the changes. Generally, men are finding it rewarding to have an intimate relationship with a child. Women, by and large, are finding it satisfying to have a job and contribute financially to the family. By and large, are you satisfied with your life? By and large, do you feel that you have adjusted to living in a new country?

***on occasion*** (page 272, lines 35–36)

On occasion, some people may yearn for the "good old days when men were men and women were women." In other words, these people sometimes wish they lived at a time when roles were more fixed and people did not have to think so much about what they wanted from their lives. On occasion, especially when one is having problems, it is natural to want to go back to an easier time. On occasion, do you wish you were back in your own country? Do you feel homesick on occasion?

***come of age*** (page 272, line 41)

A person comes of age when he or she legally becomes an adult. In the United States, citizens can vote at the age of eighteen. In most states, however, people cannot order alcoholic beverages unless they are twenty-one years old. In some states, people must be eighteen to obtain a driver's license, but in other states, they only have to be sixteen. Coming of age legally is one aspect of becoming an adult; another aspect is psychological. What indicates that a person has come of age psychologically?

## Gerunds or Infinitives

In each of the following sentences, choose either the gerund (*-ing*) form of the verb or the infinitive (*to* plus the simple form of the verb). If you want to check your answers or if you have any difficulties, refer to Chapter 7 (page 148) for gerund guidelines and Chapter 10 (page 211) for guidelines for infinitives.

1. The new and improved model of the male is expected _____

_____ in breadwinning and child rearing and be both
  (to share, sharing)
tender and tough.

2. The man has to be prepared _____ in the home as well
                                (to work, working)
   as in the office.

3. Women appreciate _____ they will have a helpmate in
                      (to know, knowing)

   life when they agree _____ the man of their choice.
                         (to wed, wedding)

4. Some men find that they actually enjoy _____ and
                                            (to cook, cooking)

   _____ after they finish _____ because it helps
    (to clean, cleaning)                (to work, working)

   them learn _____.
               (to relax, relaxing)

5. In many relationships, couples decide _____ the
                                           (to share, sharing)
   childbirth experience. As a result, 4 out of 5 men want

   _____ with their wives when their babies are born. Usu-
    (to be, being)

   ally these men would like _____ their babies minutes after
                              (to hold, holding)
   birth.

6. Men who hold on to the old macho ways often miss _____
                                                      (to get, getting)
   involved in these remarkable moments of sharing.

## Pronouns

As a review exercise, paragraph 7 of the article has been reproduced below with all the pronouns removed. Read the sentences
carefully and fill in the appropriate pronouns. Refer to the article to
check your answers.

Men in _____ 50s and 60s also have a hard time coping on

occasion. Some reach the verge of retirement only to find that

_____ wives have decided _____ want to go to work. Psychologist Canter tells of a 57-year-old man who initially supported _____ wife's desire to get a job. But when _____ was promoted from office worker to a management post and began to travel, _____ world started to crumble.

## Prepositions

As a review exercise, paragraph 12 of the article has been reproduced below with all the prepositions removed. Read the sentences carefully and fill in the appropriate prepositions. Refer to the article to check your answers. If your answers differ from those in the original article, show your answers to your teacher or to a classmate. In some cases, there is more than one right answer. (In the preceding pronoun exercise, there was only one right answer for each blank. However, some rules for prepositions are more flexible than the rules for pronouns.)

Studies show that, slowly and sometimes painfully, men are adjusting. The Institute _____ Social Research _____ the University _____ Michigan found that _____ 1965 and 1981 men _____ the 24-to-44-year age group increased the amount _____ time they devoted _____ housework _____ 20 percent. Many now take a major role _____ their children's lives _____ the day _____ birth. A survey _____ Levi Strauss & Company found that 4 out _____ 5 fathers are present _____ the delivery room as compared _____ only 27 percent a decade earlier. The study also found that most fathers now change diapers. Anxious _____ excel _____ their new roles, some are enrolling _____ fathering courses that are burgeoning nationally.

## Commonly Confused Words

**who's/whose**

Read the following paragraph, noticing the use of *who's* and *whose*.

The man *whose* wife returned to work only to find herself receiving many promotions is an interesting case. *Who's* to say that she would have responded the same way if he had started to get promotions and had to begin traveling? *Whose* problem is worse, hers or his?

Going by what you observed in the paragraph, complete the following definitions.

_____ means "who is" or "who has."

_____ means "belongs to whom."

Now use *who's* and *whose* in sentences of your own.

# Sentence Skills

## Present Continuous Tense

Draw rectangles around the subjects in the following sentences. Then draw circles around the verbs. The first one has been done for you.

1. People today are living in a changing world.

2. He is experiencing changes in his relationships with women at present.

3. Still, change in real life is happening more slowly than in the movies.

4. "I am trying to be a successful businessman, a good husband, and a loving father."

5. We are now attending classes to help us deal with our new responsibilities.

6. "You are all experiencing new demands and new possibilities."

Let's use these sentences to examine the present continuous tense.

In this tense, the *to be* verb *(am,* _____, or *are)* is followed by

the _____ form of the verb. Some words that are used with the present continuous tense are *now, right now, at this moment,* and *at present.*

As a class or in small groups, answer the following questions using the present continuous tense.

The present continuous tense is used to describe actions that are happening right now or at the moment of speaking.

1. What are you doing right now?
2. What are two things that you are not doing right now that you would like to be doing?

The present continuous tense is used to describe things that are happening around us or in the world right now.

3. What do you think is the most interesting thing that is happening in the world right now?
4. Are you changing in relation to sex roles, to the things we have read about in this chapter?

The present continuous tense is used to describe things that are happening in the near future.

5. When you watch the news, what are you waiting to find out about?
6. Are you doing anything special this weekend?

There are certain verbs that are not usually used in the continuous tenses (present continuous, past continuous, future continuous, present perfect continuous, and so on). A list of these verbs follows:

| | | | |
|---|---|---|---|
| appear | have | own | smell |
| appreciate | hear | possess | sound |
| be | know | prefer | taste |
| believe | like | recognize | understand |
| cost | love | remember | want |
| dislike | mean | see | |
| hate | need | seem | |

These verbs can be divided into three basic categories:

1. *Words that relate to feelings*

   For example, "I hate you" or "I love you" are treated as permanent states of being, not just present moment feelings, although "I am feeling sick today" is correct. In this case, the verb is expressing a temporary state of being.

2. *Words that relate to ownership or possession*

   For example, "I own a green convertible" or "I have a house in the country" are regarded as permanent, although "I am having some people over to dinner tonight" is correct. In this case, the verb is not used to express a permanent state of being.

3. *Words that relate to perception*

   For example, "I see the blue sky above me" or "I smell the potatoes burning" are not treated as continuous actions, although "I am hearing Bach for the first time" is correct, since it expresses a perception that takes place at the moment the sentence is spoken and refers to an event that takes place over a period of time.

## Simple Present Tense

In the following sentences from "The American Male," the present tense verbs have been omitted. Fill in each blank with the correct form of the verb. Refer to the article to check your answers.

1. Men today _____ a world in which macho no longer is
                  (face/faces)
   enough.

2. Psychologists _____ some men respond to the current
              (say/says)
   confusion by fleeing commitment and rejecting pressure from women to be more open.

3. In some ways, says Tufts University historian Donald Bell, the

   current shift _____ a return to America's agrarian past,
             (mark/marks)
   when "there was much sharing of work, emotional roles and child rearing."

4. But change in real life _____ far more complicated than
             (is/are)

   in the movies, especially when men _____ few clear role
              (have/has)
   models to follow.

5. Even the modern tough guy Clint Eastwood _____ a
(display/displays)
new sensitivity on the screen in "Tightrope" as the divorced father of two.

In the following exercise, fill in each blank with either the simple present tense or the present continuous tense of the verb.

1. Women today _____ the changes that men have made
(appreciate)
in relation to sharing housework.

2. Many men _____ for their identity in this confusing new
(search)
world.

3. Men _____ few role models to follow.
(have)

4. The modern family _____ more time together.
(want)

5. Most recent research _____ that men and women
(indicate)

_____ to the changes.
(adjust)

## Present Perfect Tense

The verbs have been removed from the following sentences from the article. To review the present perfect tense, fill in each blank with either *have* or *has* plus the past participle of the verb. Then refer to the article to check your answers.

1. Males in their 30s and 40s—"the transitional generation"—

_____ the most.
(suffer)

2. All of these changes _____ the eyes of advertisers.
(catch)

3. Some reach the verge of retirement only to find that their wives

_____ they want to go to work.
(decide)

Now change these sentences into questions using the present perfect tense. Write the questions in the following blanks.

_____

_____

_____

_____

## Indirect Speech

We use quotation marks when we use the exact words that someone has said or written. This is referred to as direct speech. If we are expressing someone's ideas without using quotation marks or the exact words, this is called indirect speech or reported speech.

"Men are confused and searching for their identity," says Mathilda Canter, a psychologist in Phoenix.

This is an example of _____.
　　　　　　　　　　　　(direct speech/indirect speech)

a. Mathilda Canter, a psychologist in Phoenix, says that men are confused and searching for their identity.

b. Mathilda Canter, a psychologist in Phoenix, said that men were confused and searching for their identity.

Underline any words that are different in these two sentences. These

are examples of _____.
　　　　　　　　　　(direct speech/indirect speech)

"By and large, women are more sure of where they are and where they are going," says New York psychologist Herbert Freudenberger.

This is an example of _____.
　　　　　　　　　　　(direct speech/indirect speech)

a. New York psychologist Herbert Freudenberger _____ that women are usually more sure of where they are and where they are going.

b. New York psychologist Herbert Freudenberger said _____

women were usually more sure of where they were and where

they _____ going.

Underline any words that are different in these two sentences. These

are examples of _____.
　　　　　　　　　　(direct speech/indirect speech)

"Many of them married with one set of rules and now feel that the rules
have changed," says Graham Spanier, a sociologist at the State University of
New York at Stony Brook.

This is an example of _____.
　　　　　　　　　　　　　(direct speech/indirect speech)

a. Graham Spanier, a sociologist at the State University of New York

　at Stony Brook _____ _____ many men married with one set

　of rules and now feel that the rules have changed.

b. Graham Spanier, a sociologist at the State University of New York

　at Stony Brook _____ _____ many men had married with one

　set of rules and then felt that the rules had changed.

Underline any words that are different in these two sentences. These

are examples of _____.
　　　　　　　　　　(direct speech/indirect speech)

"They recognize that men are involved in the home in ways that were
unheard of 10 years ago," says Alice Goldberg, director of research services
for Benton & Bowles, a New York advertising agency.

This is an example of _____.
　　　　　　　　　　　　　(direct speech/indirect speech)

a. Alice Goldberg, director of research services for Benton & Bowles,

　a New York advertising agency _____ _____ advertisers rec-

　ognize that men are involved in the home in ways that were un-

　heard of 10 years ago.

b. Alice Goldberg, director of research services for Benton & Bowles,

　a New York advertising agency _____ _____ advertisers recognized that men _____ involved in the home in ways that had been unheard of 10 years before.

Underline any words that are different in these two sentences. These are examples of _____.
<u>(direct speech/indirect speech)</u>

**EXERCISE**

We usually use *says that* if the fact or event reported is still true or is still going on. We usually use *said that* and a verb in the past tense if the fact is no longer true or the event is over. However, the change of verbs is often optional. Change the following sentences from direct speech (using quotation marks) to indirect speech (no quotation marks).

1. Samuel Osherson, a Harvard University psychologist, says, "He tried to satisfy both without great success."

2. Dan Logan, who heads a Washington, D.C., organization called Free Men, says, "The motto of the movement is be yourself."

3. University of Vermont psychologist Phyllis Bronstein says, "We're at the awkward stage right now."

# Paragraph Skills

## Special-Feature Paragraph

**transitions and tenses**

The following paragraph is the introduction to a *Newsweek* article entitled "Playing Both Mother and Father." For easy reference, the sentences have been numbered. Underline all the transitions used in the paragraph. In the spaces provided after the excerpt, list the transition words in each sentence and the tense in which each sentence is written. Then answer the questions. The first one has been done for you.

¹<u>In recent years</u> a virtual separate republic of single-parent households has formed in the country's midst. ²Following the domestic upheavals of the 1970s, when nearly one of every two mar-

riages broke apart, the divorce rate appears to be leveling off in the 1980s—kindling hopes of some renewed stability in the stormy latitudes of the family. [3] But the marital devastation has already been great; its impact on the country's social fabric has only just begun to be measured. [4] According to the Census Bureau statistics of 1984, single parents headed 25.7 percent of the families with children under 18 in the United States. [5] Experts predict that one of every three families, possibly even one out of two, will be headed by a single parent in 1990. [6] They estimate that a quarter of the now married mothers and fathers with children will be single parents sometime in this decade. [7] And approximately half the children born in the 1980s will spend part of their childhood living with one parent.

*Sentence 1*
Transition words <u>in recent years</u>
Verb <u>has formed</u>
Tense <u>present perfect tense</u>
Why did the author use the present perfect tense? <u>This tense shows indefinite past, probably extending to the present and maybe the future.</u>

*Sentence 2*
Transition words <u>Following the domestic upheavals of the 1970s</u>

Verb _____

Tense _____
Transition word/s <u>in the 1980s</u>
Verb <u>appears</u>

Tense _____
Why did the author begin with the past tense, and then use the present tense in the second part of the sentence? (Look at the transition

words.) _____
*Sentence 3*

Transition word/s _____
Verb 1 <u>has been</u>

Verb 2 _____

Tense _____

Why did the author use this tense in this sentence? (Look at sentence

1.) _____

*Sentence 4*

Transition word/s _____

Verb _____

Tense _____

Why did the author use this tense in this sentence? What year is the

sentence telling us about? _____ What year is it now? _____

*Sentence 5*

Verb 1 _____

(*Predict* is a special word that has a future meaning and is used in
the present tense to refer to future possibilities.)

Verb 2 _____

Tense _____

Transition word/s    in _____

Why did the author use *predict* and the future tense? What period of
time is the author telling us about?

_____

*Sentence 6*

Verb 1 _____

(Like *predict, estimate* used in the present tense informs the reader
about future possibilities.)

Verb 2 _____

Transition word/s in this _____

Which decade is the writer making predictions about? _____

Explain why the writer used *estimate* and the future tense in this sentence.

_____

*Sentence 7*

Transition word/s _____

Verb _____

Tense _____

What time period is the author writing about? _____

Why did the author use this tense? _____

We have analyzed the structure of this paragraph so that you as writers can understand how and why writers change tense within a paragraph. What are some of the reasons?

_____

_____

As readers, we are also interested in the content of the paragraph.

1. What is the main idea of this paragraph?
2. How did the writer develop the paragraph?
3. Would you be interested in reading more about this subject? In other words, did the introduction engage you?
4. Prediction is an important part of writing. It helps us to move through the text with understanding. What did you think would come next?
5. Were you able to understand the main idea of the paragraph even if you did not know every vocabulary word? Did you use context clues to help you with unfamiliar words, instead of interrupting your reading to look up each unfamiliar word in the dictionary?
6. Compare this introduction with the introduction to "The American Male." Which introduction do you prefer? Why?

The technique that we used with this paragraph is one that you can use with other reading material—newspapers, news magazines, textbooks, and so on. It can help you to understand how a piece was written and how the author made certain decisions. Moreover, it can help you with your own writing and your reading.

## Editing Skills Paragraph

The following paragraph is an unedited first draft. By this time, you should have enough experience to be able to edit material like this without being told what the errors are. Rewrite the paragraph, correcting the surface errors. If you have any difficulties, discuss them with a classmate. To check your answers, turn to page 348.

The article on "The American Male" made me think about what it means to be a men. I grown up thinking that been a man meant that you had to be tough, people told me it was wrong to cry and I believe them. I remember went I was very young and my favorite aunt died. I really wanted to cry then. But I didn't. I held back the tears and everyone said I was a real man. It made me feel good. Then anyway. Now I am starting to wonder if been a real man means being able to let yourself go and feel that's what I wonder now. Believe it or not. I cried the other day in front of my girlfriend and then we both cried together. It made us get even closer. Overall, been a real man seems to me to be about being able to be yourselves. Getting in touch with the real you behind all the things we used to use to impress the world.

# Essay Skills

## Persuasion

When we write, we have many different purposes. We may be trying to teach someone how to do something. We may be telling a story. We may be describing something to someone who has never seen it. We may be writing for our own enjoyment so that we can understand ourselves better. Another very common reason why we write is to convince other people of our opinion on a particular subject. We argue in our writing; we try to persuade the reader at least to rethink a subject.

The techniques for writing a persuasive or argumentation essay are part of the earliest tradition of writing. First, the problem should be clearly stated. Along with this statement there should be a proposed solution to the problem. This part of the essay is usually contained in the introduction.

Next, the writer gives the details, the evidence to support the argument. The details should be clear to your reader. You should provide as much explanation as possible so that your reader will be able to follow your thinking process.

The presentation of the evidence is one of the most important parts of a persuasive essay. There are two basic methods: deduction and induction. We will first examine deductive reasoning. In this method, the writer presents an idea or general statement and then backs it up with evidence. Although generally we examine an entire essay to see how it is developed, the examples that follow refer to the deductive method as it is used in paragraph development.

Little more than a generation ago, life was far simpler for the American male. More often than not, he was family patriarch and breadwinner. His wife catered to his needs and raised his children. His word around the home was law.

The following example, from Chapter 2, also begins with a generalization that is then supported with details or evidence.

Over a billion people in the world speak more than one language fluently. In the Philippines, for example, many people must speak three languages if they are to engage fully in their community's social affairs. They must speak the national language, Pilipino; one of the eighty-seven local vernaculars; and English or Spanish. In small countries, such as the Netherlands or Israel, most children are required to study at least one foreign language in school, and sometimes several. Most adults in the Netherlands speak German, French and English in addition to Dutch. Even in the United States, whose inhabitants are notoriously unconcerned about languages other than English, about 10% of the residents usually speak at least one language in addition to English in the course of their daily lives (National Center for Education Statistics, 1978). Throughout much of the world, being able to speak at least two languages, and sometimes three or four, is necessary to function in society.

In the preceding examples of deductive reasoning, draw a circle around the generalization and underline each of the supporting details. Then fill in the blanks in the following sentence. In deductive reasoning, the writer begins with a _____ and then _____ this with _____.

In inductive reasoning, on the other hand, the writer begins in much the same way that a mystery writer does. The writer gives the reader evidence, which then leads to a conclusion.

She stays up half the night copying over the notes she took in class, hoping the repetition alone will help her absorb the English. She keeps long lists of vocabulary words and has not missed a day of school since she began. She gets all her assignments done early—including the report on "Death of a Salesman," but after reading the play at least four times, she is still not sure who the salesman is.

And Khan Duong, who is 20 years old, is failing at Newtown High School.

The author begins with the evidence and leads the reader to the conclusion that this student is failing and that this student, like many others, needs some special help with English.

Adolescent girls were given many housekeeping duties. Because they had not even a slight hope of education beyond high school (who could afford it?) and because jobs were so scarce, they concentrated on a domestic future. Middle-class girls whose families had suffered severe losses tended to marry early. In the roaring 20s, the feminist movement had flowered. The great prosperity and liberal social norms of that decade had encouraged young women to think of their future in terms of education and career. The Depression greatly constricted these possibilities. Young women were forced by social circumstances to adopt a more traditional female identity as homemaker and mother.

In this selection from Chapter 5, the authors have begun with the evidence and ended with the thesis statement. Underline the evidence and draw a circle around the thesis statement.

The preceding two paragraphs are examples of inductive reasoning. In inductive reasoning, the _____ is presented first and this leads to a _____ about the subject.

Both inductive and deductive reasoning are used in the writing of persuasive essays. However, deductive reasoning is used more commonly since it utilizes the type of development often emphasized in formal writing. The main idea or topic sentence is presented first and the supporting details are presented next. Finally, the paragraph may restate the main idea as its conclusion. Experiment with these techniques in your writing. This adds to your ability as a writer.

**EXERCISES**

1. Read the following paragraph. Is it based on inductive or deductive reasoning? Underline the supporting evidence. Circle the thesis statement. Then rewrite this paragraph using the other type of reasoning discussed above. Which version do you prefer?

According to the Census Bureau statistics of 1984, single parents headed 25.7 percent of the families with children under 18 in the United States. In addition, it has been predicted that one of every three families will be headed by a single parent by 1990. A quarter of now married mothers and fathers will be single parents sometime in this decade. It is believed that about half of the children born in the 1980s will spend some part of their childhood living with just one parent. The American family is in trouble and if it is to be saved, some steps must be taken immediately.

2. Look through the readings in the book and classify them as inductive or deductive.

3. Read a newspaper or news magazine and select paragraphs or articles that you can classify as inductive or deductive. Share them with your classmates.

4. Reread some of the persuasive essays you have written and classify them as inductive or deductive.

## Suggested Writing Topics

1. "The American Male" attempts to define the new man. Define what you think a man should be. Give examples and evidence to support your point of view.

2. "The 'new male' is purely an American phenomenon. In other parts of the world, men know what they are and women know what they are." Do you agree or disagree? Support your point of view with your experiences and observations.

3. "As men become less work oriented and more family oriented, there will be fewer divorces and there will be better family relationships." Analyze this statement on the basis of the article you have read and on your experiences and observations.

4. Compare men in your native country with American men. Or if you prefer, compare women in your country with American women.

    The following questions are based on "Playing Both Mother and Father" (pages 288–289).

5. Many people believe that the life of a child living in a single-parent household is not as secure and not as psychologically healthy as that of a child living in a two-parent household. Do you agree

or disagree? Support your opinions on the basis of your observations or readings. (You can use facts from the original article.)

6. Imagine that you are a single parent. What is a typical day in your life? How do you make sure that your child has a fulfilling and productive life? What do you do to make sure that you have a fulfilling and productive life as well?

7. Imagine that you are involved in a divorce case. Convince the judge that you should be the one to get custody of your child. Cite the reasons why you would be a better parent and explain to the judge the kind of life you can offer your child. Keep in mind education, social life, religious life, family values, and so on.

## Revising I

When you have finished writing your essay for this chapter, reread "The American Male" and pay close attention to the types of evidence the authors have used. Then, when you have had at least a ten-minute separation from your writing, return to it. Treat your work as though you were viewing an uncut movie. You are the editor and you want to delete any unnecessary, repetitive parts. Yet you also want to add details that will make the movie, or in your case the writing, clearer. You want the audience to know what you believe. Don't be afraid to cut, and don't be afraid to add. When you have completed this process, you may want to share your essay with a classmate. As you read each other's essays, think about what can be deleted and what can be added to make the essay even more effective.

## Revising II

**patchwork-quilt revising with a classmate**

In Chapter 5, you practiced the patchwork quilt method of revising an essay. In this exercise, you will do the same thing with a classmate's essay. Follow the same directions as on page 113. This time give your sentences to a classmate and take that classmate's sentences. Arrange the sentences until the essay is clear. If you have any problems, discuss them with the writer of the essay. When you have finished, tape the newly arranged essay together and return it to the writer. You will receive your own taped essay. Reread it and discuss the new arrangement with the student who worked on your essay.

# CHAPTER FOURTEEN

# Biological Differences

*In "Biological Differences," excerpted from* To Be Human: An Introduction to Anthropology, *Alexander Alland, Jr., presents some surprising and disturbing facts about the biological origin of some of our notions about the differences between males and females.*

**M**en on the average are larger and physically stronger than women. The latter fact has to be clarified immediately, however, by noting that this strength only applies to short-term physical activity. Over the long haul women have better physical endurance than men. Women live longer than men, they have lower frequencies of heart attack, and less hypertension. This female superiority may be related to such biological factors as natural stress resistance in women and such cultural factors as the particularly high stress that men face in the business world.

Women on the average have a better sense of smell than men. There is some evidence that they hear better, at least at the upper range of the scale. Women are more resistant to cold than men. Sexually based differences in the nervous system may also exist. The central nervous system of all mammals works in combination with the endocrine hormonal system. Nerves work fast, but their action extinguishes° rapidly. The endocrine system is slower acting but is more sustained. Together, these two ways of mobilizing behavior form a single integrated unit known as the neuroendocrine system. The endocrine system itself is one of the chemical bases of sexual differentiation. Although the hormones found in men and women do not differ completely (both sexes carry both male and female sex hormones), the ratios of these hormones do differ in normal men and women. Since endocrines affect many aspects of normal physiology, differences in hormonal balance have some effect on behavior.

Because hormones, like genes, act only in combination with the environment, we can expect evolutionary pressures to favor different behavioral phenotypes in both sexes under different environmental circumstances. Culture is a major part of our environment.

°is put to an end

**297**

It must, therefore, have a strong influence on behavioral differences. Research on sexual differences runs into the same difficulties 30
as any research that attempts to separate out genetic and environmental effects. The only thing we can say at present about behavioral differences based on sex is the following: The average female
at birth is potentially different from the average male at birth. Although we do not know what these average potential differences might 35
°change     be, we do know that they will be subject to modification° by culture.
Potential sexual differences in behavior, although real, may be
overridden by cultural factors.

From a purely biological perspective men are more expendable
than women. We do not have to be reminded that it is females and 40
not males who bear children, but what is not so obvious is that a few
males can sexually service many females. In so many instances among
°dull     other species selection has produced gaudy males and rather bland°
females—particularly bird species. Birds have color vision and rely
°showy, flashy     on visual cues for mating. The gaudy° male is the sexual target of 45
the female, but because he is highly visible, he is also the target of
°creatures that feed upon     predators.° The female is camouflaged° or at least unobtrusive.° Her
other animals
°disguised, concealed     survival chances are higher, therefore, than those of the male. This
°does not stand out or     makes sense, of course, since it is she who must ultimately produce
force self on others     the next generation.     50

Paradoxically, sexism may derive in part from the value biological
evolution and culture places on females. When this value is translated culturally, men may convert women into objects. The first step
in this process may have occurred with the emergence of hunting as
a male task. This aspect of the division of labor protects women from 55
unnecessary danger. The incest taboo (prohibitions on marriage with
certain relatives) universal in all societies, stimulates the exchange of
women in marriage. The process of exchange increases the proba-
°people used to advance     bility that women will become valuable objects, the pawns° of matri-
another's purposes
    monial exchange. If women are seen as valuable objects they are 60
°deprived of human quali-     treasured and protected, but may also be dehumanized.° When women
ties
    become objects, sexism is born. As in the case of race, sex becomes
the basis of social discrimination. Obvious external biological characteristics are taken as evidence for unproven behavioral differences. The only way we shall ever come to know which behavioral 65
differences, if any, are characteristic of specific groups is when our
society develops full social equality. For only then will the environment allow individuals to express their full genetic potential.

# Vocabulary Development

### words relating to biology and medicine

As we have discovered in previous chapters, each discipline has its own particular jargon or terminology. In "Biological Differences," we find many words that relate to biology and medicine.

### Paragraph 1

*hypertension:* high blood pressure

### Paragraph 2

*endocrine:* the internal secretion of a gland

*endocrine gland:* one of several glands such as the thyroid, the pituitary, or the suprarenal glands whose secretions are released directly into the blood or lymph

*hormone:* the secretions of the thyroid, the pituitary, and suprarenal glands, which are carried to other parts of the body by the blood or other body fluids

*neuroendocrine system:* the nerves and the endocrine system working together

*physiology:* the science that deals with the processes and mechanisms by which animals and plants function

### Paragraph 3

*gene:* the fundamental unit of heredity, which is a segment of DNA molecules that carry instructions for the production of single proteins

*genetic:* of or produced by genes

*environmental:* all of the external circumstances, conditions, and things that affect the existence and development of an individual, organism, or group

*phenotype:* the characteristics of an organism, resulting from the interaction of its genetic makeup with the environment in which it develops

The debate over the interaction of genetic makeup and environmental factors is sometimes referred to as nature versus (vs.) nurture. Are we what we were born to be based on our genetic makeup, or does our upbringing, our environment, determine the person we become? Many scientists believe it is not one or the other but a combination of the two that produces the person that each of us becomes.

These words from the selection are difficult, but they are words that you will undoubtedly meet again throughout your educational experience. To help make their meaning clearer and more useful to you, underline these words wherever they appear in "Biological Differences."

# Reading and Thinking Skills

## Comprehension Questions

1. Alland compares men and women. According to the article, in what ways is man superior to woman?

2. In what ways is woman superior to man?

3. Alland makes a comparison between birds and human beings. What is the major difference that species selection has produced in the bird world?

## Discussion Activities

### Analysis and Conclusions

1. If you accept Alland's belief that species have changed through evolution, can you think of any reason why a woman's hearing, especially at the upper range of the scale, the higher pitches of sound, might be better than a man's? Why would a woman need this ability?

2. Why does Alland believe that men are more expendable than women?

3. What is sexism? How does Alland suggest that it can develop from the value biological evolution and culture places on women?

4. Why did men develop to be physically stronger than women? What purpose does men's strength serve in society as we know it?

### Writing and Point of View

1. The Alland excerpt is difficult to read. What creates this difficulty—the vocabulary, the ideas, or both? Explain.

2. In sentence 2, what is "the latter fact"?

3. In line 17, to what does "these two ways" refer?

4. Who is "we" in paragraphs 3, 4, and 5?

### Personal Response and Evaluation

1. In almost all societies, women live longer than men. Why do you think this is so?

2. More women are working at stressful jobs in the business world than ever before. Do you think this will affect their health? Will more women begin to have hypertension and heart attacks, or do you think women have a natural immunity?

3. Are boy babies treated differently than girl babies? Describe some differences in treatment that you have observed. Keep in mind the colors that babies are dressed in, the toys they are given, how much they are held, and how they are played with.

4. Do you think babies of different sexes should be brought up differently? Explain your point of view with your observations and experiences.

## Debate

While working on this chapter, it might be interesting to have several class debates. Divide the class into men and women, or use any other division that seems to work. Each group is given a point of view on a topic. Together the group members create an argument based on facts and observations. Then the actual debate can begin. It might be useful to audiotape or videotape the debate for later class discussions.

The following are some points of view that might be considered for debate:

| *Team A* | *Team B* |
| --- | --- |
| Women are the weaker sex. | Men are really the weaker sex. |
| Children should be brought up as equals; there should be no differences in treatment. | Boys and girls should be brought up differently. This is necessary for their future roles in life. |
| Women are not psychologically equipped to hold positions of power. | Women can deal with positions of power as well as men can. |
| There can never be true equality between men and women. | Men and women must develop true equality for there to be peace in the world. |

## Note Taking

For practice in taking notes from a lecture class, your teacher will read several paragraphs from "Biological Differences" aloud to the class. Take notes as if you were planning to study from them. Then meet in a small group and compare your notes. Discuss how you decided what to write down. What do you think are the most important ideas? Justify your choices.

## Journal Writing

Experience comes to man "as I" but it is by experience "as we" that he builds the common world in which he lives.

MARTIN BUBER, philosopher

This semester we have translated our "I" experience to a "we" shared experience through our classroom discussions, our writing, and our journals. Since this is the penultimate (next to the last) chapter in the book, this may be a good place to reflect on the journal itself. What have you learned about yourself by writing in your journal? What have you learned about your teacher and about the society around you? Have you begun to look at anything differently from the way you did when you started this semester? In what ways do you feel your writing has improved? Do you feel differently toward writing than you did? Will you continue to write in a journal once the term has ended? Would you recommend that a friend keep a journal? Write in your journal about the journal itself.

# Word Skills

## Idiomatic Expressions

Each of the following paragraphs contains a context clue that will help you understand one of the idiomatic expressions used in "Biological Differences." Underline these context clues; the first one has been done for you. Then use the expressions when you answer the questions at the end of each paragraph.

**on the average** (page 297, line 1)

"Biological Differences" claims that, on the average, men are larger and physically stronger than women. When something is reported on the average, the reader knows that no matter what is being measured there are some that rise above the average and some that fall below. Reporting something on the average tells about the middle range. On the average, how many hours do you study every night? On the average, how many times a week does it rain?

**over the long haul** (page 297, line 4)

Alland tells us that over the long haul women have better physical endurance than men. This means that women can continue doing something strenuous over a long period of time. Men may have more physical strength when they start something, but they will probably get tired before women. We can judge things in the short term, or for a short time, or we can look at them over the long haul, or over a long period of time. Over the long haul, what is more important, physical or mental stamina? Why?

*in combination with* (page 297, line 25)

Hormones act in combination with the environment. When something acts in combination with something else, there is a relationship between them. The two interact in some way. Reading in combination with writing is a good way to improve your English. Pizza in combination with soda is a popular lunch. A good way to lose weight is dieting in combination with what?

*rely on* (page 298, lines 44–45)

When you rely on someone, you know you can depend on that person. Both *rely* and *depend* are followed by the preposition *on*. When you think about relying or depending on someone, think of the act of leaning on something and that will help you to remember which preposition follows these words. How do you let someone know that you need to rely on him or her?

## Comparatives

Since this chapter discusses differences between the sexes, we would expect to find many words of comparison. Several sentences from the selection have been reproduced below with the comparatives omitted. Fill in the blanks with the words needed to make the sentences comparative. Refer to the article to check your answers.

1. Men on the average are _____ and physically
(large)

_____ women.
(strong)

2. Women on the average have a _____ sense of smell
(good)

_____ men.

3. Women are _____ to cold _____ men.
(resistant)

4. From a purely biological perspective men are _____
(expendable)
women.

5. Her survival chances are _____, therefore, _____ those
(high)
of the male.

LEFT
CEREBRAL
HEMISPHERE

Cerebral
Cortex

Corpus
Callosum

RIGHT
CEREBRAL
HEMISPHERE

Limbic
System

Thalamus

Cerebellum

Brainstem

The diagram above shows the brain, its right and left hemi-
spheres. Recent research has shown that the brains of men and women
are different. Read the following paragraphs excerpted from *The
Amazing Brain* by Robert Ornstein and Richard F. Thompson.
Underline all the comparative structures.

There do exist profound differences in men's and women's brains, differences that are present, often, before birth. There have been in recent years many bits of evidence that document differences in behavior and aptitude: girls are more verbally fluent than boys, have better fine motor control, and are less aggressive. Boys have better control of the large muscles, are more sensitive to movement, and are more aggressive. What is new is that these behavioral differences have physical expression in the brain. . . .

Only recently has an important bit of evidence on the male and female brains been discovered. While examining the corpus callosums of several brains, Christine De Lacoste and her colleagues, in work beginning at Berkeley, found that they could begin to identify individual brains by sight. . . . The women's corpus callosums are larger than the men's, and they are larger toward the back of the brain. This is the area of the brain involved in the transmission of information about movements in space and about visual space. . . . This difference appears as early as twenty-six weeks in utero; that is, it is an unborn difference in the major system of brain communication.

Whether we find more differences is another question, but now that we know that the brain becomes physically different with different kinds of experiences, different conditions in the air, different learning situations, different foods eaten, different handedness and different sexes, at least some of the pieces of the puzzle of why humans are so different from one another may be found. There are probably more differences in human brains than in any other animal partly because the human brain does most of its developing in the outside world.

These paragraphs contain some very interesting information. Answer the following questions on the basis of what you have just read.

1. What are some of the differences in the brains of men and women?
2. Are there any differences in our brains before we are born?
3. In addition to sexual differences, what other factors can cause differences in the brain? After we are born, do our brains change?
4. Why are human brains so different from one another?

Write a summary of the paragraphs you have just read. If you have any difficulty writing a summary, review page 245.

## Modals

**may/must**

Reread "Biological Differences," circling *may* and *must* each time they occur and the verb that follows each time.

What does *may* in a sentence usually mean?

What does *must* in a sentence usually mean?

Use *may* and *must* in sentences of your own answering the following questions: Why may there be differences between males and females? What must a woman be able to do for the species to survive? What must a man be able to do?

## Commonly Confused Words

**here/hear**

Read the following paragraph, noticing the use of *here* and *hear*. Then complete the definitions below.

Women can *hear* better, particularly at the upper range of the scale. The research that has been done *here* indicates many interesting possibilities. Perhaps further research will be done on hearing, and other results may be found.

_____ means "to perceive with the ear."

_____ means "at this place" or "in this case."

**when/went**

Read the following paragraph, noticing the use of *when* and *went*. Then complete the definitions below.

*When* the researchers investigated the material in the article, they *went* all over the world to make sure that their results were not culture-bound, that their results were true in different parts of the world. *When* a researcher reads of an experiment in one part of the world, he or she duplicates it to discover if the results are the same all over. On the basis of these discoveries, general statements are made.

_____ is the past tense of *go*.

_____ means "at that time."

Now use these words in your own sentences.

# Sentence Skills

## Past and Present Tenses

1. You are a scientist in the year 2400 who has recently discovered evidence about the species that once lived on earth—men and women. Rewrite paragraphs 1 and 2 of "Biological Differences" in the past tense. (In paragraph 2, "may also exist" changes to "may have also existed.") The first sentence of the rewritten article should read: "Men on the average were larger and physically stronger than women."

2. It is the year 2400, and human beings no longer exist. Your species descended from humans but is different in many ways. Instead of men and women, you have two sexes, glemb and glemen. Describe these creatures and the similarities and differences between them. You may want to refer to "Biological Differences" for some ideas.

## Sentence Combining

In this exercise, we will combine shorter sentences into longer ones, using some of the techniques we have already discussed.

Nerves work fast.
Nerve action extinguishes rapidly.

These sentences can be combined in any of the following ways. Each way is correct; for practice, you may want to try several different ways.

You can create a compound sentence:

Nerves work fast, and their action extinguishes rapidly.
Nerves work fast, but their action extinguishes rapidly.
Nerves work fast; nerve action extinguishes rapidly.

You can create a complex sentence:

Because nerves work fast, their action extinguishes rapidly.
Nerves work fast, while their action extinguishes rapidly.
If nerves work fast, their action extinguishes rapidly.

Does the meaning change in any of these sentences?
You can create a complex compound sentence.

Although nerves work fast, their action extinguishes even more rapidly, and this can create problems.

You can use the relative pronouns *which, who,* or *that.*

The action of nerves, which work fast, extinguishes rapidly.

Use these techniques to combine the following sentences. Experiment with different techniques. You should have more than one answer for each.

1a. The endocrine system is slower.
 b. The endocrine system is more sustained.

_____

_____

2a. There are potential sexual differences.
 b. The differences are between males and females.
 c. The differences can be overridden by cultural factors.

_____

_____

3a. Men are more expendable than women.
 b. Women bear children.

_____

_____

4a. Women are seen as valuable objects.
 b. Women are treasured and protected.
 c. Women may be dehumanized.

_____

_____

5a. Birds have color vision.
 b. Birds rely on visual cues for mating.

_____

_____

6a. The gaudy male is the sexual target for female birds.
 b. The male is highly visible.
 c. The male is the target of predators.

_____

_____

Another way of combining some of these sentences is to begin the sentence with the present participle (-*ing* form). In this case, the subject must be exactly the same for both parts of the sentence.

Being seen as valuable objects, women may be treasured and protected, but they also may be dehumanized.
Having color vision, birds rely on visual cues for mating.

Try this technique in the following sentences.

7a. Women live longer than men.
 b. Women have lower frequencies of heart attack.

_____

8a. Girls learn to talk earlier than boys.
 b. Girls are more social.

_____

9a. Boys have better control of the large muscles.
 b. Boys are more sensitive to movement.

_____

10a. The difference appears as early as twenty-six weeks in utero.
 b. The difference is unborn.

_____

## Articles

In the following paragraph, all the articles have been removed. Fill in each blank with the appropriate article (*a, an,* or *the*); if no article is needed, leave the space blank. Refer to the article to check your answers.

Women on _____ average have _____ better sense of smell than _____ men. There is some evidence that they hear better, at least at _____ upper range of _____ scale. _____ women are more resistant to cold than _____ men. _____ sexually based differences in _____ nervous system may also exist. _____ central nervous system of all _____ mammals works in combination with _____ endocrine hormonal system. _____ nerves work fast, but their action extinguishes rapidly. _____ endocrine system is slower acting but is more sustained. Together, these two ways of mobilizing _____ behavior form _____ single integrated unit known as _____ neuroendocrine system. _____ endocrine system itself is one of _____ chemical bases of _____ sexual differentiation. Although _____ hormones found in men and women do not differ completely (both sexes carry both male and female sex hormones), _____ ratios of these hormones do differ in _____ normal men and women. Since endocrines affect many aspects of normal physiology, differences in _____ hormonal balance have some effect on behavior.

## Pronoun Review

In the following sentences, fill in each blank with an appropriate pronoun.

1. Women have a better sense of smell than men. _____ hearing is better too, at least at the upper range of the scale.

2. The nervous system works in combination with the endocrine

hormonal system. However, _____ is faster acting than the endocrine hormonal system.

3. Differences exist in the hormone systems of men and women. It is believed that _____ must have some effect on behavior.

4. The female's survival chances are higher, therefore, than those of the male. This is because _____ must ultimately produce the next generation.

5. Research on sexual differences will continue to have problems as _____ has as _____ goal the separation of genetic and environmental effects.

---

# Paragraph Skills

## Special-Feature Paragraph

**adverbial conjunctions**
In the following paragraph, connecting words such as *however, moreover, otherwise,* and *therefore* have been left out. Rewrite the paragraph, adding these words. There are many possible ways to correct this paragraph. Share your rewritten paragraph with a classmate or with your teacher.

In this chapter, we looked at some of the ways that researchers compare men and women. Alland discussed some of the ways women are superior to men. He discussed men's superiority. Men are physically stronger than women. Women have more endurance than men. Women have fewer heart attacks and hypertension. They tend to live longer than men. Alland suggests this may be related to the stress men deal with in the business world. More women are working in stressful situations. Women may begin to develop these diseases. Women in these situations have to be studied. No one will know for sure if changes will occur. Research asks questions. Research answers questions. There will always be more research needed in this field.

We can connect these sentences with transition words such as those studied in past chapters, or we can use adverbial conjunctions. When we use these adverbial conjunctions to connect two complete sentences, we must use a semicolon.

Male birds have a very gaudy appearance; on the other hand, female birds look dull so they are not easy targets for predators.

A list of these adverbial conjunctions or joining words follows:

| | |
|---|---|
| in addition to | means "combined or associated with" |
| also | means "in addition to" |
| furthermore | means "in addition to" |
| moreover | means "in addition to" |
| as a result | means that one thing causes another |
| consequently | means "as a result" |
| therefore | means "as a result" |
| thus | means "as a result" |
| however | means "but" |
| nevertheless | means "but" |
| on the contrary | means "but" |
| on the other hand | means "but" |
| indeed | means "in fact" |
| instead | means "as a substitute or alternative" |
| meanwhile | means "at the same time" |
| otherwise | means "under other conditions" |

Let's look at some of the ways the sentences in the paragraph above could have been connected.

Alland discussed some of the ways women are superior to men. He discussed men's superiority.

We can use any of the words meaning *in addition to* to connect these sentences.

Alland discussed some of the ways women are superior to men; furthermore, he discussed men's superiority.

or

Alland discussed some of the ways women are superior to men. He also discussed men's superiority to women.

Men are physically stronger than women.
Women have more endurance than men.

We can connect these sentences using any of the words that show contrast or mean almost the same thing as *but*.

Men are physically stronger than women; on the other hand, women have more endurance than men.

or

Men are physically stronger than women; nevertheless, women have more endurance than men.

Women have fewer heart attacks and hypertension.
They tend to live longer than men.

   We can use any of the words that mean *as a result* to connect these sentences.

Women have fewer heart attacks and hypertension; consequently, they tend to live longer than men.

or

Women have fewer heart attacks and hypertension; thus, they tend to live longer than men.

Alland suggests this may be related to the stress men deal with in the business world.
More women are working in stressful situations.

   We can use the *meanwhile* connection.

Alland suggests this may be related to the stress men deal with in the business world; meanwhile, more women are working in stressful situations.

   The second sentence in the preceding example could also be connected to the sentence that follows it.

More women are working in stressful situations.
Women may begin to develop these diseases.

   We can use connecting words that mean *as a result*.

More women are working in stressful situations; therefore, women may begin to develop these diseases.

Women in these situations will have to be studied.
No one will know for sure if changes will occur.

   We can use the *otherwise* connection.

Women in these situations will have to be studied; otherwise, no one will know for sure if changes will occur.

Research asks questions.
Research answers questions.

   We can use an *in addition to* connection.

Research asks questions; moreover, research answers questions.

   We can use an *as a result* connection to end the paragraph.

Consequently, there will always be more research needed in this field.
Therefore, there will always be more research needed in this field.

Rewrite the paragraph on page 311 using some of these adverbial conjunctions. Keep the use of the semicolon in mind as you write; remember, too, that sentences can begin with connecting words. Sentence variety is important. Your paragraph should include both long and short sentences.

## Editing Skills Paragraph

As we have seen in each of the last chapters, the following first draft needs editing for surface errors. Rewrite the paragraph and correct all the errors. The answers are on page 348.

Reading about the biological differences between men and women. People can really learn a lot that will help them in there everyday life. The nature vs. nurture argument is a interesting one. No one know for sure if people are born with certain genetic characteristics. That determines there lives. They may be influenced by they're environment as much as by they're genetics. According of research, the brain changes. It can changed because of many things. Such as diet, the air, handedness, etc. It makes sense that you should take good care of yourselves by eating right, exercising and to try to live healthy lives. Despite everything people may try, however, they're will always be difference between the sex.

# Essay Skills

## Comparison/Contrast

In "Biological Differences," Alland compared and contrasted males and females. When a writer compares two things, the writer looks for the similarities. When a writer contrasts two things, the writer looks for the differences. We compare and contrast things every day. We may compare how fast the bus came this morning with how fast it came yesterday. We may contrast the experience of walking to school with the experience of taking the bus. It is a human activity to compare and contrast. We do it in our minds, and we do it aloud with our friends. For many writers, however, the comparison/contrast essay can create problems.

There are two basic patterns of organization that comparison/contrast essays may follow. The two may contain the same information, but it is presented in a different manner. In the first method, the writer follows this basic pattern:

Introduction
Body Paragraph(s) A—presents all the information about A
Body Paragraph(s) B—presents all the information about B
Conclusion         —sums up and makes final comparisons and/or contrasts

The second method involves alternating within each paragraph. It is organized as follows:

Introduction
Body Paragraph    —about one aspect of the comparison
                  Point A
                  Point B
                  Point A
                  Point B
Body Paragraph    —about another aspect of the comparison
                  Point A
                  Point B
                  Point A
                  Point B

Conclusion

Many writers find the first method, the block approach, easier to organize. In this method, all the information about one side of an issue or problem is presented, and then all the information about the other side is given. Using this method, it is also possible to present all the similarities and then all the differences. In the second method, the alternating method, a point from one side is given, then a point from the other side. This is a good method to use for longer pieces of writing because it is easy to follow. For this reason, a reader may prefer this method.

The following paragraph is from an essay that uses the block form; it presents the information about women's physical superiority. We can assume that the writer will next give us all the information about the areas of male superiority.

Women, on the average, have a better sense of smell than men. Women hear better at the upper range. Women have more physical endurance than men. They generally live longer and do not usually suffer from hypertension and heart disease.

Using the alternating method, the writer of an essay about male and female differences makes the comparison within the paragraph itself. The paragraph that follows uses the alternating method to compare the health problems of men and women.

Women, on the average, have a better sense of smell than men. Men, however, have keener eyesight. Women hear better at the upper range, whereas men often have more acute hearing at the lower range. The estimated life span for men is 74 years of age; for women it is 78 years of age.

The comparison/contrast essay is a popular form of writing. "Biological Differences" is written in the comparison/contrast mode. Does

it follow the block pattern or the alternating pattern? _____

*The Amazing Brain* (page 305) is also written in the comparison/contrast mode. Does it follow the block pattern or the alternating pattern? Experiment with both styles in your own writing.

In comparison/contrast writing, we use special transition words:

| *To compare* | *To contrast* |
|---|---|
| also | but |
| as . . . as | not as . . . as |
| as well as | however |
| likewise | nevertheless |
| similarly | on the other hand |
| too | in contrast |

**EXERCISES**

1. Write a paragraph comparing and contrasting the behavior of the dog with that of the cat.

2. Write a paragraph contrasting living in a city with living in the country.

3. Write a paragraph comparing and contrasting a book with the movie made from that book.

4. Write a paragraph comparing and contrasting the teaching methods of two teachers you have had.

## Suggested Writing Topics

1. Write an essay comparing and contrasting the way girls are raised with the way boys are raised. Use your own observations and experiences as evidence.

2. Write an essay comparing and contrasting the teaching methods in your native country with those in the United States.

3. What are some of the differences between men and women? Include information from the Alland article, as well as your own observations and experiences.

4. The characteristics that a person looks for in a friend may be very different from the ones that are important in a future husband or wife. Compare and contrast these characteristics.

5. Each language is unique, although there may be some similarities between certain languages. Compare and contrast your first language with English. Consider such characteristics as the following: the ways in which questions are constructed, where adjectives are placed, the use of articles, how nouns are made plural, whether or not the language is phonetic.

6. We have read several research studies in this book. If you were a scientific researcher, what would you research and why? Give the details of your research proposal. Imagine that your reader gives grants of money to researchers, and you are trying to convince that person that your idea is worthwhile.

## Revising

The type of writing we did in this chapter requires organization and clear thinking. Before you began writing, you probably made notes in order to make sure that you considered all the points of comparison and contrast. When you revise, look first at your notes and then at your piece of writing. Read your writing as though you were looking at it for the first time. Are there enough details and is there enough evidence to make your points? Do you like the sound of your essay? Does it seem to be adequately developed? Consider these points as you read and revise.

# CHAPTER FIFTEEN

# Foreigner

This excerpt, entitled "Foreigner," is from the novel of the same name by Nahid Rachlin, an Iranian woman who now lives and writes in the United States. It is about a woman returning home to Iran after fourteen years. She has to learn to deal with changes in herself, her family, and her country.

**A**s I boarded the plane at Logan Airport in Boston I paused on the top step and waved to Tony. He waved back. I pulled the window curtain beside me and closed my eyes, seeing Tony's face falling away, bitten by light.

In the Teheran airport I was groggy° and disoriented.° I found my valise° and set it on a table, where two customs officers searched it. Behind a large window people waited. The women, mostly hidden under dark chadors, formed a single fluid shape. I kept looking towards the window trying to spot my father, stepmother, or stepbrother, but I did not see any of them. Perhaps they were there and we could not immediately recognize each other. It had been fourteen years since I had seen them.

A young man sat on a bench beside the table, his task there not clear. He wore his shirt open and I could see bristles of dark hair on his chest. He was making shadow pictures on the floor—a rabbit, a bird—and then dissolving the shapes between his feet. Energy emanated° from his hands, a crude, confused energy. Suddenly he looked at me, staring into my eyes. I turned away.

I entered the waiting room and looked around. Most people had left. There was still no one for me. What could possibly have happened? Normally someone would be there—a definite effort would be made. I fought to shake off my groggy state.

A row of phones stood in the corner next to a handicraft° shop. I tried to call my father. There were no phone books and the information line rang busy, on and on.

I went outside and approached a collection of taxis. The drivers stood around, talking. "Can I take one of these?" I asked.

The men turned to me but no one spoke.

°dazed, half awake  °confused  °suitcase

°came from

°items made by skilled hands

"I need a taxi," I said.

"Where do you want to go?" one of the men asked. He was old 30 with stooped shoulders and a thin, unfriendly face. I gave him my father's address.

"That's all the way on the other side of the city." He did not move from his spot.

"Please . . . I have to get there somehow." 35

The driver looked at the other men as if this were a group project.

"Take her," one of them said. "I would take her myself but I have to get home." He smiled at me.

"All right, get in," the older man said, pointing to a taxi. 40

In the taxi, he turned off the meter almost immediately. "You have to pay me 100 tomans for this."

"That much?"

"It would cost you more if I left the meter on."

There was no point arguing with him. I sat stiffly and looked out. 45 We seemed to be floating in the sallow° light cast by the street lamps. Thin old sycamores° lined the sidewalks. Water flowed in the gutters. The smoky mountains surrounding the city, now barely visible, were like a dark ring. The streets were more crowded and there were many more tall western buildings than I had remembered. Cars 50 sped by, bouncing over holes, passing each other recklessly, honking. My taxi driver also drove badly and I had visions of an accident, of being maimed.°

We passed through quieter, older sections. The driver slowed down on a narrow street with a mosque at its center, then stopped in front 55 of a large, squalid° house. This was the street I had lived on for so many years; here I had played hide-and-seek in alleys and hallways. I had a fleeting sensation that I had never left this street, that my other life with Tony had never existed.

I paid the driver, picked up my valise, and got out. On the cracked 60 blue tile above the door, "Akbar Mehri," my father's name, was written.

I banged the iron knocker several times and waited. In the light of the street lamps I could see a beggar with his jaw twisted sitting against the wall of the mosque. Even though it was rather late, a 65 hum of prayers, like a moan, rose from the mosque. A Moslem priest came out, looked past the beggar and spat on the ground. The doors of the house across the street were open. I had played with two little girls, sisters, who had lived there. I could almost hear their voices, laughter. The April air was mild and velvety against my skin but I 70 shivered at the proximity° to my childhood.

A pebble suddenly hit me on the back. I turned but could not see anyone. A moment later another pebble hit my leg and another be-

---

°yellowish
°medium-sized bushy trees

°crippled

°dirty and neglected

°nearness

hind my knee. More hit the ground. I turned again and saw a small boy running and hiding in the arched hallway of a house nearby.        75

I knocked again.

There was a thud from the inside, shuffling, and then soft footsteps. The door opened and a man—my father—stood before me. His cheeks were hollower than I had recalled, the circles under his eyes deeper, and his hair more evenly gray. We stared at each other.   80

"It's you!" He was grimacing,° as though in pain.

°making a twisted facial expression

"Didn't you get my telegram?"

He nodded. "We waited for you for two hours this morning at the airport. What happened to you?"

I was not sure if he was angry or in a daze. "You must have gotten   85 the time mixed up. I meant nine in the evening."

My father stretched his hands forward, about to embrace me but, as though struck by shyness, he let them drop at his sides. "Come in now."

I followed him inside. I too was in the grip of shyness, or some-   90 thing like it.

"I thought you'd never come back," he said.

"I know, I know."

"You aren't even happy to see me."

"That's not true. I'm just . . ."                                  95

"You're shocked. Of course you are."

He went towards the rooms, arranged in a semicircle, on the other side of the courtyard. A veranda° with columns extended along several of the rooms. Crocuses, unpruned rosebushes, and pomegranate trees filled the flower beds. The place seemed cramped, un-100 tended. But still it was the same house. Roses would blossom, sparrows would chirp at the edge of the pool. At dawn and dusk the voice of the muezzin would mix with the noise of people coming from and going to the nearby bazaars.

°porch

We went up the steps onto the veranda and my father opened the105 door to one of the rooms. He stepped inside and turned on the light. I paused for a moment, afraid to cross the threshold. I could smell it: must, jasmin, rosewater, garlic, vinegar, recalling my childhood. Shut doors with confused noises behind them, slippery footsteps, black, golden-eyed cats staring from every corner, indolent°110 afternoons when people reclined on mattresses, forbidden subjects occasionally reaching me—talk about a heavy flow of menstrual blood, sex inflicted by force, the last dark words of a woman on her death bed.

°lazy

My father disappeared into another room. I heard voices whis-115 pering and then someone said loudly, "She's here?" Footsteps approached. In the semidarkness of a doorway at the far end of the room two faces appeared and then another face, like three moons, staring at me.

"Feri, what happened?" a woman's voice asked, and a figure stepped 120 forward. I recognized my stepmother, Ziba. She wore a long, plain cotton nightgown.

"The time got mixed up, I guess." My voice sounded feeble and hesitant.

A man laughed and walked into the light too. It was my step- 125 brother, Darius. He grinned at me, a smile disconnected from his eyes.

"Let's go to the kitchen," my father said. "So that Feri can eat something."

They went back through the same doorway and I followed them. 130 °one in front of another   We walked through the dim, intersecting rooms in tandem.° In one room all the walls were covered with black cloth, and a throne, also covered with a black cloth, was set in a corner—for monthly prayers when neighborhood women would come in and a Moslem priest was invited to give sermons. The women would wail and beat their chests 135 in these sessions as the priest talked about man's guilt or the sacri- fices the leaders of Islam had made. They would cry as if at their °cannot be canceled   own irrevocable° guilt and sorrow.

We were together in the kitchen. Darius, Ziba, my father—they seemed at once familiar and remote like figures in dreams.   140

---

# Vocabulary Development

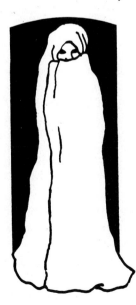

**words relating to Iran and the religion of Islam**

"Foreigner" introduces us to the special vocabulary of the country of Iran and the religion of Islam. As you read about different coun- tries and peoples, you will be exposed to such new vocabulary.

*chador:* a dress that Iranian women wear, which is draped around the body, across the shoulders, over the head, and across the lower part of the face

*tomans:* Iranian money

*mosque:* a Moslem place for the worship of God

*muezzin:* in the religion of Islam, a crier who calls the faithful to prayer

*Islam:* the religion taught by the Prophet Mohammed in the A.D. 600s (Mohammed, who was born in Mecca in A.D. 570, taught the worship of one God, Allah, and proclaimed that he, Mo- hammed, was Allah's messenger. *Islam* is an Arabic word that means "submission." Islam is the faith of approximately one- fifth of the world's population.)

*Moslems (Muslims):* those who believe in Allah and accept Mo- hammed as God's messenger (In Arabic, *Moslem* means "one who submits to God.")

**EXERCISES**
1. If there is a Moslem student in the class, that student might inform the other class members about the Islamic religion and traditions.
2. You might want to consult your library to find out more about Islam or about other religions. Write a short paper to hand in to your teacher or present to the class.

# Reading and Thinking Skills

## Comprehension Questions

1. Why doesn't anyone come to meet Feri at the airport?
2. What happens when she tries to phone her family? When she tries to take a taxi?
3. What is her first impression of the neighborhood and street in which she grew up?
4. She has been away from home for fourteen years. Has her father changed? Has her home changed?
5. When Feri enters her home, she has sensual memories—memories of sights, sounds, smells, tastes. What are some of these memories?

## Discussion Activities

### Analysis and Conclusions

1. Do you think Feri is wearing a chador, or is she dressed in Western style? Do you think this affects the way she is treated by the men at the airport and the little boy throwing the pebbles?
2. What are some of the details from the story that suggest that Feri feels like a foreigner in her own country?
3. Each story creates a mood for the reader. There is something dreamlike about this story. What words and incidents make this story seem dreamlike?
4. Her father stretches his hands forward as though to embrace her, and then he drops his hands. Why does he drop his hands? How does this make her feel?

### Writing and Point of View

1. Compare Nahid Rachlin's style of writing with Kate Chopin's. Which do you prefer and why?

2. Like Hemingway, Rachlin uses dialogue throughout the story. Do you enjoy stories in which there is dialogue? Why or why not?

3. "A Mortal Flower" is excerpted from an autobiography; "Foreigner" is excerpted from a novel. Are there differences in the styles of writing? Are there any indications that "Foreigner" is fictional? If so, what are they?

**Personal Response and Evaluation**

1. Rachlin says that the veranda seems "cramped and untended." Sometimes when we return to a place that we knew as children, it seems cramped and smaller than we remember it to be. Have you ever had that experience? Why do you think this occurs?

2. What do you think will happen next in the story?

3. Will Feri remain in Iran, or will she return to her life in the United States? What in the story helps you to decide?

4. Have you ever had an experience similar to Feri's? How did it make you feel?

## Role Playing

1. Act out the story in class with students playing the parts of Feri, the taxi driver, the father, and the other characters. One student should read the background narration. Students might want to bring tape recorders to class on the day the story is acted out; the tapes will help students develop such skills as listening, acting, and intonation. Each new contact with the story will also make the experience with it even richer.

2. In addition to acting out the story, you might also rewrite it as a play. You may want to collaborate as a class and write a second act telling what happens next to Feri and her family.

3. Invite another class to observe your class's performance of the play. Afterward, the performing class should answer the other class's questions about the story, the play, the characters, and so on.

## Journal Writing

What is writing, if it is not the countenance of our daily experience: sensuous, contemplative, imaginary, what we see and hear, dream of, how it strikes us, how it comes into us, travels through us, and emerges in some language hopefully useful to others.

M. C. RICHARDS, *Centering: Poetry, Pottery and the Person*

In this, the last chapter in the book and the last journal writing experience, you may want to think of Feri, a foreigner in her own country. In some ways, we are foreigners in our own minds until we can begin to translate our experiences into a language we really understand. Writing can help us to do this. Our journals throughout this term have tried to serve that purpose, to offer a place to record impressions of the world and to make sense of them with our words. Sometimes we have recorded dreams and sometimes real events; regardless, we have tried to use our journal entries to deepen our understanding of ourselves and, at the same time, to improve our writing.

When we write this time, think of dreams, of returning to places we have thought about and had mixed feelings about. Before you write, you might want to cluster (see page 61) around the word *foreigner* or *dream*. You may want to write a story, a poem, or prose (writing that is not a poem). A short poem by the Russian poet Olga Berggolts may help you to reflect on these ideas and stimulate your mind and pen.

### To My Sister

I dreamt of the old house
where I spent my childhood years,
and the heart, as before, finds
comfort, and love, and warmth.

I dreamt of Christmas, the tree,
and my sister laughing out loud,
from morning, the rosy windows
sparkle tenderly.

And in the evening gifts are given
and the pine needles smell of stories,
And golden stars risen
are scattered like cinder above the rooftop.

I know that our old house
is falling into disrepair
Bare, despondent branches
knock against darkening panes.

And in the room with its old furniture,
a resentful captive, cooped up,
lives our father, lonely and weary—
he feels abandoned by us.

Why, oh why do I dream of the country
where the love's all consumed, all?
Maria, my friend, my sister,
speak my name, call to me, call . . .

# Word Skills

## Idiomatic Expressions

Each of the following paragraphs contains a context clue that will help you understand one of the expressions used in "Foreigner." Underline these context clues; the first one has been done for you. Then use the expressions when you answer the questions at the end of each paragraph.

*no point* (page 319, line 45)

When Feri gets in the taxi and the driver turns off the meter, she realizes that there is no point arguing with him. There is <u>nothing to be gained</u> from arguing with him. When we play games, we score points. If we do not score, we make no point. This expression is used outside of the sports world, as we see in this story. Have you ever avoided an argument because you realized that in the end there would be no point in arguing?

Some other idioms that use *point* are:

**beside the point:** not concerned with the subject being discussed

For example:

Your friends are talking about ordering food for dinner and you mention how much you enjoyed your vacation the summer before. They may tell you that what you are talking about is <u>beside the point</u>.

**make a point of:** stress; treat something as if it were important

For example:

You <u>make a point of</u> explaining to your friends why you brought up your trip. You learned to make fried chicken then and you would like to make it for everyone.

**stretch a point:** make an exception to a rule

For example:

They tell you that no one is allowed to cook in their parents' kitchen, but they will <u>stretch a point</u> in your case and let you cook dinner.

*in a daze* (page 320, line 85)

Feri's father seems to be in a daze when she first arrives. He seems confused, as if he doesn't know whether to be angry or happy. Have you ever had an experience when you felt like you were in a daze (registering for school or arriving at the airport, for example)?

***in the grip of*** (page 320, line 90)

Feri feels like she is in the grip of shyness. Shyness has taken over her feelings at the moment. One can be in the grip of anger, sadness, sorrow, silliness, and so on. This happens when a feeling takes you over, and your responses are governed by that feeling. Have you ever been in the grip of a feeling as is Feri and her father in the story?

The following is another expression that uses *grip(s)*.

**to come to grips with:** to deal with something, especially a problem

For example:

The family had to come to grips with the fact that they had lost their passports.

Now use these idiomatic expressions in sentences of your own.

## Prepositions

**review**

In the following sentences from the story, the prepositions (words like *of, in, at, on, by*) have been removed. Fill in each blank with the appropriate preposition. Refer to the story to check your answers. If your answers differ from those in the story, show them to a classmate or your teacher. In some cases, there is more than one correct answer.

1. As I boarded the plane _____ Logan Airport _____ Boston I

   paused _____ the top step and waved _____ Tony.

2. The driver slowed down _____ a narrow street _____ a mosque

   at its center, then stopped _____ front _____ a large, squalid
   house.

3. This was the street I had lived _____ for so many years; here I had played hide-and-seek _____ alleys and hallways.

4. He went _____ the rooms, arranged _____ a semicircle, _____ the other side _____ the courtyard.

5. _____ dawn and dusk the voice _____ the muezzin would mix _____ the noise _____ people coming _____ and going _____ the nearby bazaars.

6. We went _____ the steps _____ the veranda and my father opened the door _____ one _____ the rooms.

7. He stepped _____ and turned _____ the light.

8. Darius, Ziba, my father—they seemed _____ once familiar and remote like figures _____ dreams.

## Modal Auxiliaries

**past time**
In paragraph 3 of the story, *could* means "had the ability to." It is often used as the past tense of *can*.

He wore his shirt open and I could see bristles of dark hair on his chest. (lines 14–15)
I could almost hear their voices, laughter. (lines 69–70)

**EXERCISE**

Answer the following questions, using *could* plus the simple form of the verb to describe moments in your past.

1. When you were a child and you looked out your window, what could you see? _____

2. When you started school, what couldn't you do that you can do now? _____

3. When you started school, what could you do that you can't do

now? _____

Reread the story, underlining *could* each time it appears and the verb that follows it. Notice how the word *could* is used.

## Modal Auxiliaries

**past possibility**

*Could have* plus the past participle ⎤ refer to past possibility. The
*May have* plus the past participle ⎬ speaker or writer is not sure
*Might have* plus the past participle ⎦ whether something happened.

I entered the waiting room and looked around. Most people had left. There was still no one for me. What *could* possibly *have happened?*

In the space provided, answer this question for Feri, using *could have, may have,* and *might have* plus the past participle. The first possibility has been filled in for you.
They could have gotten stuck in traffic.

_____

_____

*Must have* plus the past participle refers to past probability. The speaker or writer is almost certain that something happened in a particular way.

He nodded. "We waited for you for two hours this morning at the airport. What happened to you?"
I was not sure if he was angry or in a daze. "You *must have gotten* the time mixed up. I meant nine in the evening."

Here are some other examples; you fill in the blanks.

1. Feri arrives in Teheran; everything looks very different. She must

have _____ .

2. You look out the window and the street is all wet. It must have

_____ .

3. You meet a friend and his hair is shorter than it was the day before. He must have _____.

4. You are asleep and you hear a buzzing sound. You wake up. The alarm must have _____.

In the following blanks, write two of your own sentences using *must have* plus the past participle.

_____

_____

### other past-time modals

*Ought to have* plus the past participle

*Should have* plus the past participle

refer to actions that were advised but not acted upon.

Feri *ought to have made* the time clearer to her family.

Did she make the time clear to her family?

She *should have brought* their telephone number with her.

Did she bring their telephone number with her?

In the space provided, write three other things that Feri ought to have or should have done.

_____

_____

_____

*Would have* plus the past participle refers to a past preference that was not fulfilled.

Her father *would have been* happier if Feri had visited before fourteen years had gone by.

Had Feri visited before fourteen years had gone by?

The men *would have treated* her differently if she had worn a chador.

Was she wearing a chador?

Write three more sentences about Feri and her family, using *would have* plus the past participle.

_____

_____

_____

## Special Use for the Word *Let*

*Let* is sometimes used as an auxiliary verb, usually in the imperative, which means making a request, a command, a suggestion, or giving instructions. *Let's* is a contraction of the words *let* and *us*. It is used for the first and second persons together (you and I, or us).

"Let's go to the kitchen," my father said.
Let's talk about that.
Let's not talk about that.

Now use *let's* in a sentence of your own.

## Commonly Confused Words

### cloth/clothes
Read the following paragraph, noticing the use of *cloth* and *clothes*.

*Cloth* is a piece of fabric used to sew with. You make *clothes* out of *cloth*. *Cloth* is not singular for *clothes*. *Clothes* refers to the items that we put on our bodies when we dress. Men's and women's *clothes* are very different in some parts of the world. In Iran, for example, women wear very different *clothes* than men do. In the United States, on the other hand, some *clothes* that men and women wear are very similar.

Fill in each of the following blanks with *cloth* or *clothes*.

1. I bought some _____ to make some _____.

2. A designer buys beautiful _____ to put together a new

   line of _____.

3. Because there was no door, the heavy dark _____ hung in front

   of the _____ closet.

Write two more sentences using these words.

# Sentence Skills

## Tense Review

**Simple Past Tense** In the following sentences from "Foreigner," the past tense verbs have been removed. Fill in the correct form of the verb. If you have difficulty, see page 349 for a list of irregular verbs. Refer to the story to check your answers.

1. I ＿＿＿＿＿＿ my valise and ＿＿＿＿＿＿ it on a table,
   　　(find)　　　　　　　　　(set)

   where two customs officers ＿＿＿＿＿＿ it.
   　　　　　　　　　　　　　(search)

2. I ＿＿＿＿＿＿ looking towards the window trying to spot my
   　(keep)

   father, stepmother, or stepbrother, but I ＿＿＿＿＿＿ not see
   　　　　　　　　　　　　　　　　　　　(do)

   any of them.

3. A row of phones ＿＿＿＿＿＿ in the corner next to a handi-
   　　　　　　　　(stand)

   craft shop.

4. I ＿＿＿＿＿＿ outside and ＿＿＿＿＿＿ a collection of taxis.
   　(go)　　　　　　　　　(approach)

5. I ＿＿＿＿＿＿ the driver, ＿＿＿＿＿＿ up my valise, and
   　(pay)　　　　　　　　(pick)

   ＿＿＿＿＿＿ out.
   　(get)

6. A pebble suddenly ＿＿＿＿＿＿ me on the back.
   　　　　　　　　(hit)

7. I ＿＿＿＿＿＿ nine in the evening.
   　(mean)

8. My father ＿＿＿＿＿＿ his hands forward, about to embrace
   　　　　　(stretch)

   me but, as though ＿＿＿＿＿＿ by shyness, he ＿＿＿＿＿＿
   　　　　　　　　(strike)　　　　　　　　　(let)

   them drop at his sides.

**Past Perfect Tense** Fill in the following blanks. If you have any difficulty, see Chapter 12, page 259.

The past perfect tense is used when we want to write about more than one event that occurred in the _____. We use the _____ tense to describe the event that happened first and we use the _____ tense to describe the event that happened next.

The past perfect tense is formed with _____ plus the past _____.

Examine the following examples from the story.

I entered the waiting room and looked around. Most people had left.

Which happened first—Feri entering the room or the people leaving? _____

Why did Rachlin use the past perfect tense for the second sentence? _____

The streets were more crowded and there were many more tall western buildings than I had remembered.

Why does Rachlin use "had remembered" in this sentence? _____

_____

His cheeks were hollower than I had recalled. . . .

When had Feri last seen her father? _____

Why does Rachlin use "had recalled" in this sentence? _____

_____

## Sentence Combining

Using some of the techniques from earlier chapters, combine these short sentences into longer ones. Keep in mind that there are many correct ways to create new sentences. Try several combinations and share them with a classmate.

1a. I boarded the plane at Logan Airport in Boston.
  b. I paused on the top step.

c. I waved to Tony.

___

2a. I found my valise.
 b. I set it on a table.
 c. Two customs officers searched it.

___

3a. I kept looking towards the window.
 b. I was trying to spot my father, stepmother, or stepbrother.
 c. I did not see any of them.

___

4a. We went up the steps.
 b. The steps led to the veranda.
 c. My father opened the door.
 d. The door led to one of the rooms.

___

5a. A man laughed.
 b. He walked into the light.
 c. He was my stepbrother.
 d. His name was Darius.

___

## Indirect Speech

**review**

In Chapter 13, we examined indirect speech—expressing what someone has said or written without using quotation marks or the exact words. This is also called reported speech.

| Line 29: | "I need a taxi," she said. | direct quotation |
|---|---|---|
| | She said that she needed a taxi. | indirect speech |

Notice the pronoun change from direct quotation to indirect speech. *I,* the person speaking, changes to *she.*

| Line 30: | "Where do you want to go?" one of the men asked. | direct quotation |
|---|---|---|
| | One of the men asked where she wanted to go. | indirect speech |

Notice the pronoun change from *you* to *she*.

| | | |
|---|---|---|
| Lines 83–84: | Her father said, "We waited for you for two hours this morning at the airport." | direct quotation |
| | Her father said that they had waited for _____ for two hours that morning at the airport. | indirect speech |

Notice the change from *this* in the direct quotation to *that* in indirect speech.

| | | |
|---|---|---|
| Line 120: | "Feri, what happened?" a woman's voice asked. | direct quotation |
| | A woman's voice asked her | indirect speech |

Notice that the speaker is identified before the reported speech begins.

| | | |
|---|---|---|
| Lines 41–42: | "You have to pay me 100 tomans for this," said the taxi driver. | direct quotation |
| | The taxi driver said that _____ had to pay _____ 100 tomans. | indirect speech |
| Line 82: | Feri asked, "Didn't you get my telegram?" | direct quotation |
| | Feri asked if they had _____ telegram. | indirect speech |

Notice how the question form changes in reported speech.

**EXERCISE**

1. For more practice, change the following direct quotations to indirect or reported speech.
   a. "I am happy to see you," she said to her father.
   b. "Things have really changed here," he told her.
   c. "Do you have a phone?" Feri asked her brother.

2. For extra practice, change other direct quotations in the story to indirect speech.

**EXTRA PRACTICE**  1. Rewrite the paragraph that begins at line 63, changing it to the third-person singular *(she* instead of *I).*

2. Rewrite the paragraph that begins at line 13, changing it to the simple present tense.

3. Rewrite the paragraph that begins at line 105, changing it to the future tense using *will.*

# Paragraph Skills

Transitions of Place

Rachlin moves her reader by using transitions of place, which she locates at the beginnings of the paragraphs. To illustrate, we will examine the first lines of several of the paragraphs. As we examine the words of transition, think about why Rachlin might want to make the reader very conscious of place.

As I boarded the plane at Logan Airport in Boston . . . (paragraph 1)
In the Teheran airport I was groggy and disoriented. (paragraph 2)

What happens between paragraph 1 and paragraph 2? _____

_____

Does the author tell the reader much about Boston? _____

Which place do you think will be more important in this story—Boston or Teheran? Why do you think this?

_____

A young man sat on a bench beside the table. . . .
I entered the waiting room and looked around.
A row of phones stood in the corner next to a handicraft shop.
I went outside and approached a collection of taxis.

Where has Rachlin taken us in these paragraphs? _____

_____

What do we know about Teheran at this point? _____

_____

How do you think Feri feels about Teheran? What does Rachlin say

that makes you think that way? _____

_____

We passed through quieter, older sections.
I followed him [her father] inside.
He went toward the rooms. . . .
We went up the steps onto the veranda. . . .
My father disappeared into another room.
They went back through the same doorway and I followed them.
We were together in the kitchen.

Is Feri happy to be home? How does the reader know?

_____

Did Feri have a happy childhood? How does Rachlin use words about
place to let the reader know the answer to this question?

_____

Rachlin has taken us on a tour of Feri's life using the transitions
of place. We have followed her from Boston to Teheran. We have
followed her through the confusing airport to the expensive taxi that
drove her through streets familiar yet strange. We have arrived at
her street and seen the mosque, the house of old playmates, and
finally her old home, which looks frighteningly similar to the way it
had looked when she left fourteen years before. Once in the house,
Rachlin leads us through a maze of a veranda, into the "rooms."
Finally we end up in the kitchen.

Why do you think the author used these transitions of place? How
does reading them make you feel?

_____

According to the story, how does Feri see her world?

_____

Look back at the other stories we read. Do any of them use place
in the way that Rachlin does?

## Images

To understand how images can create a feeling or understanding on the part of the reader, let's examine some of the images Rachlin uses.

In the Teheran airport, Rachlin tells us about the relationships between men and women.

The women, mostly hidden under dark chadors, formed a single, fluid shape.

What does this sentence tell us about the women in the airport?

_____

Do you think Feri is wearing a chador? Why would Rachlin want the reader to know if Feri were wearing a chador?

_____

A young man sat on a bench beside the table, his task there not clear. He wore his shirt open and I could see bristles of dark hair on his chest.

Contrast these two descriptions. What is Rachlin telling us about the differences between men and women in Teheran?

_____

The April air was mild and velvety against my skin but I shivered at the proximity to my childhood.

There is an interesting contrast of images in this sentence. What does it tell the reader about Feri's childhood?

_____

## Mood

Rachlin creates a dreamlike mood with her choice of descriptive words.

We seemed to be floating in the sallow light cast by the street lamps.

"Floating" creates a very dreamy feeling. "Sallow light" is a shadowy light, as contrasted with a bright, sunny light.

The smoky mountains surrounding the city, now barely visible, were like a dark ring.

"Smoky mountains" conveys an image that is vague, cloudy, and dreamy. "Barely visible" gives the reader the same feeling.

Read through the story, looking for any other images that suggest dreams.

Rachlin has used many delicate poetic images to convey strong feelings. What do you think Rachlin wants the reader to think about

Feri? _____

What do you think Rachlin wants the reader to think about Feri's

family? _____

What do you think Rachlin wants the reader to think about Te-

heran? _____

Poets use words very carefully. They are always looking for exactly the right word to convey meaning. Poets work with fewer words than prose writers do; however, prose writers must also be concerned with finding the right word. The above examples illustrate some of the ways in which Rachlin was able to influence the reader's view of her characters and the city she describes. When you write, keep in mind the power of words. Search for the right word to help your reader better understand what you have written.

## Editing Skills Paragraph

The following paragraph is a first draft. It contains many surface errors. Edit and rewrite the paragraph, correcting the surface errors.

Returning home can be very difficult. As we see in Nahid Rachlin's story "foreigner." People return to their home countries they find many changes. The streets may not look the same. People they remember do not recognized them. If they go back to there own childhood house. The house may look very different. It may appear small and cramped. A women returned to her neighborhood and their house was gone. In it's place was a little store. No one remembers her. She is extremely depressed. It is also possible to return to a place wear everyone remember you. That makes a person feel happy inside; in least you where not forgotten.

For the answers, turn to p. 348.

# Essay Skills

## Visualization

In this, the last chapter of the book, we will examine another way to stimulate interesting and creative writing. Using this technique, the writer visualizes or sees what is going to be written about. The writer totally enters the life or the world of the piece of writing. As writer Katherine Mansfield describes her writing process,

When I write about ducks, I swear that I am a white duck with a round eye, floating on a pond fringed with yellow-blobs and taking an occasional dart at the other duck with the round eye, which floats beneath me. . . . In fact the whole process of becoming the duck . . . is so thrilling that I can hardly breathe, only to think about it. . . . I don't see how art is going to make that divine spring into the bounding outline of things if it hasn't passed through the process of trying to become these things before recreating them.

*Letters of Katherine Mansfield*

Mansfield describes a process that is similar to the one we will use. Once you have decided on the topic you will write about, close your eyes and try to enter the world of that topic. You can use experiences that you have had in your life to help you see more clearly. Mansfield wrote about the duck because when she was a little girl, she saw a duck killed that she had loved. The duck was to be made into dinner, but young Mansfield was unaware of this as she went down to the water's edge with some other children. The duck's head was chopped off in front of the impressionable child, and the duck ran around headless until it finally died. Mansfield never forgot this moment, and she was able to use her feelings for the duck to make her writing come alive.

When you visualize, use any experience or observation you have had and try to bring it alive inside your head. By the time you actually begin to write, you should have the sights, sounds, smells, and feelings inside your head. If you are writing a comparison/contrast essay, visualize the ideas until they come alive inside you. If you are writing a persuasive essay, persuade yourself first by totally immersing yourself in the topic.

If you have trouble getting started, use the clustering technique discussed on page 61. Begin to cluster around a word, and when an image starts to come to you, close your eyes and try to make the image as vivid and alive as possible.

**EXERCISES**

1. Visualize someone or something else's world. Mansfield visualizes being a duck. You can visualize yourself as your sister, your father, a dog, a cat, or a tree on the street. Try to re-create in its entirety the world of that person, creature, or thing.

2. Visualize as completely as possible your first day in this country or any other important day in your life. Re-create your experience, and then write down as much of it as you can in the next twenty minutes. Don't worry about spelling or grammar for this exercise.

3. By yourself or with a classmate, create your own visualization exercise.

## Suggested Writing Topics

1. Write the next chapter in Feri's life.

2. Feri is a foreigner in her own land. Have you ever felt this way? Have you ever felt foreign and strange anywhere? Describe the situation in which you felt this way and what you did to change the experience.

3. Feri describes the feeling of going home. Maria Muñiz writes in Chapter 4 (page 67) of returning to Cuba. Do you think Muñiz's experience will be similar to Feri's? Imagine that you are Muñiz returning to Cuba. What will your experience be like? Compare it to Feri's. (If you prefer, you can visualize yourself returning home.)

4. Imagine that you are Feri and it is your first night home in Teheran. Write a letter to Tony in Boston telling him about your experiences.

5. "Childhood is not always the happy, peaceful time it is usually pictured to be." Do you agree or disagree? Support your point of view with your experiences or observations.

6. In the poem by Olga Berggolts on page 324, the poet describes dreaming of Christmas in the old house where she spent her childhood years. Visualize returning to your childhood house at holiday time. Describe in detail what you see, smell, hear, and taste. What about it seems different now that you are no longer a child?

7. Rachlin describes Feri's family house very vividly. Write a description of a place that meant a lot to you as a child. Include details about how it looked, smelled, and felt to you then.

## Revising

Use the technique of visualizing for revising as well. Try to imagine your essay as a total unit. Without looking at the page, try to imagine what it looks like. In your visualization, see the essay—the length of the paragraphs, the overall pattern of the essay. Then when you feel you are clear about the essay, look at the paper in front of you. See how well it matches your imaginary essay. Revise your essay until it is as close to your imagined essay as possible.

## Conclusion

As you have tried the various exercises related to prewriting and revising, some have probably worked for you better than others. Each writer is individual, and there is no one correct way to write. Experiment with the various methods until you find the best ones for you. In the meanwhile, the best method to improve your writing is simply to write.

# Answers to Exercises

**Chapter 1:**

*page 16*

Thousands of men, women, and children have left Vietnam to come to the United States. They have had to leave their parents, friends, and families behind. When these people arrived, they suffered many crises; often they found their lives were difficult. They had to attend classes to learn the new language, and they often had to move to overcrowded cities in order to get job opportunities. Traditionally, people have come to the United States from countries all over the world. Despite the many difficulties of adjusting, these immigrants give a vitality to the country, and the country offers many possibilities to these newcomers.

*page 21*

All the students from Mr. Alexander's English class in Barrett College spend time in the library. Every week each student borrows a book and reads it in order to do the homework. One student has read four books on children because she wants to be a child psychologist. Another student has an interest in economics and has read many books on that subject. The whole class seems to be benefiting from its library experience.

**Chapter 2:**

*page 39*

Sung Hee moved to Massachusetts from Korea. She attended Boston University and lived in a dorm with her cousin. She began to work on Saturday night in Filene's, a big department store, and she practiced English with her customers. On Sundays Sung Hee usually rented a little Chevrolet from Avis. Carrying a tourist book called *Inside Massachusetts,* she visited such historic sites as Plymouth Rock and Old North Church. She spent hours at the Boston Public Library looking at the John Singer Sargent murals. She met Tony at a midnight showing of *Casablanca* and last Christmas they said "I do." Now she is teaching Tony Korean and planning to travel home to introduce him to her family.

*page 40*

When Martin and Fatima volunteered to work one afternoon in the Westville College Post Office, they were in for a surprise. In one corner, there were many boxes piled high. They found three heavy cartons of English jam and jelly addressed to Professor Honey White, now of the Ford Foundation. She had left the school back in February and had moved to New Jersey. Fatima accidentally opened a box filled with the Wordstar programs needed for the college IBM computers. "Mr. Smith, this post office is a mess," Martin told the postmaster. "I know it, son. We just have to get a little more organized. The U.S. mail has to go through and we will do it. Soon." Martin and Fatima left there wondering if the college mail would ever get through.

*page 41*

Marie learns languages very easily. She was born in Haiti and has spoken French and Creole all her life. Now Marie also knows English, Spanish, and Italian. She has a special technique that always works for her. At night she goes to sleep by hypnotizing herself as she stares at a poster of the stained glass window in Notre Dame in Paris. Her Sony Walkman tape deck is on her head, and she listens to a different language tape each night.

**Chapter 3:**

*page 52*

inside, surface, specific

*page 60*

Ernest Hemingway's story "A Day's Wait" tells about a young boy who is afraid of dying. He hears the doctor say, "His temperature is one hundred and two degrees." He remembers his friends at school in France saying, "Schatz, you can't live with a temperature over forty-four degrees." The boy's temperature is very high. "You don't have to stay in here with me," he tells his father, "if it bothers you." His father doesn't know what's really bothering the boy. When he finds out he says, "Schatz, it's like miles and kilometers." Schatz believes his father, but still he doesn't relax for several days.

*page 61*

My sister, Hilda, lives in an apartment on the top of a high hill in San Francisco. She works as a computer operator in a big bank there and when she looks out her window, she sees the Golden Gate Bridge. She loves heights. She even flew in a private airplane over the Rocky Mountains. Once she said to me, "I saw both the Pacific and the Atlantic Oceans in one day." She would like to fly around the world some day.

**Chapter 4:**

*page 74*

He, it, his
I, you
I, you
I, my
it, it
he, his, he
he, your

*page 84*

I came to the United States when I was fifteen. My homeland is Haiti, and I miss all the beautiful beaches and the people I knew there. When I arrived in Minneapolis, Minnesota, on a Tuesday in January, it was colder than any day I had ever known in my whole life. Even my poor suitcase seemed to shiver that day. I remember my first tear froze to my cheek. Although I tried very hard to speak English, no one seemed to understand me. Since I first arrived in this country, many things have changed. Because I have a good job now, I have a warm down jacket and furry earmuffs to protect me from the cold. My mother and father are here too, and we all laugh at those first weeks and all the problems we had back then.

**Chapter 5:**

*page 110*

Although getting engaged has changed Samia's life, she doesn't want to marry now. Ahmed, her boyfriend, wants to get married right away, but she disagrees. She likes showing her girlfriends her diamond ring. She enjoys discussing her future wedding with them when she is in school. She knows that she makes her friends jealous such as when her best friends made a real effort not to review their homework with her in the cafeteria as they usually did every afternoon. Samia claims that she likes being engaged, but she doesn't want to get married. Being a housewife doesn't sound like too much fun to her.

**Chapter 6:**

*page 134*

Like Pablo Casals, Marc Chagall was a remarkable man. He also lived a long and productive life. He was born in 1887, and he died in 1985. Chagall lived for almost a century. He was a great painter whose paintings make people feel happy. They usually show dancing figures such as flying cows and pigs, playful lovers, and brightly colored flowers. Chagall was born in Russia in the Jewish quarter of the town of Vitebsk. He had eight brothers and sisters. Chagall knew he wanted to be an artist when he was a little boy; however, he did not become famous until he was in his fifties.

**Chapter 7:**

*pages 153–54*

Ullman wanted to ask a student in her class on a date, but she had a problem. The student was a man and Ullman was a woman. She grew up in a family that had traditional values. They did not believe their daughter should ask a man on a date. They believed the man should ask the woman out. At the same time, Ullman saw her friends asking men on dates. They felt good about it, and they said the men did too. They said it took some of the pressure off the men. One of her friends met her boyfriend this way. Women and men in Ullman's college go on casual dates, and often the women ask the men out. The arrangement worked well and everyone seemed happy— everyone, that was, except Ullman. At last, she tried it herself. She asked out the man she liked and he told her he would like to go.

*page 156*

Asking someone on a date can be risky. If the person says "no," you may feel rejected and embarrassed. However, it's important to keep in mind that rejection is not always personal. There are many reasons why someone cannot accept your offer. It's not always as simple as it seems. Once someone refused when I asked her to go out the first time. She said she had to take care of her younger brothers and sisters. I felt angry until I saw her at the movies. There she was with four little children. When she smiled at me, I realized she had been telling the truth. I asked her out again the next week, and she agreed if her younger sister could come with us.

**Chapter 8:**

*page 174*

Sociologists examine how people live in groups. They examine phenomena such as people's behavioral patterns in relation to love and marriage. They want to know if people in France celebrate marriage in the same way as people in the Philippines. Their studies show that some customs and traditions are similar from place to place. For example, people usually get married with some kind of ceremony. They usually get dressed up for their wedding. However, there are some differences. In some places, marriages are arranged. In other places, people meet and fall in love. In general everyone hopes that the marriage will be happy and long-lasting.

**Chapter 9:**

*page 193*

March 14, 1894

Dear Aunt Millie,

 I think you should sit down before you read this letter, and I think you should have a handkerchief handy. Louise, your favorite niece, died last night. I hated to come right out and tell you like that, but I didn't know how else to say it. All of us who loved her feel terrible. We all knew her heart was bad, yet none of us expected this so soon, so suddenly. I guess I should tell you what happened, shouldn't I? Well, it is a strange story. There was a bad railroad accident, and we all thought Brently was killed. When Louise got the news, she acted very odd. She went up to her room and she locked the door. She wouldn't open it up, not even for me. When she finally let me inside, she looked peculiar. Even though I knew she had been crying, her face was bright, shiny, and beautiful. As she grabbed me around the waist, she stared deep into my eyes. Then we went down the stairs together. Suddenly, the door opened. Holding his old suitcase, Brently came in. I screamed and Louise fell down. Just like that, she was dead. By the way, she left a letter saying where she wanted her things to go. She left you her armchair, her ivory pen, her crocheted shawl, and her love.

Always,

*page 197*

Because she allowed herself to feel free, Louise Mallard felt guilty. She heard her sister knocking on the door, yet she did not answer. She wanted to sit in her room where she felt comfortable. Josephine and Richards were waiting for her downstairs. They wanted to see her, to hear her, and to know that she was all right. Their voices bothered her. When she finally opened the door, Josephine was there. Louise could not explain the way she felt to her sister because she did not think she would understand.

**Chapter 10:**

*page 222*

Don found out that when people work for their family, often they have to work harder than when they get a job from someone else. Don didn't want a job as a bookkeeper, but it was the only job his uncle could give him. The bills would arrive every day and Don would pay them. Many times, however, he lost them. His uncle talked to him about how he could help Don organize himself better, but it never worked. Working as a bookkeeper was only temporary, but for Don, it felt like forever. When his uncle's bookkeeper came back from vacation, Don said that his uncle was glad to see him go.

*page 222*

Looking for a job can be difficult. There are many different types of problems. For one thing, the interviewee is never sure what to bring on the first interview. I usually bring too much. This can be confusing to the interviewer. From now on, I will bring only the necessary documents such as my résumé, my birth certificate, and my high school diploma. In addition, I try to impress the interviewer by dressing very neatly and never chewing gum. I always look directly into the interviewer's eyes. I want the interviewer to believe that I can be trusted. If I remember to follow my own advice, I believe I will get a job very soon.

**Chapter 11:**

*page 242*

even though, but, still, otherwise, however, instead of, on the other hand, although, yet, in contrast

*page 244*

According to Oskamp, there are many factors involved in job satisfaction. People have to feel their jobs are meaningful and interesting. They have to offer the workers a mental challenge. Even though there are individual differences in what people think is important, most people agree that the jobs should offer some challenge. Pay has greater importance for individuals who cannot gain other satisfactions from their jobs. Jobs which offer external recognition, good pay, and a mental challenge are sought by most people. Each person wants a feeling of fulfillment.

**Chapter 12:**

*page 258*

Trying to get a job at the Rockefeller Foundation is difficult for a girl who does not have pull. Finally, the morning postman brings the letter. She is to go for an interview at Peking Medical College, to the comptroller's office. She prepares her clothes and goes to the East Market to buy face powder to cover her pimples. The next morning, she goes with her father to Yu Wang Fu Palace to the administration building. They cross the marble courtyard and go into the entrance hall. Her father leaves. She finds the office and meets her future employer, Mr. Harned. His bald head reminds her of a temple on the hill in North Sea Park. She takes a typing test and gets the job.

*page 262*

The first thing, Most of all, The best thing, The biggest advantage, Finally, The basic reason

*page 265*

One thing Bob always has trouble with is whenever he gets a new job, he gets nervous and he is late. This time though he bought a noisy alarm clock and set it the night before. Then, of course, there was a power failure in his building and the time was wrong. He jumped out of bed when the alarm sounded. He ran into the shower, and he was ready to leave on time. He thought he had a lot of time, so he walked slowly down the street looking in all the store windows. When he walked into the job, his boss was looking at her watch, shaking her head. He couldn't figure it out until he got home that afternoon and realized his clock was wrong.

**Chapter 13:**

*page 292*

The article on "The American Male" made me think about what it means to be a man. I grew up thinking that being a man meant that I had to be tough; people told me it was wrong to cry and I believed them. I remember when I was very young and my favorite aunt died. I really wanted to cry then, but I didn't. I held back the tears, and everyone said I was a real man. It made me feel good, then anyway. Now I am starting to wonder if being a real man means being able to let go and feel. That's what I wonder now. Believe it or not, I cried the other day in front of my girlfriend and then we both cried together. It made us get even closer. Overall, being a real man seems to me to be about being able to be myself. I am getting in touch with the real me behind all the things I used to use to impress the world.

**Chapter 14:**

*page 314*

Reading about the biological differences between men and women, people can really learn a lot that will help them in their everyday life. The nature versus nurture argument is an interesting one. No one knows for sure if people are born with certain genetic characteristics that determine their lives. They may be influenced by their environment as much as by their genetics. According to research, the brain changes. It can change because of many things such as diet, the air, handedness, etc. It makes sense that people should take good care of themselves by eating right, exercising, and trying to live healthy lives. Despite everything that people may try, however, there will always be differences between the sexes.

**Chapter 15:**

*pp. 338*

Returning home can be very difficult as we see in Nahid Rachlin's story "Foreigner." When people return to their home countries, they find many changes. The streets may not look the same. People they remember do not recognize them. If they go back to their own childhood house, the house may look very different. It may appear small and cramped. A woman returned to her neighborhood and her house was gone. In its place was a little store. No one remembered her. She was extremely depressed. It is also possible to return to a place where everyone remembers you. That makes a person feel happy; at least the person was not forgotten.

# Principal Parts of Irregular Verbs

| BASE | PAST | PAST PARTICIPLE |
|------|------|-----------------|
| awake | awaked, awoke | awaked, awoken |
| be | was, were | been |
| bear | bore | borne |
| beat | beat | beat, beaten |
| become | became | become |
| begin | began | begun |
| bend | bent | bent |
| bet | bet | bet |
| bind | bound | bound |
| bite | bit | bit, bitten |
| bleed | bled | bled |
| blow | blew | blown |
| break | broke | broken |
| breed | bred | bred |
| bring | brought | brought |
| build | built | built |
| burst | burst | burst |
| buy | bought | bought |
| catch | caught | caught |

| Base | Past | Past Participle |
|------|------|-----------------|
| choose | chose | chosen |
| come | came | come |
| cost | cost | cost |
| creep | crept | crept |
| cut | cut | cut |
| deal | dealt | dealt |
| dig | dug | dug |
| dive | dived, dove | dived |
| do | did | done |
| draw | drew | drawn |
| dream | dreamed, dreamt | dreamed, dreamt |
| drink | drank | drunk |
| drive | drove | driven |
| eat | ate | eaten |
| fall | fell | fallen |
| feed | fed | fed |
| feel | felt | felt |
| fight | fought | fought |
| find | found | found |
| fit | fit, fitted | fit, fitted |
| flee | fled | fled |
| fly | flew | flown |
| forbid | forbade | forbidden |
| forget | forgot | forgotten |
| freeze | froze | frozen |
| get | got | gotten |
| give | gave | given |
| go | went | gone |
| grind | ground | ground |
| grow | grew | grown |
| hang (an object) | hung | hung |
| hang (a person) | hanged | hanged |
| have | had | had |
| hear | heard | heard |
| hide | hid | hidden, hid |
| hit | hit | hit |
| hold | held | held |
| hurt | hurt | hurt |
| keep | kept | kept |
| kneel | knelt, kneeled | knelt, kneeled |
| knit | knit, knitted | knit, knitted |
| know | knew | known |
| lay (put) | laid | laid |
| lead | led | led |

| BASE | PAST | PAST PARTICIPLE |
|------|------|-----------------|
| lean | leaned, leant | leaned, leant |
| leave | left | left |
| lend | lent | lent |
| let (allow) | let | let |
| lie (recline) | lay | lain |
| light | lighted, lit | lighted, lit |
| lose | lost | lost |
| make | made | made |
| mean | meant | meant |
| pay | paid | paid |
| prove | proved | proved, proven |
| quit | quit, quitted | quit, quitted |
| read | read | read |
| rid | rid, ridded | rid, ridded |
| ride | rode | ridden |
| ring | rang | rung |
| rise | rose | risen |
| run | ran | run |
| say | said | said |
| see | saw | seen |
| seek | sought | sought |
| sell | sold | sold |
| send | sent | sent |
| set | set | set |
| shake | shook | shaken |
| shine | shone, shined | shone, shined |
| shoot | shot | shot |
| show | showed | showed, shown |
| shrink | shrank | shrunk |
| shut | shut | shut |
| sing | sang, sung | sung |
| sink | sank | sunk |
| sit | sat | sat |
| sleep | slept | slept |
| slide | slid | slid, slidden |
| speak | spoke | spoken |
| speed | sped, speeded | sped, speeded |
| spend | spent | spent |
| spin | spun | spun |
| split | split | split |
| spread | spread | spread |
| spring | sprang, sprung | sprung |
| stand | stood | stood |
| steal | stole | stolen |

| BASE | PAST | PAST PARTICIPLE |
|------|------|-----------------|
| stick | stuck | stuck |
| sting | stung | stung |
| strike | struck | struck, stricken |
| swear | swore | sworn |
| swim | swam | swum |
| swing | swung | swung |
| take | took | taken |
| teach | taught | taught |
| tear | tore | torn |
| tell | told | told |
| think | thought | thought |
| throw | threw | thrown |
| wake | waked, woke | waked, woke, woken |
| wear | wore | worn |
| weave | wove | woven |
| weep | wept | wept |
| win | won | won |
| wring | wrung | wrung |
| write | wrote | written |

# Models for Tenses

## Active Voice

### Simple Present Tense

| SINGULAR | PLURAL |
|---|---|
| I go | we go |
| you go | you go |
| he goes | |
| she goes | they go |
| it goes | |

### Simple Past Tense

| | |
|---|---|
| I lived | we lived |
| you lived | you lived |
| he lived | |
| she lived | they lived |
| it lived | |

### Simple Future Tense

| | |
|---|---|
| I will learn | we will learn |
| you will learn | you will learn |
| he will learn | |
| she will learn | they will learn |
| it will learn | |

### Present Continuous Tense

| SINGULAR | PLURAL |
|---|---|
| I am helping | we are helping |
| you are helping | you are helping |
| he is helping | |
| she is helping | they are helping |
| it is helping | |

### Past Continuous Tense

| | |
|---|---|
| I was sleeping | we were sleeping |
| you were sleeping | you were sleeping |
| he was sleeping | |
| she was sleeping | they were sleeping |
| it was sleeping | |

### Future Continuous Tense

| | |
|---|---|
| I will be playing | we will be playing |
| you will be playing | you will be playing |
| he will be playing | |
| she will be playing | they will be playing |
| it will be playing | |

**353**

## Active Voice

*Present Perfect Tense*

| SINGULAR | PLURAL |
|---|---|
| I have seen | we have seen |
| you have seen | you have seen |
| he has seen | |
| she has seen | they have seen |
| it has seen | |

*Present Perfect Continuous Tense*

| SINGULAR | PLURAL |
|---|---|
| I have been trying | we have been trying |
| you have been trying | you have been trying |
| he has been trying | |
| she has been trying | they have been trying |
| it has been trying | |

*Past Perfect Tense*

| SINGULAR | PLURAL |
|---|---|
| I had jumped | we had jumped |
| you had jumped | you had jumped |
| he had jumped | |
| she had jumped | they had jumped |
| it had jumped | |

*Past Perfect Continuous Tense*

| SINGULAR | PLURAL |
|---|---|
| I had been running | we had been running |
| you had been running | you had been running |
| he had been running | |
| she had been running | they had been running |
| it had been running | |

*Future Perfect Tense*

| SINGULAR | PLURAL |
|---|---|
| I will have left | we will have left |
| you will have left | you will have left |
| he will have left | |
| she will have left | they will have left |
| it will have left | |

*Future Perfect Continuous Tense*

| SINGULAR | PLURAL |
|---|---|
| I will have been getting | we will have been getting |
| you will have been getting | you will have been getting |
| he will have been getting | |
| she will have been getting | they will have been getting |
| it will have been getting | |

## Passive Voice

*Simple Present*

| SINGULAR | PLURAL |
|---|---|
| I am given | we are given |
| you are given | you are given |
| he is given | |
| she is given | they are given |
| it is given | |

*Present Continuous*

| SINGULAR | PLURAL |
|---|---|
| I am being taken | we are being taken |
| you are being taken | you are being taken |
| he is being taken | |
| she is being taken | they are being taken |
| it is being taken | |

*Simple Past*

| I was brought | we were brought |
|---|---|
| you were brought | you were brought |

*Past Continuous*

| I was being carried | we were being carried |
|---|---|
| you were being carried | you were being carried |

## Passive Voice

*Simple Past*

| **SINGULAR** | **PLURAL** |
|---|---|
| he was brought | |
| she was brought | they were brought |
| it was brought | |

*Present Continuous*

| **SINGULAR** | **PLURAL** |
|---|---|
| he was being carried | |
| she was being carried | they were being carried |
| it was being carried | |

*Simple Future*

| SINGULAR | PLURAL |
|---|---|
| I will be found | we will be found |
| you will be found | you will be found |
| he will be found | |
| she will be found | they will be found |
| it will be found | |

*Present Perfect*

| SINGULAR | PLURAL |
|---|---|
| I have been offered | we have been offered |
| you have been offered | you have been offered |
| he has been offered | |
| she has been offered | they have been offered |
| it has been offered | |

*Past Perfect*

| SINGULAR | PLURAL |
|---|---|
| I had been loved | we had been loved |
| you had been loved | you had been loved |
| he had been loved | |
| she had been loved | they had been loved |
| it had been loved | |

*Future Perfect*

| SINGULAR | PLURAL |
|---|---|
| I will have been seen | we will have been seen |
| you will have been seen | you will have been seen |
| he will have been seen | |
| she will have been seen | they will have been seen |
| it will have been seen | |

"The Social Context of Identity Formation," K. W. Fischer and A. Lazerson, from *Human Development,* by K. W. Fischer and A. Lazerson. W. H. Freeman and Company. © 1985.

"Age and Youth," *Joys and Sorrows: Reflections by Pablo Casals* as told to Albert E. Kahn. © 1970 by Albert E. Kahn. Reprinted by permission of Simon and Schuster, Inc.

"Will You Go Out With Me?" Laura Ullman, *Newsweek,* © 1984 by *Newsweek,* Inc. All rights reserved. Reprinted by permission.

"Love and Marriage," Leonard Broom and Philip Selznick, *Sociology: A Text with Adapted Readings,* 6th edition, © 1977, Harper and Row. Reprinted by permission of Leonard Broom.

"I am a Bunch of Red Roses," translated by Reza Baraheni and Zahra-Soltan Shokoohtaezeh, from *A Book of Women Poets from Antiquity to Now* edited by Aliki and Willis Barnstone, © 1980, Schocken Books.

"Jobs of the 1990s," Gwen Kinkead, *Fortune,* © 1983 Time Inc. All rights reserved.

"The Work Itself," Stuart Oskamp, *Applied Social Psychology,* © 1984, pp. 180–182. Reprinted by permission of Prentice-Hall, Inc., Englewood Cliffs, New Jersey.

"A Mortal Flower," by Han Suyin. Reprinted by permission of Han Suyin.

"The American Male." Reprinted from *U.S. News & World Report* issue of June 3, 1985. Copyright, 1985, U.S. News & World Report, Inc.

"Biological Differences" from *To Be Human: An Introduction to Anthropology* by Alexander Alland, Jr. Copyright © 1980 by Newbery Award Records, Inc. Reprinted by permission of Alfred A. Knopf, Inc.

From *The Amazing Brain* by Robert Ornstein and Richard F. Thompson. Text copyright © 1984 by Robert Ornstein and Richard F. Thompson. Reprinted by permission of Houghton Mifflin Company.

"Foreigner" selection is reprinted from *Foreigner* by Nahid Rachlin, by permission of W. W. Norton & Company, Inc. Copyright © 1978 by Nahid Rachlin.

"To My Sister" by Olga Berggolts, translated by Daniel Weissbort, from *A Book of Women Poets from Antiquity to Now* by Aliki and Willis Barnstone, © 1980, Schocken Books.

# Index